Readers Say...

"Marrs is a kindred spirit to each of us in business who has had the nagging thought, 'there must be a better way.' He shows how it's possible to create a successful life based on a deeply felt sense of spiritual truth. What a gift!"

David Langer, President
Global Alliance for Transformational Entertainment (GATE)

"Perfect for those who are trying to find real meaning in their work lives. A truly inspired work."

Ron Scolastico, PhD
Author, Doorway to the Soul

"*Executive in Passage* takes us through the crisis many people experience these days when they feel a conflict between material success and their most central values. It's beautifully written with raw honesty, courage, and inspiring possibility about creating a fulfilling personal and professional life."

Sarah Edwards, LCSW, PhD
Psychologist

"Intensely personal and inspirational, this book gives us all hope that we can come into full alignment with our own true natures."

James Weil
Retired Executive, MetLife

"Reading this book makes me recognize that my career was part of a larger pattern of transformation—of me, of business, maybe even of the world itself. I wish I'd had it 10 years ago."

Karen File
Professor of Marketing

"I recommend this book to anyone feeling conflicted or dissatisfied in their career. Marrs' credibility as a businessman and his search for authenticity make this book a vital resource for both professionals and individuals in the career/life planning process."

Marti Beddoe
Career Counselor

"A courageous journey of a man willing to do whatever was needed to grow, expand, and live a totally honest life. I felt the experience throughout my being and was profoundly affected."

E. P., Los Angeles, CA

"Never has a book offered such complete comprehension of my journey and such loving support."

M. A., Denver, CO

"I was about halfway through my 'Subtle Agenda' journey when I found your book the first time. I cannot even begin to tell you the comfort it gave me. I just finished reading it again, and it, again, is a passage of light. Now I realize I do not need to leave a field that I love to lead a spiritual life and continue a spiritual journey."

J. G., Marina Del Rey, CA

"*Executive in Passage* fell off the shelf at the local bookstore. I couldn't put it down and ended up reading it from cover to cover within a day. Not only was it a validation of my process, (there were times I thought I was crazy) it was a voice of hope. I laughed, I sighed, I cried—I cried a lot! It was more than the story that moved me, it was your ability to so clearly and poignantly capture the essence of it all."

M. J., Boulder, CO

"If I hadn't known otherwise, I would have thought you were describing parts of my life. The story is mesmerizing—each night I picked up your book and read for several hours until I fell asleep. It was so compelling I finished it after only a few nights."

E. O., Los Angeles, CA

"I read *Executive in Passage* a few days before we left on a long camping trip. I brought it along and read it aloud to my husband during the long hours we spent driving through the Northwest. Some nights after dinner we would be sitting in beautiful places in the mountains or woods and I'd read aloud to my husband and step daughter. I would see my husband sit in awe at a passage or tears would come to his eyes at those times when you spoke to his soul."

S. R., Orange County, CA

"From the moment I picked it up I knew it would be my 'path through the wilderness.' In a way I feel you wrote the book for me. I felt your journey was mirroring mine. You give me such hope."

N. A. M., Southfield, MI

"The candor and integration of 'business' and 'private' aspects of your experience give the book a compelling quality—for the general reader, I imagine, and certainly for me as a researcher/writer interested in questions of corporate responsibility."

M. E., Cambridge, MA

"Every executive pounding the pavement today wondering 'what the hell hit me' should be reading your book before they waste their time trying to find a job that won't satisfy them anyway."

B. D., PhD, San Diego, CA

"Your story shot straight to my gut and both gripped my mind and touched the spirit within me. I now understand what my *Subtle Agenda* has been struggling to reveal ... that the mechanics involved in a career and life change are far less important than the deeper comprehension of the inner self and where it can lead."

C. G., Dallas, TX

"I've just finished reading your wonderful book for the second time. I was profoundly touched by your sensitivity and courage to pursue your heartfelt desires without compromise. Like you, I'm searching for meaning in my life. As I read your book I could feel your love, courage, and pain coming through every page."

B. W., Coursegold, CA

"I must admit that this is the first time a book has had such a significant impact on me. It enabled me to identify the processes and events that have shaped my life over the past six years and helped me gain a better perspective of my journey, as well as understanding and coping with the trials of transformation."

P. S., Irvine, CA

"Whenever I have a bad day I still refer to your book. It is so comforting to know I am not crazy and others like yourself have taken the journey and survived."

S. V., Scottsdale, AZ

"Your story is mine as well. Your authenticity and your courage to lead from your exposed weakness will give heart to others like myself."

G. J., Nashville, TN

"This book served as an incredible mirror and road map that traced my life down a path I'm still following—from uneasiness and contradictions in values to calm clarity and peace of mind ... a very moving experience and a priceless message from a man who did it."

L. H., Mercer Island, WA

"Bless you for writing your book! It is the first time I have found anything in print which so closely parallels my own journey, and it has provided me with great comfort, assurance, and a wonderful lift up to the Bigger Picture of what's going on!"

L. M., Reading, MA

"Your story is inspiring to those of us attempting to combine our knowledge of the material world with our hard-won spiritual awareness. Thank you for sharing your journey."

S. B., Dexter, MI

"Your message is one for the heart, not the head, and in the constantly accelerating world we live in, your voice I feel will serve as a beacon to corporate leaders willing to take that leap back to their values and to people and things they really love."

G. J., Denver, CO

"Your book has helped to facilitate a turning point in my life that has opened me to pure joy, understanding and creative expression."

S. M., Shorewood, WI

"I really commend you for the frank and honest discussions that are of such importance to so many of us, especially men who are in the business and professional world."

J. G., Oakland, CA

EXECUTIVE
IN
PASSAGE

*Let yourself be silently drawn by the stronger pull
of what you really love.*

Rumi
The Essential Rumi

EXECUTIVE IN PASSAGE

When Life Lets You Know
It's Time to Change,
Let That Knowing Lead You

Donald Marrs

with Paige Marrs, PhD

BARRINGTON SKY PUBLISHING • SANTA MONICA, CA

Executive in Passage:
When Life Lets You Know It's Time to Change,
Let That Knowing Lead You

ISBN: 978-0-9258870-0-9
Library of Congress Control Number: 2013916820

Published by

Barrington Sky Publishing
212 26th Street, Suite 239, Santa Monica, CA 90402
connect@bsky.com

Book production by Stacey Aaronson

Printed in the USA

*To all who desire a more meaningful and fulfilling life
and have the courage to answer the call.*

☯

In loving memory of Ron Scolastico, PhD

ACKNOWLEDGEMENTS

I originally wrote this book because my life insisted I do so. It has been my great fortune that so many people found the telling of my story useful to making sense of and navigating their own. Over the years, my connections with readers and others on the journey have inspired me, moved me, and helped me find even deeper understanding of my own path. To all of them, I am grateful.

In the fragile early stages of this work, there appeared a single person who by being so moved by what she read, breathed new dimension into it. Paige made extensive green pencil edits in the margins and by "just opening the buds" helped make the book what it is now. Since I shared that early draft with her, she has become my beloved, my co-writer, my wife, and one to whom I am deeply indebted for the many outrageously happy years we continue to enjoy together.

Many others who contributed to the first edition of this book were acknowledged at that time of those printings. However, we'd like to again mention David Erramouspe who painted the cover while sitting under the stars on Mulholland Drive to illustrate Los Angeles at night. Hidden in the image is my home in the Hollywood Hills where much of these experiences were lived. That house and surrounding landscape unwittingly provided important supports during those year, along with my dog, Stray.

We wish to thank Elizabeth and Rick Moody for their generous feedback. Elizabeth shared her insightful understanding of the larger mystical possibilities of this story, and Rick, who understands the human journey as the window to the divine like no other person we know, asked just the right questions. Together they contributed richly to the shaping of new material.

We are particularly indebted to Susan and Ron Scolastico, beloved friends for so many years, who remain persistently encouraging at every stage of each new venture we share with them over decades of dinners. We are deeply grateful for the many ways they contribute to our emotional and spiritual lives and so lovingly nourish the creative environment in which we flourish.

We also appreciate the many talents and skills of Stacey Aaronson, who transformed a hard bound book into a beautiful new soft cover and a luminous ebook to enable us to reach a new world of readers.

Last, and in some ways first, I wish to acknowledge my daughter, Sarah, who contributed herself to this story, and who never lost her loving connection to me despite my wandering out of her life for a time while I searched for a life of my own.

CONTENTS

THE RETURN

WHEN ONE
DOOR CLOSES ...

Keep listening to that wee small voice.

Leo Burnett

Don't let the noise of others' opinions
drown out your own inner voice.
And most important,
have the courage to follow your heart and intuition.
They somehow already know
what you truly want to become.

Steve Jobs

When I set out to resolve the conflict between my values and my work, and to heal the split I felt in myself, I knew one door was closing and fully expected another would soon open. It didn't. Not even close.

What happened instead is illustrated succinctly by a T-shirt Paige and I found in a little shop on Maui shortly after we started leading workshops for people going through difficult transitions. The shirt is solid black except for two big, white, perplexed-looking eyes staring out from utter darkness with a dialogue balloon that says:

"I know that when one door closes
another one opens
but man, these hallways are a bitch!"

1

If your life has been pushing you to change, and you've landed in one of those dark hallways, then we have something important to talk about. I only wish that someone who knew the bends and twists of this passage—and the location of its hidden light switches—had reached out to me. Surely I would have learned from their mistakes and breakthroughs rather than stumble around so much on my own.

I've since learned that a "dark hallway" can start in many ways. For some people, it's abrupt. One day your life hits a wall with little or no apparent warning. For others, there's a growing sense that something is off, that something needs to change, but the signals can be so subtle that it's hard to interpret them or know what to do differently. For me, the early signals were subtle, and I didn't pay real attention until they got deafeningly loud.

My first suspicion that life was letting me know it was time to change was a vague sense of emptiness in my work. I was becoming more uneasy and less fulfilled by the day, but I kept shoving those feelings aside. My success in advertising was accelerating, and it was utterly intoxicating to be creating television ads for high-profile, multinational brands. There was no room for self-doubt in that environment.

"It's just the normal stresses," I told myself, as I tried to soldier on.

This strategy worked for a while. I even felt stronger for bearing the pressure. But the inner alarms grew louder, and I kept ignoring them until one day it all fell apart.

Actually, I fell apart while presenting the next round of Doughboy commercials to a roomful of Pillsbury executives. I completely blanked. I'd been creative director on that account for almost a decade, but I suddenly didn't even recognize the adorable squishy guy in the chef's hat on the storyboards behind me.

In that moment, a door decisively closed—slammed shut really—and into a dark hallway I went. It was obvious that I needed to change my approach to my work or try something entirely new, but I was not sure which—or even what or how. I certainly didn't realize there was a hallway to traverse, although I did have a strong sense that losing it at Pillsbury was part of a larger language. My life was speaking to me, in this case quite vehemently. I just didn't know how to decipher the message. I was unclear what it wanted me to understand, or how much to value it, if at all.

When I first decided to reset my career, I could not have foreseen that what began as a crisis in my work would become so much more than the closing of one door and the opening of another. The dark hallway in between was like the cocoon for the caterpillar who does not yet know it's becoming a butterfly. Unlike the caterpillar, however, who I imagine has no choice but to go along with the metamorphosis, I had to find the courage to engage the struggle head on. This story admits embarrassing miscalculations, painful failures, and what it took for me to finally attune to life's hidden language and let wisdom lead the way.

It was worth it, though. My subsequent successes far surpassed what I achieved before, but that's the least of it. My entire life became stunningly more love filled and expansive than I could have anticipated. The new door that ultimately opened turned out to be the threshold of an entirely different level of awareness, an initiation into a more meaningful, more productive, and extraordinarily more fulfilling way of being in life.

Of most enduring benefit, this process forced me to become fluent in the multifaceted language of inner guidance—the source of a most intimate knowing—which turned out to be my wisest mentor and most trusted guide. I believe that developing and refining my relationship with that larger wisdom is what gave me access to vast and magnificent capacities that lie within us all.

These learnings unfolded in a sequence of phases that are highlighted within the text to illuminate significant but often misunderstood turning points in this journey. I hope you find them useful. From listening to the stories of others "in passage," it is obvious that each of us is heir to these gifts.

NEW IN THIS EDITION

I've learned a lot since this book first came out. Time and experience, plus comments from readers and clients, have made me even more aware of the transformational power and universality of the process written about here. Now that it's being re-released as both paperback and e-book, I decided to use the opportunity to make a handful of changes.

For instance, Paige, who is also my wife, is now listed as co-author. This gives her proper recognition for the clarity of human and spiritual depth she contributed to the original manuscript and to this edition. The prologue and epilogue have been updated, and you'll find an "Afterword" that shares important new insights, the kind that can only be attained with the passage of more time. There are a few other changes within the text, including calling my daughter by her real name, Sarah, who I'm proud to say has just become a published author herself!

The change I'm most excited about, though, is the opportunity to share two of the most significant experiences of my life. Both are of a spiritual nature, and both were purposely omitted from the initial writing. At the time, each felt too tender, too sacred, and if I'm fully honest, too "out there" to reveal, so I convinced myself that the story could be told just as well without them.

I now know that I was wrong in that decision. If you asked me today to describe the two or three most significant experiences that were pivotal to the success of my passage, ones that others might find useful to hear, these two would be paramount.

The first event radically altered my career path, literally turning me away from the contemplative life of a monk to the competitive life of a Fortune 500 advertising executive. This transformation took place at dawn in the chapel at the Abbey of Gethsemani in Kentucky, where I had planned to study with Thomas Merton, who was in residence at the time. This story is told in Chapter Four.

The second was a quantum leap into what I can only describe as a state of expanded consciousness and bliss. In this altered knowing, I was taken out of myself and immersed in the underlying essence at the core of true success, happiness, and love. This life-altering encounter, which appears in Chapter Twenty-Nine, occurred at my home in the Hollywood Hills in the aftermath of a business debacle that made the disastrous presentation at Pillsbury seem gentle.

My hope is that the sharing of these experiences will stimulate sincere and valuable insights about the language of your inner wisdom and about the fulfillment this journey can bring you. Perhaps you'll better understand what your life wants you to know and how to tap the inner resources you need to achieve what you most passionately and uniquely desire.

I also hope you'll use this book well—get messy with it even. Make notes, write questions, jot down new awarenesses, and share them with us if you like:

don@executiveinpassage.com

or

paige@executiveinpassage.com

If you let this story illuminate your passage, you might discover that you are reading about your own journey, and more importantly, that you are advancing and uplifting your own path of wholeness, awakening, fulfillment, and love.

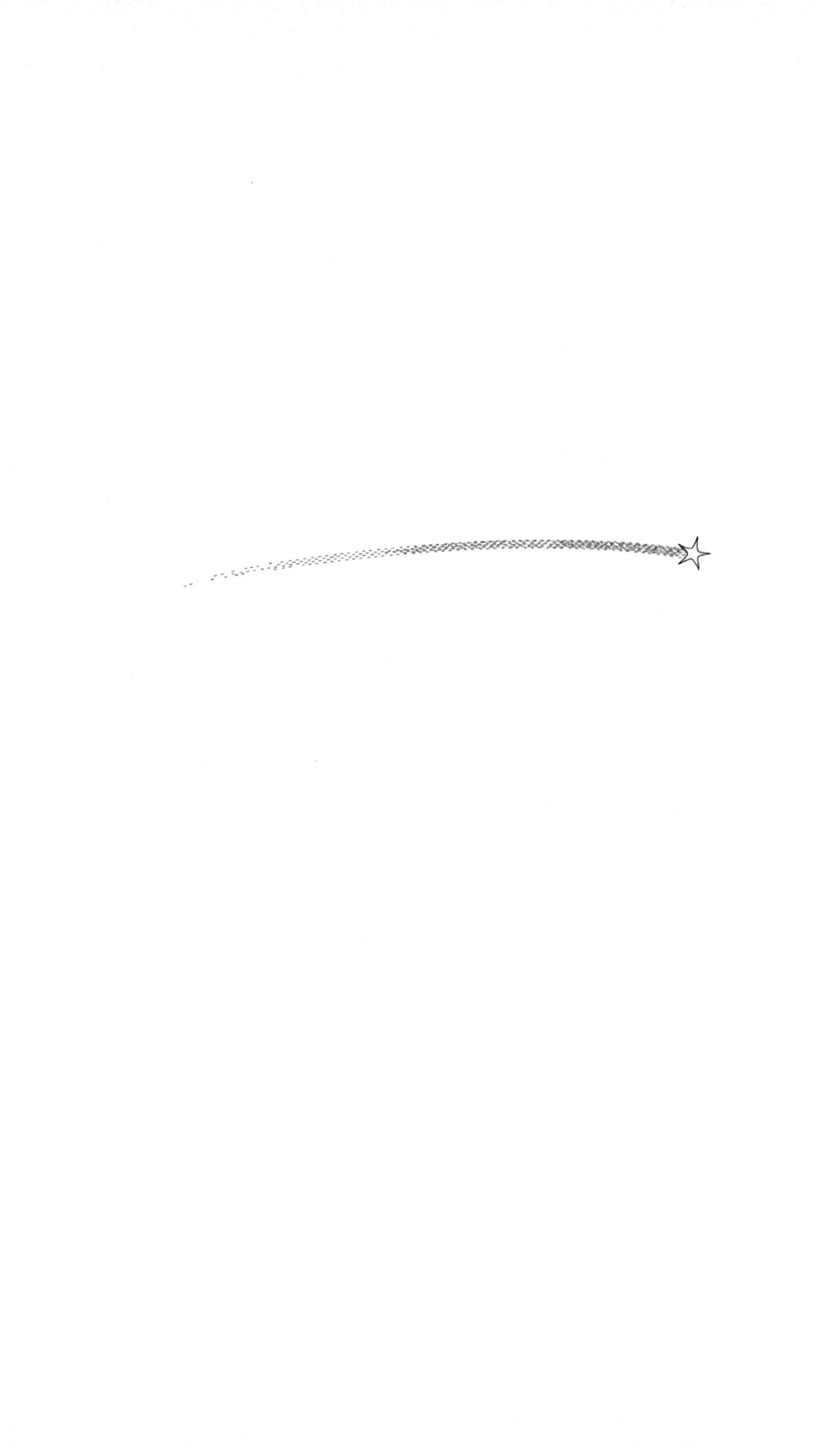

THE CALL

But whether small or great, and no matter what the stage or grade of life, the call rings up the curtain, always, on a mystery of transfiguration—a rite, or moment, of spiritual passage, which, when complete, amounts to a dying and a birth. The familiar life horizon has been outgrown; the old concepts, ideals, and emotional patterns no longer fit; the time for the passing of a threshold is at hand.

Joseph Campbell
The Hero with a Thousand Faces

ONE

LINCOLN PARK

I'll start with what I saw as a hairline crack that appeared in my life one day, much the way it does in a fine porcelain bowl. One day it was there, and suddenly everything changed. I saw the frailty of everything, the impermanence, the first glimpse that a once joyful thing was beginning to end.

The large elms in Chicago's Lincoln Park were still barren of leaves that morning. Mounds of sooty snow were still piled up along the sidewalks, topped with frozen dog waste. It was windy and cold, but tiny blue crocuses jutted up through the patches of bare grass, promising an early spring. My daughter Sarah was with me and we were walking to her wonderful private school a few blocks down the street from our park side apartment.

We must have been a lovely sight. Here was a cute little girl in her school clothes, walking through the park with her daddy, who was wearing his gray homburg and a tweed chesterfield coat. A successful-looking daddy, a little girl in pink, a bleak urban park, early spring, life just beginning to burst with new hope, renewal, love, and family. Everything was in its place, or so it appeared.

What no one saw was that I had tears in my eyes. As we walked along I hid them from Sarah, answering her in short, muted words so she wouldn't notice that my voice was too choked to speak without sobbing. The tears weren't just from sadness, although my sadness almost overwhelmed me. A few moments before, just after we'd entered the park, I had been deeply touched by the realization that the "ideal" life I was living might now be over, and the tears welled up out of relief, as much as out of regret.

A vulnerable place in me was beginning to crack open much the way an oyster shell splits, revealing soft, delicate flesh. As a boy, I had learned to hide my feelings and always kept myself bottled up tight. Now I could barely contain the tenderness I felt as I slogged along in the bittersweet knowledge that I would not be walking Sarah to school this way much longer.

Everything had come to a climax that morning, but the seeds had been sown on countless earlier mornings. My wife, Joan, and I had had another fight, but this one felt worse than the rest. I don't remember how it started anymore. I just remember the jaggedness in my gut. I only remember the despair.

It was becoming clear to me that I was living with my own worst enemy. It was as if I had engaged someone to destroy me. After seven wonderful years of marriage, the person I had loved more than anyone had come to represent so much pain that I couldn't stand being around her anymore.

At first, I noticed small things. Women I encountered during the course of a day seemed kinder than my wife usually was. Then I'd go home at night and she would be complaining about one thing or another, and it was usually my fault. How late I was working, how little money we had, how often I had to travel, how little attention I paid to her.

The more unhappy she was with me, the more closed off I became. She was frightened and had become critical in an attempt to reach me again. But it had the opposite effect. I felt so stung by her criticisms that I retreated further and further away.

Everything seemed upside down. What was once love had become pain. What was once exciting was now repulsive. The bond of marriage we had made so lovingly now felt like a double suicide pact.

When I took Sarah's hand to walk her to school after the argument that morning, my mood was as sullen and dark as an Illinois thunderstorm. As we left the apartment, I carried my pain and hurt hidden deep in my gut, expecting they would disappear as usual once I got to work. I could always depend on getting through even the worst fights of my marriage by just ignoring them and withdrawing into my creative projects. I would work the whole day, not sharing the pain with anyone, and if Joan and I hadn't talked to resolve the argument, we'd barely speak that night. We'd even go to sleep angry, then get up the following morning still holding our silence. The trick for both of us was not to give in.

Now just a block from Sarah's school, I was still deep in my thoughts. Something was different that day. I had fallen into some dark hole, and in on top of me fell all the past months of sadness, hurt, and despair. The pain was so intense that I ached for something to come pull me out. Then suddenly my dark mood was shattered by words as soothing as a mother's speaking to her child, and they brought a flood of tears to my eyes. *You are in charge of your own life.*

These words came so swiftly and powerfully, yet so tenderly, they penetrated deep into my heart. I felt dizzy and weak, and I wanted to cry.

Before that moment, I'd had no realization that I was free to change my life. It was as if I had been trapped in a prison with no future. But now, an instant later, I not only had been given permission to change, I was being encouraged to do so. My God, I could let myself out! I couldn't believe it. It was so simple. I had suddenly awakened and found myself in charge! Why had I never felt this way before?

At the gate to the school I lifted Sarah up, hugged her tightly, and drew her fresh young scent into my lungs. In a moment she was running off with an innocence that I knew she would soon lose.

I turned and walked along the zoo with its primal animal noises, and then headed down past the farm towards the high-rises beyond.

I could think of nothing but the powerful inner voice and the truth it carried. If I was in charge of my life then I could change things. I'd had realizations like this before about my marriage, but I was always afraid to act on them. Life would go back to normal, and the impulse would fade away. But this felt different. It was a warm, powerful urge to act, and I knew I had to change things after this, or I could never hide from my cowardice.

Outwardly, I had the sophisticated gloss of male success that I had worked years to create. Inside, I was bound up in knots. My past life had such a tight grip on me that I felt helpless to change things. I felt trapped in my marriage. I felt trapped in my lifestyle. Trapped in my career. Trapped in the high-rise I lived in. Trapped in the high-rise I worked in. Trapped in my skin.

The recognition of how I'd denied my true feelings horrified me, and I knew the pain wouldn't stop unless I took my life back in my own hands. With just this awareness, I felt movement, as if I were turning a huge ship in a small harbor, trying to head out to sea.

What had held me? Perhaps it was the vise-hard image I had of myself. I had imprisoned myself in ideas of what I thought others wanted me to be. I had been more Catholic than any of the Catholic school kids I knew growing up. More embarrassed by sex. More shy. I strove to be better, and when I entered business I worked harder for success. I eliminated the parts of myself I didn't like and hid anything that seemed to be a weakness. I believed there was only one perfect way to do something, and I relentlessly worked to live out what I thought it was. But under the armor, there was a lost little boy.

I couldn't express my vulnerability to other men. In those days, men didn't usually talk about such intimate things with each other. I learned more about my male friends from my wife, who learned them from their wives, than I ever heard from my friends directly. When we got together, we discussed football, business, women, or, most of the time, local politics. This left us all pretty isolated from each other, but by some measure, it made us feel safe.

Looking up at the endless line of high-rises along the lakefront, I felt like an early Shaker who'd been catapulted into executive America. Where were the white socks I had worn here from Ohio? Where was the plain wood furniture of my youth? I hid my lack of sophistication and formal education under a cashmere scarf. Walking to work that morning was a country-bred kid, dressed up as an advertising executive. But under it all, he was aching to emerge honestly as himself. He just didn't know how.

By the time I met Joan, I had the image down pat. I had given up every last hint in my personality that I had come from a small town. My family had no money, and to get any education at all, I joined the Army for the GI bill. It bought me twenty-eight months, and I used them to buy my way into a new world.

I learned to speak the way people did on network television. I dressed like the young men who came from graduate programs in Eastern universities. And I carefully hid any evidence that I had gone to a two-year art school.

When I noticed that the guys from the Eastern schools didn't wear white socks, I went to Sears and got black ones. When I noticed that they went to Brooks Brothers, I went there too. I wanted to make it in business, and even though I didn't have all the advantages, I tried to make up for it in style, hard work, and good behavior.

I had always felt judged by other people and thought that if I just went along and did what the successful people did, then I would do well too. Now, I was finally awakening to the fact that I had constructed my entire life by responding to what others expected of me. I had lived my early years in fear of a wrathful God, denying my own desires every step of the way. When I began working, I shifted my allegiance to the corporation. Then when I got married, I submitted myself to that. So throughout my entire life, I did as either my religion, the corporation, or my marriage required of me because I wanted to satisfy them above all else. I had played by the rules and succeeded.

But to do it, I locked up the little kid from Ohio, and now, after more than fifteen years, he was finally making his move.

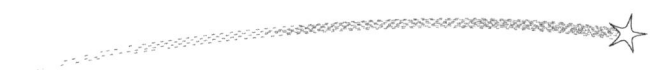

INNER STIRRINGS

The first signal of my passage came as a small cry from within. Nothing dramatic triggered the break. A small illumination had simply turned on in a dark corner of my mind, and suddenly everything was clear — one stage of life was over and another was about to begin.

I had spent the first part of my life following the expected paths, going along with others, imprisoning my spirit in order to be successful. But by withholding my true self, I had choked off my uniqueness. By following others, I had lost myself. And now, the life I had so carefully created was no longer worth the emotional cost of keeping it all together. It felt limited, unfulfilled, and even unbearable.

As the tight structure of my world loosened and moved, my once secure home felt like a house shifting in the sand. My initial responses were disbelief, anger, and panic. Then finally as I surrendered to the change, I felt an overwhelming desire to move with it and let my true self come through.

My passage had begun.

TWO

A DREAM BELOW THE DREAM

I n the days and weeks that followed, I began to realize that the "little voice" I heard while walking Sarah to school through Lincoln Park had, in many ways, released me from my past. Disengaging from my marriage slowly became more real to me, and by whatever timing, my long-indentured spirit was stirring to be free.

Perhaps I could have gone on, but trying to keep it all together was no longer worth the sacrifice. My desire to end the pain of marriage was my first halting step toward creating a life that was really mine.

I'd come to the office early to think. Plants always made me feel more peaceful, so after setting my briefcase on my desk, I watered the small palm that shivered near the icy window. This kind of palm, which flourished so well in the tropics, just never did well in Chicago. Perhaps it was as discouraged as I was by the miles of gray, frozen buildings that lay in its view.

All my life I'd followed other people's ideas. My religious fervor as a kid originally sprang from my parents' fierce commitment to Catholicism, although I confessed to a mystical bent of my own. My fierce pursuit of success was my ticket out of the Great Depression mentality with which I'd been raised. All my big decisions had been made to please other people, and now that I was feeling free of my marriage, everything else in my life began to feel vulnerable too. I was growing impatient with these bitter Chicago winters and longed to escape the towering glass and concrete buildings and return to the earth. The noise of someone arriving for work down the hallway broke into my thoughts for a brief moment.

One truth rang clear. The scales had finally tipped, and the satisfaction in my marriage no longer balanced the pain. Yet, the thought of divorce horrified me. No one in my family had ever gotten a divorce. They'd even voted against Adlai Stevenson because he had gotten one. I had been taught that only God could release the bonds of marriage, and only the Pope could grant an annulment. I was no longer religious but found the haunts and furies of childhood hard to ignore, especially as they related to life's rites of passage.

Joan and I had not married in the Church. We didn't want our wedding to be a pretense. Still, even though I'd made the break, from somewhere deep in my psyche the wrathful God of my youth was watching from the apse of the cathedral back home.

My mind raced. Could I really get a divorce? It was becoming more common, but long marriages were still the norm. Was I ready to join the ranks of men considered somewhat "flaky"? Was I so sure this wasn't working that I was willing to get a divorce? God, what would my family say?

Maybe it's just a temporary impulse, I thought. Maybe it's a delusion. We had built so much in Chicago since we were married, what would happen to our friends, our social life? Maybe I was just in an unhappy phase. I wasn't feeling good about anything anymore.

As I sat there at my desk, trying to get focused on my work, it began to dawn on me that even advertising was no longer the bottomless cup of satisfaction it once was.

What would I do if I left advertising, I asked myself. If I could create the career of my dreams, what would it be? Each time I let my imagination fly, it got cold feet and landed back in my office where it was warm and comfortable. Even it had learned to play it safe.

The only possibility that secretly excited me was to somehow work in film. My mother, who rarely left the house when I was a kid except to go to Mass or the supermarket, loved movies and movie magazines. Wouldn't she flip if I went into that business? Deep down I was too embarrassed to let people know about my closet desire to be involved in film, but it had been a part of me from the first moment I saw *Snow White* at the Plaza Theater in Cincinnati. This was before television, of course, and was one of the first color movies I ever saw. The power of that story and the impact of its giant color pictures left a permanent mark on my imagination.

Now, with a fresh ear, I heard that little voice telling me that after years of struggling to make it in advertising, I was not fulfilling my childhood dream. How could this be? I was the man that the little boy in Ohio had wanted to be. I was the successful advertising executive that the art student had longed to grow into. Why couldn't my career just continue to bloom for me as other people's did for them? Was there really another life waiting out there for me? I sorted among this faded collection of dreams and realized that hawking breakfast cereal had not been among them.

I got up, flipped the DO NOT DISTURB sign on my door, and closed it. People were arriving for work. I kicked my feet up on the frosted windowsill and thought about it more. I had to confess that I really did want to make movies, and yet, there was a dream even below that dream. My real desire was to write, although I couldn't identify it as such at the time. As I sat in my office, it was the idea of telling stories on a movie screen that fired my blood.

Walt Disney was doing what I wanted to do. He was creating wonderful stories that told of magical people in extraordinary worlds, and he was thoroughly successful doing it.

The phone jogged me out of my reverie, but as I reached for it, the button light stopped flashing. My secretary must have arrived.

Was I crazy? I had made lots of commercials, but despite how much I loved going on production trips to the West Coast, advertising was not the movie business. Here I was, reaching my late thirties, at the height of my career. Could I really give it all up for something so elusive as the movie business?

What was happening to me that made the life I'd built so carefully feel so irrelevant now? I was beginning to feel split apart and realized how much I was doing things that I no longer wanted to. What once felt like my own game now felt like someone else's.

Then what *was* my game? Was it really the movies? What would I do if I were starting over again, selecting entirely from my own desires? I didn't know because I had never given myself the chance to find out. I'd played in other people's games because I was afraid to start my own. What if I went for what I really wanted and then failed? That had always been too painful to consider.

Despite the vulnerability I was feeling, I also felt braver. The mere thought of chucking advertising for the movies put me back in touch with the daring young art student and his passion to create something of value with his life.

It felt strange to be going through a crisis of "values" when values never seemed to be an issue before. Yet now, money, power, social position, security—all paled next to this desire to create something of more personal worth. It was not simply about making movies. I needed to leave a life that felt like it was finishing. I needed to find a way to reconnect with my deepest aesthetic values and follow them wherever they led.

I was beginning to realize that I had lost touch with a part of myself that had fired me when I was younger. There was a place, deep and around the bend in my psyche, a place from which all my dreams would originate but was no longer touched in my work. I first discovered that precious place as a child, and it led me into art. Somehow I lost contact with it along the way.

Now, with cracks in my armor, my passion flickered to life again. This was not going to be just the end of a painful marriage, but possibly the end of a whole way of life. I was feeling an almost erotic urge to get back in touch with myself. In an instant, it became the most important thing.

THREE

THE GASOLINE CRUNCH

O n a bus a few days later, I read in the paper about the long lines of cars at gas stations all over the country. Relieved that I didn't own a car, I felt free of the hassles of the gas crunch.

When I arrived at the office, there was an urgent message to attend a meeting in the chairman's office later in the morning on Oldsmobile. I was working on a campaign for one of their luxury cars at the time and had a hunch the meeting might have something to do with the oil shortage.

I closed the door to be alone, something I found myself doing more frequently. My creative group resented losing their easy access to me because it slowed their getting approvals, but I needed more time for myself. I felt my own crises piling up and thought they were every bit as important as the office ones—something new for me. I sat down and absently started making small drawings on a pad of paper.

I wished I had someone to talk to about all of this. Not my parents, even though I longed to discuss it with them. In the past they had always tried to convince me to stay with what I had. "A bird in the hand is worth two in the bush" was often my father's advice. Any threat of change in my life would drive both my parents into a storm of prayers to St. Jude.

It had become clear to me that my natural shyness and my family's support of the status quo had prepared me for a "gatekeeper's" life—keeping the gatehouse for someone else's mansion. My unspoken belief that I deserved little from life (since I would get mine in the next world) had led me to work for those with more power, position, education, or money. Was I always going to be working in other people's companies and building other people's fortunes?

A gatekeeper would automatically look for a place in a successful institution and assume whatever position was given. In return, a contribution to the owner's estate was expected. Otherwise, the gatekeeper could lose his borrowed position. In a large corporation, this meant building the institution's wealth and internalizing its values—all out of a fear of being banished from the power structure.

All life appeared to work the same way. I learned that if I wanted to get along I'd have to go along. If I didn't follow the rules, a daddy in the sky would punish me. In *Jack and the Beanstalk*, the little boy breaks his mother's rules, and in doing so, discovers a vine to heaven. But just to remind the young man of his transgression, he's nearly killed by the giant who lives there. Such stories taught me respect for authority, and as I grew up, I always looked over my shoulder to make sure I was attending properly to all the known gods.

I checked my watch. It was time for the Oldsmobile meeting. I told my secretary I was leaving and took the elevator up to the sixteenth floor.

I was ushered into the chairman's office immediately. He was finishing a phone conversation, so I stood in the doorway until he motioned for me to sit near his desk. There was no one there but the two of us, and as Henry hung up the phone, he began talking about the gas crunch and the problems it was causing our Oldsmobile and Union Oil accounts.

Even though I only rented cars, I related more to the gasoline consumer than to the auto and oil companies. Instead of worrying about their sales, or even client revenues for the agency, I was more concerned about whether the country was going to continue working or not.

I began to feel uncomfortable as he spoke about the agency's need to support the interests of our clients in this crisis. Under Henry's voice I heard my own little voice urging me not to say yes too quickly. I felt the muscles tighten in my gut when I heard that someone would have to go to Detroit and receive a large assignment being offered as sort of a competition between General Motors' advertising agencies. The winning agency would receive an extra $25 million in media expenditures to keep the luxury car production lines moving through the gasoline scare. It was a whopping opportunity for me, and with the agency's 15% commission, it was a nifty way for the company to make a bundle in a very short time. All we needed was a winning campaign. Then he asked me if I would go to Detroit for the assignment.

In a flash, I recalled an earlier time when our founder, Leo Burnett, was looking for people to work on a presidential campaign. I was active in politics and was asked to help. But because I wasn't anywhere near as conservative as the candidate, my little voice had urged me to say no. I had hesitantly declined, but began to worry about having drawn a line between me and the company. I secretly promised myself not to stand in opposition to management very often, but now, again, I was having to deal with dissent from my little voice.

What saved me this time was a vicious schedule for the next week that could not be ignored. I had no heart to sell people big cars in the middle of a gas crisis, but how could I tell that to the chairman just when the agency needed so much help?

"I can't, Henry. I'm preparing for several big meetings this week. Have you checked with anyone else?"

"I'm told they're hung up on other things too," he said, "but I guess one of them will go if you can't."

I was wondering if he could sense what was going on inside of me. I apologized and went on in more detail about how busy I was. The phone buzzed and as he leaned forward to answer it, I moved toward the door. When he waved, I took it as my signal to leave.

Growling at myself on the way to the elevator, I was angry for feeling so divided. Anyone wishing to move ahead in business would not turn down a meeting at General Motors—at least not one that the chairman of the agency had personally asked him to attend.

I longed for the good old days when ads were simply ads. When I arrived at Burnett out of art school, the company had been running a major Marlboro campaign, and I loved it. Who thought about the effect of smoking on anybody's lungs? The Surgeon General wasn't yet issuing warnings about lung cancer. Creating an exciting "image" was the only thing that mattered. But now when I looked around at what we were selling, I got a knot in my stomach.

I felt trapped having to do things I no longer wanted to do. I was living in a country that gave me maximum freedom to create anything I wanted, and here I was, working on things I no longer cared about. My little voice was now whispering to me persistently that I needed to end this split.

My jaw was grinding as I paced back and forth. When the elevator arrived, I got on and slammed my fist on the button that would take me back down to the fourteenth floor.

FOUR

THE CRACK WIDENS

y wife and I did not talk again that morning. Lynn, Joan's daughter by an earlier marriage, and Sarah, who was a few years younger, were both becoming very aware of our silences. On mornings like this they'd learned to be quiet also, for fear of bringing our wrath down on themselves.

After helping Sarah off the bus at her school, I settled back in my seat and tried to read the paper. I was incapable of focusing on the news, and soon my mind was tossing among the waves that were crashing from Lake Michigan almost up to Lake Shore Drive.

The night before, Joan and I had gone to a party for a friend who was running for political office. Even though it was an opportunity to connect with people we rarely saw, I was beginning to dread evenings like this because they often triggered problems between us.

If I became absorbed in conversation with one of our woman friends, Joan would feel painfully reminded that I was becoming more withdrawn from her. If the conversation went on long, and if I looked particularly animated, she'd assume there was more going on than there was. It was true that I was becoming more withdrawn, but it was not because I was interested in other women—it was just a relief to talk to them at events like this. Between the constant pressures at work, which kept me feeling embattled, and with the stress of raising a young family, I had no chance to heal myself at home.

As I withdrew, Joan felt threatened. The more threatened she felt, the more critical she became and the more I withdrew. So what began as a mild rift between us became a raging conflict. I never had an affair, or even an ongoing friendship with another woman, but I could never convince my wife of that.

That night I was making the rounds of people I knew when I noticed "that look" on Joan's face. That look, with its frozen whiteness, always appeared when she was angry at me, and I knew I would have to answer for something when we got home. Soon I got my courage up and wandered over to her.

"Want to go?" I asked.

She turned away, not to pout, but to get her coat.

There was silence in the cab, and silence in the elevator ride up to the apartment, but I knew there would be no silence when we closed the door. As on all such evenings, we sat talking for hours until the pressure was out of the situation. I heard how unhappy she was, how unable she was to communicate with me, how closed off I was, and how provocative I was with other women. I told her how painful it was to live with someone who was so critical and unhappy, how I resented her watching my every move when we went out, and how I couldn't communicate very well with her either. As usual, we got to bed late, woke up more exhausted than before, and were in no mood to talk about it further.

The office hallways were buzzing that morning. Ads and storyboards lined the walls outside the conference rooms waiting for creative review meetings. The agency was pitching Pepsi. We didn't have a soft drink client at the time, and management was excited about the creative work that was being presented. An account like this, which ran mostly on television, was considered a plum since there was so much opportunity for sheer invention and creativity.

My group was busy with another assignment, and I was glad not to be part of it. I was hearing my little voice again. This time it told me I didn't want to sell people sugar water. I drank soft drinks myself because I liked them, and the kids did too, but there was a part of me that did not want to spend my life selling them. What was happening to me? As an employee and stockholder I was happy that the agency was working on the pitch, but I was even happier that I had nothing to do with it. It was obvious that the split was widening, and it frightened me.

A clear pattern was developing:

I had quit smoking a few months before and was feeling conflicted about working on our Philip Morris brands.

I always loved working on Kellogg's but had begun to restricting the kids' intake of presweetened cereals.

Then there was Oldsmobile. I just couldn't bring myself to sell gas guzzlers during the oil crisis.

Here were some of the largest billings in the house, the most exciting projects for creative people, and they were suddenly clashing with my values.

Feeling repelled by the biggest moneymakers in the agency was becoming a problem. My values were growing in importance, and my passion for making it in advertising was dwindling. In meetings, I would look at the other guys and wonder if they had their conflicts too, but I never spoke openly about this issue with anyone. It was simply not what the executives discussed. The corporation was in business to make money, and that was the most important consideration. Personal values could be seen as an expression of weakness as well as a liability if they got in the way of business.

As I hung up my coat, my secretary came in and reminded me about a product taste-test starting soon in the kitchen. Before I went, I checked my little palm tree and found that it, like me, was wilting. I couldn't quite see where my split was taking me, but on a subtle level, I began to get the creepy feeling that my career was ending and that I just hadn't fully realized it yet.

When I arrived at the kitchen, muffins were coming out of the oven. New products are the lifeblood of consumer-oriented companies and are always a good source of extra revenue for agencies too. So everybody encouraged new products along, and our own people were no exception.

"Notice how much taller they are than the normal muffins," coaxed the home economist.

The account supervisor jumped in.

"What's special about this muffin is that it has this new buttery color. See that?"

He broke one open. Sure enough, it had a golden center.

"Is that color from butter?" asked Pete.

I loved Pete. He was one of my most rebellious writers and always liked to ask the questions that would be most embarrassing for an authority to answer.

"No," came a tentative response from one of the account executives. "It's food coloring." Several people laughed, and a smile crept across my face.

Here was a product "improvement," as we liked to call a new idea that was not strong enough to stand alone as a new product. It was the agency's job to take these "improvements" and present them to the public in the best possible light.

I caught Pete's eye, and since he was the one who would have to write about it, we both burst out laughing. Once we got started, it was like trying to stop laughing in church. The more we tried to hold it back, the worse it got.

It was funny how when I got an idea, I suddenly saw reflections of the same thing all over the place. For years and years it seemed that everyone was trying to get into the agency, trying to get jobs, trying to succeed, and trying to accumulate stock. Now I was becoming aware of people looking for ways to change their lives. One of the cereal account executives had left a couple of years before, and I heard later that he had surfaced as a north suburban church minister. It had struck me as rather unusual, but now I knew what he must have felt. Another executive left behind our national insurance account and went back to law school.

For a long time, working at Leo Burnett was like being in Mecca. Now it felt like a little trickle of pilgrims was journeying to other places.

In high school, I began going on retreat to a monastery, the Trappist Abbey of Gethsemani in Kentucky. This was to fulfill my childhood belief that if life was really about reaching heaven, and if we have only one shot at it, why not go all the way? Why not devote my whole life to the pursuit of my spirit?

At the end of my senior year, I reached a three-pronged fork in the road. Would I be a monk? A painter? An advertising man? My passion for making the right choice would not let me resolve my dilemma easily. I was a born artist, and drawing came easily to me. I won several national art awards when I was in grammar school but found painting a touch boring. Even though I could do it well, it was like poking through ashes. My desire to be a painter felt already spent, and something more meaningful was pulling at me.

In grade school, my wanting to become a priest made me popular with the nuns, plus it was a source of great pleasure for my parents. I liked the privileged status it gave me, but I liked even more how true it felt. It sparked in me a deep sense of being in touch with very large things. I loved the air of destiny my spiritual ambitions gave me.

Now with three lives in front of me—pursuing the arts, pursuing the soul, and pursuing business—advertising, which combined two of them, should have been the obvious choice, but it wasn't. Those weekend retreats as Gethsemani exerted an indescribable pull. On one of those trips, I was climbing a set of stairs, following the retreat master. Suddenly a monk came hurrying down, and I hardly had time to throw up my arms to catch him as he sailed into me. He smiled an apology (he had taken a vow of silence) and hurried off. The retreat master asked if I knew who that was. When I said no, he told me that the monk was Father Louis and that I might know him as Thomas Merton. I was overwhelmed at having had such close contact with the man whose books had brought me there.

Simply being at the monastery fulfilled me in some mysterious way, and I relished my walks around the grounds. Passing the rows of simple iron crosses on the burial plots and watching the monks work in the fields lifted my heart in ways that nothing else did. I sensed I had lived this life before.

One weekend, shortly after my graduation, I went there to imagine I was entering the monastery. If it felt right, I would make the choice to go in. If it felt wrong, I would go to art school and learn advertising design.

Knowing I was there to make that choice, the novice director took me to parts of the monastery that were off-limits to weekend retreatants. When I was shown their private quarters, I imagined myself in one of the simple cells. It felt familiar and wonderful, but also narrow and tight.

After my tour, the novice director asked if I would like to attend early services with the resident monks. He wanted me to have the experience of spirit as they lived it, and I was thrilled at the opportunity. Well before dawn the following day, he quietly escorted me to the balcony of their chapel and left me there in silence.

The church looked more grand at that hour than it probably was. In the semidarkness, it was tall and elegant, built on the Gothic bones of past centuries. Below me lay rows of parallel pews that lined both sides of the center aisle. The first hint of the rising sun appeared through a row of tall, arched windows.

I knelt in reverence as monks filed into the chapel below me. They were clothed in white hooded robes that seemed to glow in the early light. The scene was soon cast in soft pinks and oranges streaming down through the windows. As the chanting began, the sounds welled up around me and embraced my heart and soul. I let myself be absorbed into the place, and I knew that I could spend my life there.

Then amidst the incantations, I was suddenly startled by a voice. I turned to find that no one was there. The voice had come not from outside me but from deep within. It was silent yet present, and so audible it was as if spoken by someone next to me.

"You've done this and done this," the voice said. "In this life, do it in the city."

This was shocking and disturbing, but also comforting. It was strange but familiar. It was not a thought or an intuition, but rather a disclosure from an awareness quite separate from my own, one that knew me so well it revealed a vision of my life I could not have known or articulated. The words neither asked nor commanded an action from me. I was simply informed that to discover my true path in this lifetime, I needed to go into the clamor and chaos of the city, not into the quiet of the monastery.

I was only vaguely aware that some people believed in past lives and had never considered such a thing for myself. I thought of it as a vaguely interesting artifact of other religions. Yet, when I heard the words and felt the gravity of the message, I knew it to be true.

In that rosy dawn light, with a background of hypnotic chanting, I accepted this guidance that the life I was witnessing before me would not be mine, not this time.

With that single utterance, my desire to live a dedicated, sacred life was gently redirected by an unseen guide. I can still feel the dry taste that this shocking revelation left in my mouth that morning.

Those few moments, which felt as if they happened beyond time, set a course that would take many years to fulfill. It was the first of several significant interventions of guidance at pivotal moments by a consciousness within me, yet other than my own.

CRISIS OF VALUES

This phase was wrought with a growing sense of alienation from everything that had once been familiar and supportive. Yet at the same time, a new burst of idealism flooded me with a strength and passion that could not be denied.

Every day, I saw evidence of how I'd smothered my impulses and how my values conflicted with the life I'd built. Feelings of discord were magnified by the sense that no one else seemed to be having the same problem. Everyone around me was living life as usual, while my world had turned inside out. The more these feelings of crisis escalated, the more intensely I desired to start all over again.

Externally, life was in full bloom, but internally I was dying. Yet it was the isolation of this phase that forced me to shift my focus from the outer world to an awareness of subtle impulses from within.

This shift was not completely unfamiliar. In drawing and other creative work, I'd always followed a sense of personal "knowing," a quiet feeling that one thing was somehow better than another. Now I found myself trusting this personal sense as a source of guidance that could help me make choices about my life. Listening to these gentle proddings became the bridge of light that carried me forward.

FIVE

LOCKED OUT

Spring had turned to summer, and the biting twenty-below-zero winds had turned to damp, billowing mugginess. I was feeling exhilarated about my career—something I hadn't felt in a long time—because new job opportunities suddenly abounded. It felt good to have other companies pursuing me, and it made me wonder if my conflict of values was more about changing jobs than about advertising itself. The sudden rash of offers also led me to consider how much money I could generate by cashing in my stock and profit-sharing trust, which were considerable by ordinary standards. I began to realize that I had money to live on if I needed it.

Things were popping inside Leo Burnett also. Over the years I had successfully made the switch from being just an art director to being a writer, and then moved up to becoming a creative director. Rumors began floating around that I was about to be made a vice president, which excited both me and the little boy from Ohio who was still watching from inside.

Yet, despite the new opportunities, the work itself was getting less and less interesting. I found that when my heart wasn't in a project, I couldn't override myself like I used to.

My body felt heavy, but I wasn't gaining weight. It was taking more effort to get my work done, and the schedule didn't help. The weeks were often six days long, and we would also work several nights. In some weeks, I would go to Cincinnati for a creative presentation, to New York for a meeting, and to Minneapolis for something or other. In between, we would put together the creative material to be presented in these and other meetings. Then, to make things worse, my people also had West Coast television productions and other meetings of their own, and even occasional sick days which, to my chagrin, they seemed to take often.

Life at home was no escape. Each time Joan and I tried to talk about what to do, it turned into a fight, ending in no communication at all. At times we interrupted our silences to make love, and then got up the following morning and barely spoke. As long as we were able to make love, even as brittle as it was sometimes, we believed we might have a chance. But as the bond between us disintegrated, our social life began to crumble too, bringing further torture to an already fragile situation.

By the time August came, I was exhausted. We had rented the beach house in the Michigan dunes again, and I was looking forward to just lying in the sand. But just before we left, I was asked by management to go to Los Angeles for a couple of days toward the end of my vacation, and if I would, I could take a few extra days after Labor Day. The idea appealed to me and I agreed, thinking that it might actually be better not to have to move the family back on a holiday. It also seemed it might be better for Joan and me if I got out of those close quarters for a few days—even if it took me out of town on my birthday.

So all during August we lazed around the summer house. It was nestled down on the water and near a creek that flowed through the dunes to the lake. I took Sarah and Lynn hiking up Thunder Mountain, a giant dune that rose up behind the house, and we swam and took a little sunfish out sailing. Things between Joan and me did not improve, but they didn't deteriorate either.

When it came time for me to leave for Los Angeles, we drove the rented station wagon to Benton Harbor airport. I got out, put my overnight bag down on the cool morning tarmac, kissed Lynn and Sarah, and caught Joan's cool eyes as I kissed her and turned away. She did not like my leaving.

The little feeder-airplane roared its engines and bumped down the runway. My life seemed to be taking a new course, but I hadn't quite figured out what it was. I looked down and saw the station wagon, tiny as a toy, moving slowly down the country road. Beyond through the haze, as the airplane banked, I could see the towers of Chicago.

On the following day, the meetings were going well and Paul, the account executive from the agency, and I decided that we had had enough of the clients. We were staying at the hotel where the meetings were, but decided to check out and move closer to the airport to make it easier to leave the following morning.

We had a wonderful dinner of steak and lobster right on the water overlooking the Marina. He toasted me on my birthday, we got a little loaded on good French wine, and I went to bed early.

Back in Chicago the following day, I stopped by the apartment to pick up some clothes before taking the train back to the beach house. When I got to the door of our apartment, I unlocked it, but when I turned the knob and pushed, it was still locked. It felt locked from the inside, which was curious since there should have been no one there. I had the uneasy feeling that something was wrong, but I didn't know what. When the superintendent of the building arrived with his master key, even he could not open it. Finally, he went downstairs to get the tools to take the door off its hinges.

Just as he returned, Joan opened the door, her face cool with rage. She managed a laugh and told him that she had been running the vacuum and couldn't hear the door. He looked at me puzzled, glanced once more at Joan, then left.

I hated moments like this. It was like standing on a volcanic slope with quiet rivers of smoldering rage rolling down around us, threatening like the depths of burning hell, raw with the heat of fear and anger. I sat down, and Joan let her fury run free as she stormed about. When things calmed down, I heard what had happened.

It seems that she had called the hotel to have a bottle of champagne sent to my room on my birthday and found that I had checked out. Since I was not due home until the following day, she jumped to the conclusion that I was spending the night with another woman. She felt so sick about it that she left the girls with a friend at the beach house and came home. That morning, she was still so angry, she had called an attorney to talk about starting a divorce.

The anguish we were feeling had somehow splashed out of ourselves, like acid spilling from a bowl. I shrank back from it, having never experienced anything like this before. We had let the fury out, and it now had a life of its own. Somehow we had lost control.

When I heard the words *divorce* and *separation*, they were like hot swords entering my stomach. Hearing them spoken shocked me, even though I had been feeling much the same way since I knew how far our troubles had gone. Yet I was surprised at Joan's courage in confronting a bad situation. As awful as things were, I was feeling too guilty about divorce to force it myself. Perhaps it was because she had been through one before that she was better able to do what she did. As painful as it was, part of me was relieved that Joan had taken the first step, because I also knew it was finally time to face the surgeon.

When the passions quieted, we talked about what had happened. What I felt most guilty about—guilt was one of the few things I was able to feel at that time, guilt and loss—was that on the day of the meetings, as we rushed out of the hotel, I had failed to call her. I'd had a quick feeling that I should call, but there was a part of me that just let it pass. It was that one choice that had brought our conflicts to a head.

The marriage was in its final stages after that and we could not reverse the slide. I became more closed off at the office and began to hide behind double vodkas when I arrived home. Joan and I finally decided to file for separation and set the legal process in motion as soon as we could prepare the kids. But first we wanted to give the kids, and perhaps ourselves, one last Christmas.

SIX

THE HOLIDAYS

Even Christmas carols made me sad as I shopped the crowded aisles of Marshall Fields. I would pick up something that one of the kids might like, then feeling guilty about leaving them, I'd put it down and move away.

My forebodings about leaving the marriage were draped over me like a dark shroud. The only peace each day was the first instant I awakened. In that moment my mind would take a quick inventory, remaining free until it fastened on the horrible realization that I was breaking up my family. Sometimes I felt like a wrecked ship, creaking and groaning, aground on the back of a huge whale. It was as though an outside force was shaking us and changing our lives, one that we hadn't chosen and could not stop, or even understand. Preparing for the holidays was the worst.

I always hated moving, I thought, as I went through the revolving doors out to Madison Street. Down at the corner, the sound of bells mingled with a Salvation Army choral group. Shopping was too difficult, so I headed up toward Wabash Avenue to catch the bus home.

As I walked, I remembered having gone a few years before to a benefit at the Chicago Institute of Psychoanalysis when they were moving to their new headquarters. There was an audiovisual presentation about the psychological problems of separation as part of their moving day celebration, and I had eagerly watched as the first slide came up. It was a female nude in late pregnancy, with a vast mound of her flesh looming up like a mountain before us.

"This is our first home," said the presenter, "and each time we have to move after this, the trauma of the first time is restimulated."

What followed were slides of an infant being discharged into the world, a violent slap on the butt, and cries of fright in the night. While the entire audience squirmed and groaned, my mind raced over all the times I'd moved and how difficult it had always been.

For me, any kind of separation was traumatic. I hadn't been able to stay overnight away from my parents until I went to summer camp in the sixth grade. It was a constant embarrassment for all of us. I even refused to stay with my grandparents, whom I loved dearly, and who lived right across the street. It was simply so painful for me that I would get sick to my stomach. I felt sick again when I left home to go into the army at eighteen, and the last time I felt the same kind of upheaval was when I disconnected from the Church. Leaving my parents made me sick physically, but leaving my religion was a wrenching of my spirit.

As the bus moved past the traffic on Michigan Avenue and headed up the inner drive, I decided to get off and walk past my first apartment, which was on Cedar Street.

Joan believed in God, but not in sin, and certainly not in any organized religion. She had somehow overcome the fundamentalist background she grew up with in southern Indiana. When I first met her I was shocked that someone as bright and sensitive as she had no formal set of spiritual laws. "What keeps you from murdering people?" I would ask seriously, but she would only laugh.

It was my religious guilt about sex that was most transformed by meeting her. I always had deep conflicts about sex, naturally enough, because I had been taught that even a small act was a mortal sin, punishable by eternal fire. My body ached to hold a woman, but guilt and fear would rise up and join with my shyness and I would be overwhelmed.

The closest I got to having sex when I was a kid was listening to Protestants talk about it. My most delicious evil encounters were having bad thoughts while listening to their dirty stories. Bad thoughts were a venial sin and not as serious an offense as having sex. Real sex was a mortal sin and could put you away forever if you didn't get to confession on time. When I went to confession I had loads of venials, but years went by before the mortals began to show up.

As I got a little older and was willing to risk committing mortal sins, I would schedule them close to confession, which was usually heard late Saturday afternoons and early evenings. I scored my first masturbation between innings of a Saturday afternoon Cincinnati Reds/Dodger game, and after watching the finish on television, I ran off to confession to get the sin removed in case I died.

One of my favorite teenage fantasies was to have some kind of government researcher come to my house and ask if I would have sex with some woman because they wanted the semen for research purposes. I thought God would forgive me if it was for medicine.

Maybe that's why they used to joke about Catholics making such good lovers. All the while they're making love, they see the fires of hell burning around them, and it just heightens the whole experience.

As I got older, I could never reconcile myself to the idea that sex was wrong, since it felt so wonderful and came from such a true place inside myself. I began to read a lot about how the rules about sin had changed over the centuries, and slowly the fixed laws of my youth began to loosen their stranglehold. Yet deep in my emotions lay a bastion of guilt that I had not yet overcome.

When I reached my old apartment house I stopped a moment to reflect.

Joan would visit me here after her modeling jobs. She was a photographic fashion model in New York and Europe before she came to Chicago. She had completely erased her southern naïveté and manner, and was an extraordinary beauty. But what had the greatest impact on me were her intelligence and sophistication. It was through Joan that I eventually found myself at home in the heart of a major city. She opened me to the art galleries, the night life, and fine dining.

After we became more intimate, I got up the courage to ask her to help me exorcise my guilt. I thought that if I could do something to consciously merge loving and sex, I could erase my conflicts. I asked if she would tell me, again and again, that she loved me, all the while we made love.

What a moment that was. To look into the eyes of another human, aglow with love for me. To look into that face. To hear her love for me and to feel such bliss. Not pain, bliss. Not guilt, love.

There in that tiny apartment, Joan and I performed a ritual that forever freed me from believing that sex and love were anything other than pure and wonderful. That day, I exorcised more than my guilt—I exorcised my attachment to religion because of its inability to go with me as I opened myself to loving.

Now, I ached from the loss of everything we once had. What was it that was pulling me out of all this? I turned away from the building and headed back to the bus stop.

As I waited in the blustering wind, I shuddered at the painful times Joan and I had struggled through.

Then I began to feel fatigue for how hard a trek it had been for the shy young boy within me. I remembered stuttering as a child and my brother teasing me about it, calling me "machine gun" when I c-c-c-c-couldn't get the words s-s-s-started on my tongue. I stuttered all during grade school and learned not to s-s-s-s-start sentences with w-w-w-w-words that began with "c," or "s," or, "w," or any sound that teased the tongue. I simply wouldn't speak if what I wanted to say began with one of those sounds, but in less tense situations, I hunted for a word that I knew I could pronounce. I still had the stutter by high school, but I read somewhere that if I put a pebble under my tongue it wouldn't flutter so badly. So each morning as my brother and I waited for the school bus, I would secretly pick up a few pebbles and slip them under my tongue. Half way into the first year of high school, I was cured.

As the number 76 bus splashed to a stop in front of me, I climbed on and stared absently at the little Italian Christmas lights twinkling on the trees along Lake Shore Drive.

I was about to leave Joan and all I could think of that night was how important she had been in my life. Before I met her, I was the raw kid from Ohio. I bought my first bottle of French wine at her suggestion, and her continental home-cooking blew any concepts I ever had about food. She would have made a wonderful diplomat's wife. She loved giving dinner parties and hosting almost any kind of gathering. Living was one of her arts.

As the bus circled through the snow-covered streets of Lincoln Park, I remembered the summer evening we entertained several Russian bankers. Joan thought a picnic would be fun, and we each carried things across the street to a little hill overlooking a pond. They marveled at the food, the wines, the candelabras, and the white linen tablecloth spread on the grass. Who but Joan would have had the courage to pull that one off? As I watched the city lights twinkling in the pond nearby, I saw how far I had come from being the shy country man/boy she first met.

When I got off the bus, I glanced at our little picnic hill now covered with snow, and realized how much of me had been opened up by Joan's ability to make an art out of living life.

SEVEN

THE LAST NIGHT

Finally the holidays were over, and the first week of January brought with it our last evening together.

During the day, Joan had gone to the store to shop for dinner. While she was there, she bought me a new toothbrush, toothpaste, shampoo and conditioner, and a new deodorant. Trying to be civilized and thoughtful to each other seemed the most natural thing in the world. It was the way we had decided our divorce would be. But it brought up all the associations I had when I had first gone off to summer camp. I felt sick to my stomach at the thought of leaving.

We had prepared well for this last day. We had consulted with two different child psychoanalysts, one for each of the girls, so they would have their own points of view represented. Out of these meetings came the formality of the past month. We each had our own time with each child as we told them we were separating. We reassured them they would be taken care of. I would continue supporting them and seeing them all the time, and much would be the same. I would have my own apartment, though, and would take a few things with me, including some of their things for them to play with when they stayed over.

I thought of the times during the final month that Joan and I cried together, and reconciled, and fought again, and somehow we had gotten through to today. I put the toilet articles on top of the clothes in my suitcase near the bed.

Joan had made dinner and we had tucked the kids in bed early so we could have the late evening to ourselves. We put the jelly-smeared, well-worn records on the funny little phonograph we owned and opened another bottle of wine. And as we had done so often before, we drank and danced to our favorite records and let the thread of our memories together run off the spool. We danced ourselves into a sweaty exhaustion, and I sank, very tipsy, into a sitting position on the floor near the record player.

Suddenly I felt a cold liquid hit the top of my head and splash down around my shoulders. It was like being jolted from the depths of sleep. Then a pungent sweet smell smashed my nostrils, and I couldn't get away from it. While I was sitting there in a puddle of memories, Joan had gotten a bottle of cologne, and with it she was anointing me. She was anointing the loss of her man, the end of her brave second family, the death of love. She was anointing a corpse, baptizing a stillborn marriage, christening a battlefield. She was draping a garland over two warriors who had fallen, but who had fought with all their hearts. She was also baptizing a new life for herself, and for me, that would soon start with the new light. I think she was also offering a sacrifice to the gods, as women do—who know ritual like no man can—by ending the battle with an ablution.

EIGHT

WILLIAM BLAKE

I always thought something would save our marriage as it had always saved us before. But nothing did. We slid down and away from it as freely as a sailor's body being buried at sea.

A protective net had been taken away, and my life was suddenly vulnerable in a way it had never been before. It was sobering—the shattering of the family dream—and frightening to be starting once again in a small apartment, alone.

Did this pain mean I should go back? Was this a sign I had gone too far? Yet, as painful as it was, under it all I felt faint, hesitant feelings that I was moving in the right direction and that a new life was indeed beginning.

I moved into a subleased apartment that my lawyer had found for me in his building. It was decorated with heavy green drapes, velvet overstuffed chairs, and other baroque touches that made me feel as though I had moved into another time period. It was an awful start in many ways.

I spent more and more time alone or at the office, and twice a week I had a night with my daughter Sarah. Lynn, who was about fifteen and in her mother's second divorce, decided that she had had enough of me and fathers leaving, and preferred to sit this one out. It would take years for us to move through this knot in our feelings for one another.

One night, after about a month of separation, in a mutual flight of hope, Joan came over to my apartment. When she'd called earlier and asked to talk, it seemed all right despite the fact that both of us had been told that lawyers could use any intimacy between us as evidence that we were not sure we wanted a divorce. Because my lawyer lived in the apartment below, I secreted Joan in the back way.

She had come with the hope that we might reconcile. She was having as hard a time emotionally as I was, but she had two additional issues to deal with. She wanted me to return home, go into therapy with her, and help her raise the girls. If I returned, she could go back to school for her doctorate and get the house help she needed. She had earned her B.A. but had postponed graduate school until Sarah was older, and now there wouldn't be enough money.

This was another collision of values. There wasn't enough income to maintain the household for Joan and the girls just the way it was, and a small apartment for me, plus two private school tuitions, and two psychoanalysts (I had one and Lynn was going), and have enough left over to create two completely new lives. Something had to give.

As a man, a husband, and a father, it ripped me apart to leave this woman and two young girls. Even though I was not abandoning them, at some level I felt I was. There was something primal, something deep in my male bone marrow, that rose up my spine, pushing me back to the family. It was an urgent call back to the cave that spoke to the protector in me. To resist such a call felt as though it would rend my spirit.

Finding the courage, or the selfishness, or the audacity, to stand fast despite that blood-call was my first conscious choice to override traditional laws of proper conduct and respond to what was in my heart instead.

As I looked deep into myself and asked for truth, my little voice told me that this part of my life was indeed over. The choice was made. I had summoned the courage to act, but with it came an agony all its own. I was causing pain for those I loved most, but I couldn't go back. Joan and I would have to muddle forward as best we could, being as good to each other as we could possibly be.

When we planned the separation and divorce, we very much wanted to be kind and loving to each other and sincerely believed we could succeed in doing so. But that lovely, passionate, painful visit changed everything. I told her the truth. I could not do more than I was already doing financially, and I could not move back to the apartment.

We might have gotten by without a rift if that was all we had tried to handle that night, but there was one more request. If I would not come back, would I at least finance her education? She asked me to guarantee enough support money to get her doctorate. I asked how long it might take. Given her schedule, it might take ten years, she thought.

I couldn't do it. I couldn't offer any more than I already was. And I couldn't guarantee her future, since my feelings about advertising were changing so dramatically.

As I watched her lonely figure pass under the street light outside, there was a part of me that wanted to return and make everything whole again, and help everybody's lives work the way they wanted.

But I'd seen the fury in her face as she left, and I knew in my gut that we were heading for the fight of our lives. When I would not promise the money she wanted, she said she'd churn it up in legal fees. I tried to swallow my fear of the fight I saw beginning, but I could not back down.

That night I felt like an outcast. I had unilaterally acted against some inner image of what an "honorable" man should do. I had broken lifetimes of inner codes. I even felt I had somehow shamed my family to have acted so independently of what "others" wanted.

Later I agreed to have one session with Joan and her Jungian therapist to find out if there was any last chance that we could resolve our conflicts. Joan had pretty well decided to become a Jungian therapist herself, and I agreed to meet with her and her doctor. The session itself led nowhere, mostly because I had no real desire for it to work, but I will forever be grateful to Joan for having introduced me to the therapist. It was through that meeting that I first become acquainted with William Blake, who from then on became a profound guide in my life.

Little did my third-grade nun know when she was teaching us Blake's poem "Tyger, Tyger" that this man so resisted the tyranny of churches. In his work *The Marriage of Heaven and Hell*, Blake put forth his "Proverbs of Hell," which reflected his belief in the superior value of personal action or "desire" over a collective "reason." Many theologians of the time took the position that following the path of reason led ultimately back to religion, while following one's personal desires led to isolation, despair, and finally, hell. Having just chosen to follow my individual "desire" over collective "reason," I was vitally interested in what Blake had to say.

In *The Marriage of Heaven and Hell*, he described how blind it was for people to automatically accept the collective view of morality as "good," while considering individual action as something "evil."

> All Bibles or sacred codes have been the causes of the following errors:
>
> 1. That Man has two real existing principles Viz: a Body & a Soul.
>
> 2. That Energy, call'd Evil, is alone from the Body; & that Reason, call'd Good, is alone from the Soul.

3. That God will torment Man in Eternity for following his Energies.

But the following Contraries to these are True:

1. Man has no Body distinct from his Soul for that call'd Body is a portion of Soul discern'd by the five Senses, the chief inlets of Soul in this age.

2. Energy is the only life and is from the Body and Reason is the bound or outward circumference of Energy.

3. Energy is Eternal Delight.

I loved hearing Blake contradict the theologians idea that "reason" was man's highest expression and individual "energy" was inferior. His belief that the body's individual energy was an expression of the soul on earth gave me insight and courage when I was struggling to trust my own values over those of the collective.

I would take Blake to lunch and sit at the crowded counter downstairs trying to keep my salad dressing off the text. As I fought to overcome my guilts, he was my favorite luncheon partner. What he felt was what I felt. His ideas harmonized with mine and helped me trust my deep internal impulses and my little voice over rational judgements when I had to evaluate what was good versus bad. Here was a large, new step for me—not just to tolerate my desires, but to honor them as a triumph!

Also in *The Marriage of Heaven and Hell*, Blake reaches his simplest and most provocative stance, regarding his "Proverbs of Hell," and he does so almost playfully.

> As I was walking among the fires of hell, [I was] delighted with the enjoyments of Genius' which to Angels look like torment and insanity. I collected some of their Proverbs of Hell, [which] shew the nature of Infernal wisdom better than any description of buildings or garments.

Among them are the following:

- The road of excess leads to the palace of wisdom.

- He who desires but acts not, breeds pestilence.

- No bird soars too high if he soars with his own wings.

- If the fool would persist in his folly he would become wise.

- Prisons are built with stones of Law, Brothels with bricks of Religion.

- You never know what is enough unless you know what is more than enough.

- As the caterpillar chooses the fairest leaves to lay her eggs on, so the priest lays his curse on the fairest joys.

The sense of purpose that I received from Blake was what I needed to resolve my conflicts about leaving my marriage, so it seemed ironic that Joan had introduced me to him.

Carrying Blake in my attaché case each day comforted me. My belief in the inherent worth of human choice was the thread that I followed out of the labyrinth of conflict once again. I had followed it out of my religion a few years before, and now I was following it out of my marriage.

With new trust, I had the sense that my little voice, speaking in creativity and love, really was a valid source of direction—even if it was leading me away from my traditional beliefs.

MAKING THE BREAK

Having the sensitivity to recognize the end of one phase did not prepare me for the onslaught of another. I had simply traded my anger for a more desperate sense of loneliness. Being separated from the comforts of the past magnified my feelings of isolation, and the lack of fulfillment in my work became more obvious.

But being alone and feeling no relief provided me an important opportunity. I had no one else to blame for my problems and was forced to develop a new relationship with myself.

I had always been aware of my inner values and ideals but had imagined them to be vaguely irrelevant to everyday life. Now I'd begun to trust them, and, as often as I could, follow them. I listened intently for inner voices, watched eagerly for internal images, and became aware of even the subtlest feelings in my gut.

With growing courage, I let myself be led by a wellspring of communication that bubbled from within, and with it came a desire for creativity, love, and greater freedom. My upbringing had warned me never to trust my "desires," but now I began to value them above all else. I saw them as the first glimpse of an inner signal that I could follow in my search for fulfillment.

It was easier, however, to identify desires than to satisfy them. It seemed impossible to keep earning a good living and still be true to my idealism. Attempting self-discovery while trying to hold my old life together felt like trying to dismantle a tower while living on the top floor. But I had undertaken the task, and I resolved to go all the way.

NINE

VICE PRESIDENT

I'd heard stories that a beard was supposed to mean something about a man, that it represented a revolution going on inside of him, or that one was about to begin—a theory that proved true in my case.

We didn't really have a dress code at the agency, but beards were few and had never been seen in client meetings. A creative guy was the first to take the chance. We all watched him grow it and wondered if management would make him shave, but when nothing happened, beards began shooting out here and there.

So, shortly after Joan and I separated, I let mine grow also. It came in black, fuzzy, thick, and itchy. I wondered what my superiors were thinking and whether it would affect how they felt about me, but having it gave me a feeling of release. It was a natural and primitive part of myself that came out during the night, and it felt good not to cut it off first thing every morning. It was exciting to awaken and let the animal stay with me as I walked around the city. To some it could mean that I no longer cared, but to me it meant that I cared more than ever.

It was noon hour as I took my scraggly, new beard into a private executive's retreat high atop our building, overlooking both

Grant Park and Lake Michigan. The sky was bright and glorious. I went to one of the windows and looked down. The Art Institute lay at the end of a strip of green carpet that spread south below us, and hundreds of white sailboats flickered nearby in the harbor.

I had raised my kids all over the map below me. I first met Lynn when she was five, right there on the Art Institute steps. How many times had I taken the girls to the Field Museum on the curve of Lake Shore Drive, and just beyond to Soldier Field, where we would ride our bikes on the Fourth of July and watch the fireworks? There was Shedd Aquarium, and beyond that the Museum of Science and Industry, where we would go as a last resort on those frigid weekends when it was just too cold to go anywhere else. It made me sad, looking at this scene, but there was high energy all around me as people started coming into the room.

I'd worked hard all these years, and this was the day one of the prizes I had been waiting impatiently for was finally to arrive. I had waited for this the way a high school athlete awaits his first monogram, or a senior officer anticipates his gold stars. Out of the three dozen offices around the world, and almost 2,000 people in our office alone, management had pulled twelve men together for lunch to announce they had been made vice presidents.

A high gaiety began lifting me toward the bar as we all ordered drinks. I nodded and smiled, taking a quick inventory of how young each one was, or how old, how many creative people, and how many business types. After measuring everyone, I took a double vodka on the rocks and touched glasses with several guys near me.

The promotion gave me a lot of satisfaction. It had been a long trip, starting when I was a kid drawing pictures of cows in the fields, continuing as I worked my way through art school, and now culminating with my making it to the fortieth floor of advertising. I felt like I had proven something to someone, but I couldn't remember who. Maybe my parents. Maybe the little kid from Ohio.

In one sense, this achievement was liberating. I felt more mobile, even more free to leave, now that I was reaching my goal. I had driven myself toward this for years and making it was like planting a flag at the top of the corporate mountain. Arriving here had made all the efforts and sacrifices along the way worthwhile.

But there was also a vague irrelevance about it. I had a nagging feeling that I wasn't going to be with these people much longer, as if I were seeing the group from a distance, and they were a mere memory. It must be what a premonition of death is like, a view of a picture that no longer has you in it. The group would be here but I would not. But where would I be? What would I be doing?

The chairman of the board took the center of the floor as we made a semicircle. He had a wide, satisfied grin on his face as he began to speak. His hand always shook from tension, and this time he was holding a drink, so I could hear the ice cubes faintly tinkle in his glass.

"Well, everyone here is a vice president except one person!" A cheer and laughter went up.

Henry must have said this very thing to every new group of vice presidents that came through, but this time I was the one who took the bait.

"Who isn't?" I asked. A hidden fear had somehow spoken.

Several guys laughed.

"Marshall," he said, and pointed to our president. I laughed nervously as an embarrassed glow bled down into my shirt.

"You guys are the future of the company, the best we have, and you'll be running the place long after I and most of top management will be retired. So we chose carefully—we have to protect our retirement benefits!"

Everybody laughed, but I heard how true that probably was. I looked around, and the initiates did look earnest, clean, and dependable.

"You can make this agency any way you want it. Just keep those retirement checks going out!" We laughed again.

With this, he handed out little boxes of business cards that said "Vice President" just under our names.

"Oh," he added, "we have flowers going out to all of your wives today so they can take part in this celebration!"

I was stunned. I didn't want Joan to get them. It would be too painful for her to get flowers for something wonderful that was happening to me but that she would not share in.

After he finished speaking, I angled over to Henry and whispered in his ear.

"I hadn't mentioned it, but Joan and I are separated, and I don't …" I trailed off, unable to speak.

He looked up in shock, first at my eyes, then at my beard. He knew Joan because we had often seen each other socially and they got along well.

"Can you stop the florist?" I finally asked.

He nodded, mumbled an apology, and seemed to make a mental note to talk to me about it later.

Sipping my drink, I studied the faces around the room and realized that several other guys were going through divorces too. I imagined us as soldiers being decorated at a hospital near the front. Then suddenly I felt sad. I had worked so hard for this and now, just as I was getting it, I was alone and couldn't celebrate with my family. I covered my feelings with another martini, which I rarely did at lunchtime, and knocked my way around the room congratulating all the wounded.

TEN

BREAKING POINT

The divorce that had begun in an affectionate mood grew more and more bitter. As the months wore on, I buried myself in my work and sought solace from the political campaigns that I loved so much. I felt myself growing weaker emotionally and physically and could tell that the continuing pressures of business and the divorce were taking their toll.

Joan's lawyers put forth proposal after proposal, each one based on the desire to guarantee her the ten years of support she wanted for her doctorate. But there were no savings, no house, and no other joint investments beyond personal belongings. I had a profit-sharing trust at the agency that extended back years before the marriage, and some company stock that had little equity because I still owed much of what I'd borrowed to buy it.

Despite the fact that there was little to negotiate, her lawyers wanted to fulfill their client's dream of becoming a therapist. And since our offer of half the value of everything, including stocks and profit sharing, plus child support and private school for Sarah, still wouldn't be enough to ensure Joan's Ph.D., they were willing to fight.

For my lawyer, the issue was to keep from mortgaging my next ten years to pay off an eight-year marriage. I couldn't guarantee more than we were already offering. I knew deep in my bones that a major shift in my life was already under way, and I could not predict where it would lead.

That's where the issues stayed frozen for the more than two years it would be before the divorce became final.

I met Carla in a political campaign. A drama school teacher, she loved politics and television. Her dream was to work as an on-air reporter for one of the networks. Another Cronkite, she would tell me. It had been almost a year and half since I had left Joan, and my heart was heavy with the stalemated divorce. Carla had been married for a short time, had a simple divorce, and was having trouble understanding why Joan and I couldn't settle our differences without the pain we were inflicting on each other.

Carla wanted a child, but I was having difficulty trusting anyone so soon after the separation. I couldn't even commit to our relationship, much less consider another marriage and more children.

"You remind me of a great Victorian house," she said at one point. "All the rooms are already full of stuff, and it seems there might not be room for anything else."

I wondered the same thing.

Over the next few months I introduced her to several producers and succeeded at helping her get on the air. But we were on again, off again, and soon I had two separations to deal with.

I did my best to hide my struggle with the divorce, and the stress it was causing me, from the people I worked with every day and from our clients. Until the divorce was settled, I couldn't leave the agency for a new job or make any other kind of move. I felt frustrated and held back. Waiting for the lawyers to reach agreement became its own kind of prison. I began stopping by the bar after work, and I wasn't getting any exercise except that blessed walk home up Michigan Avenue every night.

Our lawyers were bogged down. Joan continued to want what she wanted and was willing to wait it out, regardless of costs. Although I could understand her desires, I wasn't willing to put myself in debt to the future more than I already was. We had locked horns and only the lawyers were winning. I was getting pretty wobbly with the struggle—not feeling well, drinking a little too much, and working too hard. The worst was the waiting, having my career put on hold, and especially not knowing where my life was going.

I was constantly tired and had gained some weight, but there were a few other signs of fatigue that I allowed no one to see. I was running weaker than I was willing to admit and felt more tense when I made presentations. I didn't know anyone with whom I could unload my feelings, and every now and then I would find myself in tears, alone in my office with the door securely closed.

One busy week I went to New York on Monday, returned to Chicago for a court appearance on Tuesday, finished some Doughboy storyboards for a Wednesday meeting in Minneapolis, and was also preparing for a meeting in Cincinnati on Friday. But what happened on Wednesday in Minneapolis made all the difference in my life from then on.

The account group, some creative people, and I had arrived at Pillsbury the night before. We had too much wine and too much dinner with the client and had gone to bed late. The following morning we went to their conference room to present our fall campaign. Their president was there, along with the head of marketing and a number of other research and advertising executives. We were in good shape with Pillsbury because the Doughboy was selling plenty of product, and this new campaign was more of the same. I expected no problems.

To cover my increased stress, which sometimes came from hangovers, I had fallen into taking a couple of Valium before important meetings to hide any signs of anxiety.

The meeting began, and as my time approached I swung my chair around and began looking over the storyboards, frame by frame, to rehearse myself. I was more nervous than usual, but knew I would override the feeling once I stood up and began talking.

Making presentations and speaking in public had been difficult when I first started in business. But I had gradually learned to live with this part of my job, and then to even love it, and I often looked forward to all the theatrical aspects. But something was rising inside of me that was troubling me that day. I couldn't really connect with the commercials, and I didn't have the enthusiasm that usually helps carry the power of an idea. When it was my turn, I stood up, spread out the storyboards, and turned around.

I opened my mouth, but instead of my voice growing stronger, it started weak and stayed weak. What I was saying sounded foreign to me, and ideas that had been important earlier were now dimming as I spoke. Finally my words trailed off into silence. My mouth dried up, thick with cottony phlegm. My shirt flooded with sweat, and the light in the room darkened to gray impressions.

I couldn't remember what I wanted to say. I couldn't even remember why I was there. As I turned back to look at the storyboards, they had no meaning either. My mind had wiped clean. For a few moments, I couldn't even remember where or who I was. Things around me were familiar, but they had lost any meaning. Standing there with no words, I felt like a slow-motion train wreck that had suddenly hit the room. I became embarrassed when I saw mouths drop open, and faces turning red and white. One of the agency people tried to make light of it, but nobody laughed. I just stood there, because, after all, it was my meeting.

Finally, the president of the division asked if I would like a cup of coffee. I nodded that I would as I slowly sank into my chair and pulled the sticky shirt away from my chest. My mouth was so dry I could hardly swallow. When the coffee was poured I was shaking so much I could barely get the cup to my lips with both hands.

With nowhere to hide, and nothing more to hide from, I started to tell the group, some of whom I had been out with the night before, exactly what was happening. In front of everyone, I now confessed what I had worked so hard to conceal. I spoke softly of the court appearances, the plane trips across the country, the late nights at work, and the pain. The room was silent and everyone's attention was focused intensely on me—but not with the critical eyes of corporate executives. The veneer had dropped, and they had all welded to me as if I was their stricken brother.

Eventually, I got up to finish the presentation, but the account executive insisted that I sit down. I felt torn. I didn't want anything to go wrong with the work, but I had already blown it. Finally, I sat down and watched while one of my writers presented my part.

We all left together in a cab, but I was still a zombie by the time we got to the airport. Nobody tried to see the good side of what happened. I guess because nobody could find one.

I felt split right up the center. I couldn't let an incident like that happen ever again. I couldn't override my feelings any longer.

By the time I got back to my apartment, I was beginning to feel more myself, but the night was long and filled with images that melted like film caught in a hot projector. What the hell had happened to me? What was this trying to tell me? I was frightened and lonely, but looking down into the streets of Chicago, I could think of no one to call.

ELEVEN

THE AFTERMATH

As I reflected on things that had happened to me since the separation from Joan, I began to feel afraid that I had let some monster out of the bag. I was certainly no happier alone than married, so what had I gained? And the ordeal of trying to reach a settlement was taking a toll that didn't seem worth it.

At the same time, I felt less and less purpose in staying in advertising. It had become too much a lie to make the constant stress worthwhile. The meetings came too often and were too much like entering a bullring. I still had the Pillsbury account and it was still in good shape, but I was worried that I might blow another client meeting.

I dreamed more and more of starting over somewhere, maybe even in art, living more simply and attending to the creative muse that had been so trampled in the hard-sell world of advertising. I still felt that I couldn't make any changes until the divorce was settled, but as I considered my future options, film continued to draw me. So I went to the movies often, taking Sarah with me when I could.

Part of what was holding me was the fear of giving up my success in advertising to follow what often felt like a pipe dream.

My rational mind would think about going to another agency, but I kept remembering that nothing would really change because I would still have my basic conflict with advertising. When I let myself feel what I wanted, it was something more artistic, not something that would take me further into business.

It had always been difficult for me to give myself what I really wanted. Instead, I usually forced myself to do what seemed most reasonable. It was hard to let myself follow my desires, not just because of my religious upbringing, but because they felt like they came from a dark, mysterious pit inside me that couldn't be trusted. Only if I believed that some outside source would approve of my ideas would I give them my blessing. I just couldn't trust the urges that came from within, especially if I thought they were controversial.

I had not learned to trust my dreams, and now I could see that it was because I had not yet learned how to build a secure base inside myself. I had bought my parents' values, the agency's strategies, and even the agendas of my political friends, but I never had the guts to really follow my own. My security base, financial base, social position, and corporate identity all flowed from my work in the agency, and now I felt like it owned me. I couldn't quite get the knack of how to build a sense of purpose within myself.

I ached to be like a Picasso, who created a whole world out of his own gut, or even a Disney. Still, I felt optimistic. I could see that a brighter theme was beginning with my having the courage to leave the marriage and go for what felt right to me.

As painful as it was, when I finally acted to change my life, things began to move as if with an energy and life of their own. I could feel change moving inside, often like a stiff spring wind. As I stuck by my resolves and held fast to my courage, the grip of my past loosened and I slowly began to feel a vague movement forward. I even felt a little more in control.

A new course had been set invisibly, and I was slowly moving out of the harbor. I couldn't see the ocean yet, but a sense of adventure filled me, and I could feel the fresh salt air in my lungs.

I moved from the small, dark, furnished place where Joan had visited me, to a bright apartment in one of the Mies van der Rohe glass buildings on Lake Shore Drive. The move was another symbol of my letting myself have what I wanted. I had always admired these clear, all-glass structures but never thought for a moment I would live in one.

Each week Sarah would visit me, staying overnight, once during the week and once on the weekend. Lynn still would not speak to me. She needed to side with her mother against the enemy, and I guess to my small family I had become just that.

But during the whole tortuous divorce, Sarah stayed my friend, and I stayed hers. I always felt her support and she, I think, felt mine. We did many things together on weekends, but mostly she loved to draw with me, and we did so for hours on the living room floor in front of the giant bank of floor-to-ceiling windows. I would watch her watching me draw, and could see the innocent child still there, even though she was having to be very adult at times. She would take the marker I'd set down and put the color on the face she was drawing. I noticed that she was a more adventurous colorist than I and wondered if she, too, would become an artist one day.

We also went to a lot of movies and swam regularly at an indoor swimming club I joined mostly for her. We tried to make good on our relationship with each other, and we did.

I will always remember how Sarah stuck by me, even when she must have heard awful things about me at home. It was never what she said with words that showed me the depth of her understanding. It was in her always being there, no matter what, and without criticism.

I learned through taking care of her how to take care of the memory of myself as a child, who at the time hadn't known how to ask for love. When I loved Sarah and gave myself to her, I was giving love to the forgotten child inside me. I was re-raising the little guy who felt so lonely, finally giving him what he wanted.

I often thought about a precious moment with Sarah that happened when she was about five or six. She used to anticipate my arrival home from work by watching at the window, or sometimes by going across the street to the bus stop to wait for me. On one rainy day she was sitting at the window looking out over the park, watching for the bus that would be carrying me home. She noticed that the rain was slackening, and growing impatient, put on her yellow slicker and galoshes and trudged out to sit on the bench at the bus stop. Suddenly it began to pour.

Because it was raining so hard by the time I got near home, I got off one stop early, where it was protected by tall trees. When I got into the apartment, Joan asked where Sarah was. Concerned because I hadn't seen her, we rushed to the window to look for her in the park. There she was, beyond sheets of gray rain, sitting on the bench in her small yellow slicker waiting for the bus, soaking wet. It cut to my heart with a gentleness that took my breath away. I put my coat back on, grabbed my umbrella, and went back outside.

Rather than take this moment away from her, I went back to the earlier stop, got on a bus, and rode up to where she was waiting. I got off the bus with tears in my eyes and swooped her up in my arms, carrying her across the wet grass toward home.

"Put me on your shoulders, Daddy," she cried, "I want to be on your shoulders!"

I collapsed the umbrella, swung her up on my shoulders, and we laughed as the rain came down across our faces.

Every Saturday morning I would walk several blocks to the strategy meetings of a friend who was running for governor of Illinois. Perhaps I would not have been doing this every Saturday if it were not for the fact that I had grown quite lonely for company.

As I walked along the blustering Chicago streets, I realized this was my seventeenth political campaign. There had been a U.S. senator, a number of congressmen, a state treasurer, state senators, state legislators, aldermen, judges, and now a governor. And we'd won all but a few.

Yet these campaigns were beginning to tire me. The last one had burned me up pretty badly. After the candidate I'd been working with got the nomination, he dropped the independent support group who had won it for him in favor of the regular organization.

Until that time, I had been in politics for the fun of it and only for candidates that appealed to me. But as I discovered, politicians often chose far differently than they originally promised. So after that campaign, I lost interest. When I saw people move to Springfield or Washington to continue their careers, I couldn't see a place in it for myself. I had no desire to work in government, and when the idealism was gone, I had no reason to be there.

I made up my mind that this governor's race would be my last. I had worked on the previous campaigns for ideals, but this time it was for a friend.

It started snowing harder, so I pulled my overcoat up under my chin as I jumped across the slush in front of the Hancock Building. I was a little late for the meeting and wanted to get in out of the cold, but as I got to the revolving door I hesitated a moment and then decided not to go up. I was so tired from all the work at the office, I simply could not bear a day of work in politics. None of it felt connected to me anymore. I hailed a cab, asked the driver for his newspaper, and looked for a good movie to see. In small ways, I was learning to give myself what I wanted.

In a few months the election was held and my friend became governor. I took a month's paid vacation and served on the Governor's Transition Task Force, which made preparations for the new administration taking office. As much fun and excitement as the inauguration was, and as much pleasure as I felt in having helped elect a friend to be the new governor, it had little other meaning for me. The last time I saw Carla she was covering the inaugural festivities for network television.

TWELVE

CALIFORNIA IDEAS

One of the clients I enjoyed working with most was a winery that Nestle had bought out in the Napa Valley called Beringer. What a pleasure it was to get on a plane and go out to that rich, sunny valley, so far from the overcast skies and subzero weather of Chicago.

I felt very connected to wine. My grandfather Korb, whom I loved more than anyone else in the world, made wine in his basement each year. When I was small, I loved going down into his musty cellar with him to taste the homemade wine, sucking it through the hose from the dark keg below. All during the year I'd go to my grandparents' house to listen to the cuckoo clock, watch his wonderful gardens grow, and eat out of their amply stocked refrigerator. I'd go there to plant radishes in the spring, pick grapes in the fall, and make wine in the basement.

My grandfather died one morning at Mass after having received communion. When he was alive, he brought joy and buoyancy to our family. But after he was gone, a thick grayness seemed to descend on us that never lifted again. The only consolation my mother found was that her father had at least died in a place he loved so much.

Many years later I was repeating the ritual I had learned from him, but now it was on the twenty-first floor of a Mies high-rise. I pressed grapes into a couple of plastic garbage cans, fermented them, and corked the wine into bottles just the way I loved it as child. How I savored making wine that fall. It was as if my grandfather was visiting me, and the innocence and the contact with the earth that I felt through him returned in the process.

On the flights back from San Francisco with my bags full of California wines, I began to wonder why some people lived out there while others lived under the bleak weather back in Chicago.

I originally went to Chicago because I wanted to work on the biggest accounts in the country, in "the major leagues," I would say with a certain self-satisfaction. That meant New York or Chicago, but New York never turned me on when I was younger, and Chicago strangely did.

Now I felt that California was somehow a more exciting place to live. It was more sunny, more free, and more inventive than any place I had ever been. It wasn't like Chicago. Chicago had developed a kind of mundane dreariness for me, as if hard work, dark skies, and long rows of sooty buildings were the way my life would always be. California was warm and sunny—God it was sunny—a garden for growing things and free of the moody clouds of Midwestern winters.

Adults never went nude where I came from, but during the sixties, stories drifted back to Chicago about just how free Californians were. We read in *Time* magazine about Esalen, and about how people were being massaged naked in the open air along the ocean and having workshops in which they would hug and touch each other. Men never hugged in the Midwest when I was growing up—not even sons and fathers—and people made fun of the land of fruits and nuts. The Ohio child inside of me was shocked at the immorality and the ad man was cynical, but the newly emerging adult was quietly intrigued. I had a sense that angels were landing in California, and that some kind of liberation had begun.

It had been a horrendous winter. I flew from O'Hare Field one morning and it was almost twenty below, and when I got off the plane in Minneapolis it was twenty-five below. It was the only time in my life that I saw spit turn to ice before it hit the ground. The only good thing was that a deal was coming together with Joan. I heard rumors that she was thinking about getting married, and thought that might be why. I began to hold my breath.

Amid the usually hectic weeks we were putting in, I was asked to pitch in on a new Philip Morris product, a small cigar. I agreed because my creative group loved working on new assignments. It gave them an opportunity to shine, but my heart was not in it any more. We came up with some exciting material, and I was asked if I would go to New York personally to present it to their management. A few other campaigns were to be shown, but ours was the one chosen as the agency's recommendation.

I was living two lives. One was as a creative director who had to force himself to get the work out, and the other was a sensitive man whose guts were churning from the split he felt inside. Standing in front of people and presenting material that the creative director had developed had become almost impossible for the sensitive man. But the task could be made tolerable with a Valium, and that's how I was getting through most meetings these days. I had grown up taking medicines to quiet the various rebellions within the body, so taking them to get through work never felt unusual to me. Tranquilizers were one of the tools of the trade.

The presentation went well, and the client loved the work, but the meeting had unsettled me. They were considering marketing small cigars because Congress had passed no legislation against advertising them on television. However, I learned in the meeting that the client really had no intention of running the campaign.

It was frustrating. Each group had worked hard, investing valuable creative and personal time with no real reward. On the plane back to Chicago that night, I sat with another creative guy who'd made one of the other presentations. I didn't know it when I sat down, but he was thinking about getting out of the agency, just as I was.

"We're thinking about starting a new shop," he said, though I suspected that they had gone a lot farther than just thinking or he wouldn't be telling me about it.

"I'm thinking about splitting too," I said.

"Going to another agency?"

"No, I'd like to get out of the business entirely."

Because I had been keeping so much of what I was feeling to myself, I was surprised when I heard some of my most private thoughts come tumbling out of my mouth.

"When are you leaving?" I asked, giving myself time to consider what I had just told him.

"Actually, I'm giving my notice at the end of the week. We're going to open a place next month."

"That's wonderful!" I responded with genuine excitement for him.

I had often dreamed about starting my own agency and had even done some rudimentary planning about it with a friend who was also a creative director. But when he was given a major promotion, he lost interest. I never quite had the courage to step out alone, and I didn't know anyone else I wanted to do it with.

"What are you going to do?" he asked me.

"I'm going to California." I smiled as I listened to myself saying things that I had never put into words.

"Really! Well, congratulations. What're you going to do out there?"

"Well, I'm not sure yet."

My smile was broad as I savored what I heard myself saying. I guessed that I was going to California, but I wasn't sure how I was going to do it or what I would do when I got there.

When I got back to my apartment, it was late. I sat down and watched the city lights outside the high bank of windows.

Glancing down at the coffee table, I noticed all the film books I had bought over the last few months.

The trip to Philip Morris troubled me. As tired and busy as I was, I didn't like putting all that effort into an advertising campaign that wasn't intended to run. Most of the fun of advertising was seeing it on television and watching sales results come in.

More than that was bothering me, though. I felt used and manipulated into doing things I would have never done by choice. I had always been entirely satisfied with simply doing good creative work, but now I found myself in conflict if I couldn't believe in a project.

It troubled me that my values were separating me from a business I had loved, but I felt the clouds lift when I recalled the conversation on the plane. Going to California really excited me! Seeing myself suddenly become enthusiastic, I realized that I simply had to do what I said I would. As crazy as it sounded, I couldn't back off. The impulse had an imperative quality about it that my best creative ideas often had. I had built my career following such creative impulses, but I'd rarely followed them to plan my life. In that moment, it became the most daring thing on earth to follow that feeling, and I couldn't contain the excitement.

So it was on that plane trip, returning from New York, that I first learned that I was going to hang it up. Now all I had to do was find a way, or make a way, to do it.

The idea was so impulsive that I felt as though I had thrown myself off a cliff. Soon a more rational mind stepped in to make a plan. The most secure way was to resign as creative director and transfer to our Los Angeles office as a producer. The credibility of a long career with a major company would make financing a house and car much easier. Also, working in the business I knew so well would give me time to look around and find a way into film. But what mattered to me most was that I was going to California.

THIRTEEN

BREAKING OUT

On April Fools' Day, after twenty-six grueling months, the divorce became final with a settlement of pretty much what we had offered at the beginning.

My lawyer put his arm on my shoulder as we walked out of the courtroom. We had spent more than two years and far too much money to arrive back where we started, but it was worth it. I finally had my freedom.

"Care to get drunk?" he smiled.

"Yes," I responded, tired of the whole mess. "But I'd rather go somewhere for a long rest."

When I got back to the office I phoned the chairman, a man I considered as much a friend as a boss. My head was light from getting my personal situation settled, and I felt like I had finally severed a diseased part of myself.

"I'd like to have a few minutes with Henry," I told his secretary.

"Hold on, Don, I'll check his schedule for you."

She put me on hold for a moment, then returned. "How about tomorrow?" she asked, "About ten?"

"Great. Thanks, Sylvia."

I hung up the phone and told my secretary I was leaving for the day. Then I walked lightheartedly through the late afternoon Michigan Avenue crowds and spent the evening plotting my strategy for the next day's meeting.

Henry offered me coffee as I sat down on the sofa facing him.

"I want to go to California as an agency producer," I said as calmly as I could.

He looked at me as though I was crazy, as I had suspected he might.

"That doesn't make any sense," he said.

I blurted out the months of pent-up fatigue, the bitterness about the divorce, the conflict of values I was feeling about the business, but mentioned nothing about movies.

"But becoming an agency producer isn't going to solve that, it's still advertising," he responded. "Furthermore, we couldn't pay you what you're making here. And besides there's no future for you in production. Why don't you just take a long vacation?"

Making a big salary no longer mattered to me. The one thought on my mind was to somehow heal the split I was feeling. I told him that my mind was made up, that I'd go if I had to leave the agency to do it. This was one of the few times in my career I was willing to stand firm, flatly confronting authority for something I wanted, and now the door suddenly opened. I found myself telling him what I wanted instead of asking. When he saw that I really meant what I said, he agreed to let me go.

Henry and I had known each other for years, and he respected me both as a person and as a creative director. Why he actually agreed to the transfer, I have no idea. At first I thought it was because he figured I would go to California for a year or so and get so bored with the job that I'd come back. Perhaps it was the element of surprise.

He shook his head in disbelief as the meeting ended. No one had ever given up a top job in the home office for producing commercials in a branch office. We shook hands and I left, closing the door behind me.

After the meeting, I headed straight to personnel to let them know I was moving to Los Angeles. Then I checked the production schedule and put myself on the next pool of commercials being produced on the West Coast. I would have the better part of three weeks to get myself settled out there, and then I would come back for two months to wind things up in Chicago. With my next steps planned, I was lightheaded as I moved through the halls feeling what Alan Watts called a "vacation experience," the feeling of heightened release that comes with leaving all responsibility behind and heading for the open road.

After landing in Los Angeles, one of the first places I went after I checked into the hotel was to automobile dealers. I had not owned a car since art school because while living downtown it was more convenient to take buses, taxis, or rent cars as needed. Here, it was a different story. In Los Angeles you *are* your car, and so as a coming-out present I borrowed against my company stock to make a down payment on a Mercedes.

Soon I was driving all over Los Angeles, house shopping and trying to find a neighborhood that felt right to me. It was a city of two-story buildings and I found no place that had a community feel to it. A friend, the film critic for a Chicago newspaper, once described Los Angeles as "the only city on earth that, no matter where you are, you always feel like you're on your way to the airport." I now knew what he meant.

I felt best in the Santa Monica Mountains, so I began driving through the canyons, jotting down realtors' numbers and calling them when I got back to the hotel. I had been in apartments for the last fifteen years and after driving the canyons, I was not about to move to California and sit in another little box twenty stories off the ground.

One day, I drove into Nichols Canyon, a rustic country canyon that leaves Hollywood Boulevard and runs up almost to the top of the mountain to Mulholland Drive. At the bottom there was a dam with a small pool of water filled with rushes, so I stopped the car and walked over. There below I saw a doe and two fawns standing in the shallow water. A powerful longing for nature engulfed me. I missed the farmland from when I was growing up, and here in this canyon, a few hundred yards off Hollywood Boulevard, I found nature in its most seminal forms.

When I got back to the Beverly Hills Hotel, I had a message from a real estate agent. I called him back right away.

"You might like this one. It's higher priced than what you've been wanting, but it just came on the market this morning and I haven't shown it to anyone else yet. It has a canyon view. Do you want to see it?"

"Which canyon?"

"Nichols Canyon."

A jolt of energy went through me and we set an appointment to meet in his office as soon as I could get there.

The agent was driving, and as we wound up through the canyon I began to get more and more excited. After we had driven about ten minutes, we turned up a steep incline off the main road and I checked the road marker.

"Astral Drive?" I asked.

"Yes, Astral Drive. It has a full view of Los Angeles, and even Catalina on clear days."

Only in California, I thought.

Then we turned down a five-hundred foot driveway that ran along the mountain and dropped down into the parking area to a house that was totally secluded.

"Here it is."

My heart was beating so furiously I could hardly stand it. We had barely gotten out of the car, and already, everything inside me was urging me to take the place.

When the agent opened the front door he stepped aside to let me go through ahead of him. The walls were mostly glass, which brought the outside in. We could see the San Bernardino Mountains to the north and the canyon to the west, and there was a wonderful secluded swimming pool to the south.

"I'll take it," I said, grinning, "and don't tell me what it costs. Just tell me how much a month."

Once I was back in the agency and it was announced that I was leaving for California, things changed. The stream of power that seemed always to surge through my office was suddenly diverted to those who were now in control. My raging career had turned to a dry river bottom. I was not prepared for the impact that came from the loss of power. I had no idea how much of my ego was borrowed from the corporation. One minute I had a bloated sense of who I was, and the next moment I was nothing.

No one at the office was particularly interested in hearing that I had found a magical house in the mountains or that I'd bought a new car, so there was almost no sense of celebration. My friends, people in my creative group, others I worked with, began to ignore me. I felt as though I had crossed some invisible line and had become an outcast.

I concluded that many people had been friendly out of a need to get along at the office, so I decided to talk with a friend with whom I'd worked on political campaigns. He was stacking storyboards along the rails in the conference room when I found him. Assuming that he had heard about my move by this time, I grinned as I approached and was eager for his response. When he saw me, his mouth turned down in wry disapproval. He shook his head and said, "You asshole."

"What?" I murmured in disbelief.

"Agency producer?" The words came in a disdainful slow motion that were intended to twist in my gut like a knife. He turned away when one of his people called him, and I wandered out of the room in shock.

I must have broken an unwritten law—but I didn't know which. The only thing I could figure was that I had severed a bond that develops between corporate men. Perhaps while working together we had welded like soldiers in combat and to leave was to betray a trust.

But that couldn't be the whole truth of it. Maybe by setting myself free of the usual restraints and discarding what so many were still working for, I was causing more turmoil than I knew. Maybe some people felt threatened when I threw it all over mid-career to do what I wanted in California. Either way, it was a sour note on which to leave Chicago, and I was happy it was all over.

But some friends were pleased. The governor had invited me to dinner at the executive mansion in celebration of my going and as thanks for working in the administration. A plane was at Meigs Field in Chicago and would bring me down to Springfield.

The evening was wonderful and I was very, very happy. We recalled stories from many campaigns, I turned over my files and some photos, and when it was time to go, I was taken back to the airport.

The tiny plane took off without any difficulty, and in a few minutes we were droning northward toward Chicago again. I turned off the cabin light and watched the tiny groves of lights twinkling below. It reminded me of Ohio and the countryside I flew over to get home in the early years of advertising. Now I was almost forty and I was leaving the familiar again, and it was just as exciting and frightening as it had been many years ago.

The weekend I packed, Sarah slept over to help me. I wanted her to be part of the moving so she would feel connected to it, and so part of her could go with me in the boxes we packed.

A few weeks earlier, when I had told her I was leaving, she cried. She just broke down and cried and cried. I held her and cried too. I cried many times again during the next weeks as I sorted and packed. I cried for the loss of her. I cried for the loss of our family. I cried because I was homesick for a life that was not to be anymore. I cried as I went through my effects as though they belonged to someone deceased.

I promised Sarah she would have her own room when she visited me, and I packed her pictures so we could hang them on the walls of her new room. I promised I would have her out as soon as I could so she could swim in the pool and play on the mountain. We would discover Los Angeles together, and in the meantime, we'd write and I would send her an allowance each Monday morning, first thing.

We packed her colored markers and folded her nightie and other things into a box with my clothes. Then, one at a time, we put her toys into a box and marked it "Sarah's room" in large black letters. When I looked at her that evening, there were little tears rolling down her sad cheeks and I wondered, once again, if I was doing the right thing. I didn't know what was right anymore. I just ached to leave and ached for leaving. How do you know what is right when what you do is a kind of torture to the little spirits you've conceived and raised?

In that moment, I looked at Sarah and asked the God that made this creation why there were so many painful things, why there were so many sweet/sad partings, and why there were so few moments of real joy.

THE LEAP

This stage was a dramatic leap from the path of the familiar into an abyss of the unknown.

In this harrowing experience, I discovered that the secret was to walk through my fears rather than run from them, and that my sense of limitation dissolved with my courage to act. Learning this turned out to be one of the most important benefits of this phase, because in the full course of my journey, I would have to leap again and again.

I saw no clear path ahead, but all the signals from inside indicated that my old way of living was over. As these impulses grew, I knew that if I didn't commit to a totally new life, I would certainly die at the hands of the old one.

Once my choices were made, I began experiencing an almost heady sense of freedom. After so many years in harness, life had become urgent and real again, as if I was holding something new and precious in the palms of my hands.

There was also an awesome feeling of responsibility, a desire to make something extraordinary of the life that was now back in my charge. And floating beneath the surface of my awareness was the feeling that it was time to fulfill a special promise that I'd made to myself years before.

On the outside, I had thrown myself into a new life. On a more profound level, I'd woven the cocoon in which I would slip from one stage of life into another.

THE COCOON

After larval growth has finished comes the last larval moult. The next stage is entirely different. The pupa is an inactive, mummylike object with appendages tightly fastened down. It may have some power to wriggle its abdomen, but that is all. It remains in one spot and apparently does nothing. Internally, however, a drastic reorganization is taking place.

Alexander B. Klots
A Field Guide to Butterflies

The hero goes forward in his adventure until he comes to the "threshold guardian" at the entrance to the zone of magnified power. Such custodians bound the world in the four directions—also up and down —standing for the limits of the … present sphere, or life horizon. Beyond them is darkness, the unknown, and danger; just as beyond the parental watch is danger to the infant …

Joseph Campbell
The Hero with a Thousand Faces

FOURTEEN

NICHOLS CANYON

Moving into the house in Nichols Canyon was like moving to a magical planet. The house was on an acre of hillside land that looked across the canyon and when two adjacent acres became available, I added them for privacy. Dozens of eucalyptus trees lined the driveway and surrounded the house, the kind that have pencil-slender trunks of purple and pink bark that strips off in sheets. And there were elms and Scotch pines that whistled in the wind after the sun set.

The first night was frightening. When it gets dark up in the canyons, black is not dark enough to describe it. Night birds sang outside, which was both strange and wonderful, but they did little to calm my fear. I'd hear far-off dogs barking from some lost place in the canyon below. Owls would hoot sharply from the dark pines around the house, and coyotes would scream like hyenas as the pack ran down the driveway. After fifteen years in high-rises, this was camping in the wilderness.

I would awaken before daybreak, get up, make coffee, and shower before the pink light reached over the horizon. Then just as the sun was rising, I would walk around the mountain and see the hazy city etched in soft pinks and oranges. Emerging from shadows, I could see Universal Studios over in Studio City, and

Paramount lying asleep in the gentle smog of Hollywood. There were the old Goldwyn Studios on Santa Monica Boulevard that I could see only because I knew they were there, and 20th Century-Fox looked almost golden behind the twin towers of Century City. Beyond, if I squinted, I could see the sound stages of MGM and United Artists in Culver City.

As I walked around the mountain, many thoughts and ideas bobbed to the surface of my mind, some new and some that had lain buried under years of corporate pressure. I had begun to read books again—not popular books, but books about the nature of things—and my mind started expanding as though a tight band had been removed. I began to paint watercolor landscapes and carried home plants that I found on the mountainside. I dusted off a book on bonsai trees that I got in Chicago but had never read, and I bought two potted trees from a local Japanese gardener. One was a black pine and the other a weeping elm. I put them in the shade near the end of the pool and cared for them every day.

I felt like an exhausted sailor who, near death, had flung himself up on a tropical island after a shipwreck. I was completely spent but safe, and grateful that I had survived a desperate time to finally reach shore. And what a paradise I had found. Now that I was safe, I began to open myself to feelings I hadn't had in a lifetime. It was as though a hard, gristly part of my life had ended, and a softer, more internal time had begun. After years of self-imposed corporate exile from myself, I had managed to escape. I laughed out loud realizing that I *had* actually escaped, and the excitement of my new freedom pulsed wildly inside me. It might have appeared to some that I left the corporate world out of a lack of grit, but I was feeling like a fox who had escaped to the henhouse.

The sun's early warmth brought with it tiny bugs that danced in front of my face, and I thanked the earth for them. I celebrated seeing the polished, deep green leaves of the desert scrub, and I loved feeling the damp morning air. My heart leapt at the wildflowers in pinks, blues, and maize, and I marveled at the many mountain ranges I could count before they disappeared into the morning haze. My eyes were caught by deer tracks on the dusty fire road, and I crouched down to see them the way I had as a youngster out hunting.

Although exhausted, I felt I had pulled off a great coup. Now the corporation was working for me. I had stolen my life back and placed it in my hands again. After facing down the corporate gods I was now my own man. No longer would trying to be successful in the company dictate my every move and weigh my every decision. I was free at last.

Years before, when I released myself from the confines of my religion, I felt as if I was tearing a deeply rooted institution out of my flesh. It was as though I was finally escaping restraints that had held me for ages. Then when I left my marriage, I was leaving centuries of bad marriages, and because I had dared to face this one, I would never have to experience that again. Now that I was pulling myself out of the agency, I was escaping what felt like lifetimes of being trapped in other people's power structures, and now I felt free of them all.

The sun was finally up when I returned to the house and picked up the paper at the end of the driveway. I looked at the front page and realized that I didn't want to read about what the rest of the world was doing—I was having too much fun getting reacquainted with myself.

As radiant as my new life was, and as much as I loved the house, my heart still had a chill in it. I had lost trust in my career, in marriage, and even in loving or being loved. Yet life always seemed to have a way of giving me exactly what I needed at the very moment I was ready for it.

One Sunday morning I walked around the mountaintop before the sun was high enough to give direct light. On that dark morning I felt a tinge of anticipation in my heart, a feeling that something strange and wonderful was about to happen. I didn't see another person, as I often did on these walks, but I felt an almost mystical presence among the mountain scrub. Something was telling me to pay attention. The young hunter of my childhood became alert, but I saw nothing unusual. The light was not bright enough to let me see into the shadows—just enough to tip the edges of the leaves in pink.

I heard something rustle in the bushes ahead. Was it a coyote? There were often deer up here. I squinted at the base of a clump of bushes where I saw a shape moving and wondered if it was a tramp. I readied myself as it struggled to stand and saw that it was smaller than a man—a dog perhaps, barely able to rise to its legs. Creeping closer I saw that it was a dog, a male German Shepherd that was enfeebled for some reason. I watched the animal shake as he tried to steady himself. As I moved gently closer, I could see that he was very skinny and had bare spots on his hide. I also saw that his shyness would not let me come closer.

I began to make soft noises to him, the same noises I'd made to my collie when I was a kid. Soon I had his confidence and I took a few steps toward home to see if he'd follow me. He did follow, but never so close that he could be touched. In many ways he reminded me of myself.

When we reached the house, I gave him a bowl of whipped eggs—the only thing I had to give him that I thought a dog might like. When he was finished, still not letting me touch him, he wobbled off to sleep under the low bushes in the front yard.

For days I fed him and tried to find his owner, checking the newspapers, the dog pounds, and the posters that appeared on tree trunks along Nichols Canyon Road. But no one seemed to be looking for him. He was going to stay, it turned out, a long, long time. I had been given a living thing, and he was going to wend his way into my heart and help me open it.

I always thought that dog had a human soul. Or that in him was an angel who had come to be with me at a time when I really needed someone. Whichever, he became a friend.

But we were slow to open up to each other. From the day he arrived I called him "Stray," as though he belonged somewhere else and I was only his temporary owner. And I wouldn't let myself depend on his being there when I came home.

Each morning, he would run alongside the car all the way out to the street, watching me until my car disappeared around the bend. Still, I wondered if he would be there when I got back. But no matter when I returned, there was Stray waiting for me, sometimes at the head of the driveway and at other times, resting under the bushes in the front yard.

A full year passed before I admitted that I'd taken him into my heart. I knew I had the day I went downtown and got him a license and a dog tag with his name and my telephone number on it.

We would sit together on the deck and watch the sun go down. Stray would watch me watch the sun, and when he had my eye, he would come over and give me his nose. He'd push his shoulder up against my chest, embracing me the only way a dog can.

Here we were, the two of us, both strays. As I held him, I realized how often I'd left things. I left the farm country in Ohio, my natal city, my religion, my brother and sister, my folks, and the political party they raised me on. I left home once to go into the army, and again to go off to the city. Then after I had my own family, I left again. I left my career, my home, my wife, and I even left my child.

Now, sitting here in my house with my dog, I realized that I had come to California to heal myself, although I had no idea of what illness. I had come to California to find myself, although I had no idea how I was lost. And I had come to California to follow my little voice, although I had no idea where it was leading me.

I wondered if I had finally come home.

FIFTEEN

TAKING ROOT

There are two seats of power in advertising—one on the business side and one on the creative side. Now I found myself an agency producer, which was on neither. I felt like an officer who had resigned his commission to work in the regimental gardens. The real action was miles away, back in Chicago, or in any of the boardrooms in any of the cities where we had clients. In our company, Los Angeles was the boondocks.

I was not prepared for the loss of power. Where once people waited outside my office to see me, now no one cared I was there. Where once I had managed a creative group, now I took orders from Chicago. I had escaped the palace, but I had become a peasant in the process. For the first time in all the years I had been in advertising, I had time on my hands. I began to see what athletes must go through when their legs give out—one day they rule the world, and the next, no one knows them without their scrapbooks. I found myself telling people what campaigns I had worked on and which accounts. It was as if I had been engrossed in an elegant film, and when it stopped and the theater lights went up, there I was with no life of my own.

Despite losing the trappings of power, I was filled with the excitement of starting a new life. My little voice kept whispering that inside me was a kind of truth. Not necessarily a universal truth, and maybe not even one other person's truth, but a truth that was all mine. And if I was honest with myself, kept true to my insights, and had courage—which all by itself was brand new to me—then I would surely find the fulfillment I so deeply wanted.

I thought I had left the problems of the corporation behind me, but they had followed me here. It was an illusion that I had left them, and it reminded me of the child who wants to run away from home but is afraid to cross the street. Realizing that it was time to make something new of my life, I began talking with commercial production houses to see about becoming a director.

I met an attractive, gentle woman at one of the production houses, and from the first day we were friends. Karen had been married to a painter who was a scion of a well-known painting family back East and in New Mexico. After her separation, she came to Los Angeles from Santa Fe and found work in film. Although she longed to be a painter, she had told only a few close friends of her ambition, because she didn't want the more famous painters in her family to know.

The first time she visited me at the house was on a sunny weekend afternoon, and with her she brought a chamois bikini that fit her in every way. She had a warm, earth woman feeling about her, as though she had been bred in the western deserts, and when she walked the buckskin rode on her hips with the native grace of an Indian. I watched her swim, and fell in love with the smooth movement of her body. When she rose from the pool, the buckskin cords pulled against her back and thighs and I couldn't take my eyes off her.

I was coming to life again after a long time of wanting no closeness with anyone, and I began to look forward to our weekends together.

Karen would set up her watercolors alongside the pool, and together we would paint the flowers that grew there. I was thrilled by how beautiful she was, and how her feminine shyness reflected the soft hues and silence of the desert. I let my heart rise when I met her, and I found her easy ways very healing.

We spoke about our past marriages, and about love. I remember telling her that I didn't want anyone to say they loved me anymore because I didn't want to be owned again. "Love doesn't have to mean that," she would reply. Partly I agreed, but I was still afraid it meant she needed something from me rather than that she had something to give. She could feel the knives the divorce had left in me, so she made her paintings and asked nothing more of my words. Quietly, a sweet, unspoken love grew between us.

After talking to several commercial production companies, I was disappointed to find that they were not interested in me at all. Nearing forty years old, I was a seasoned veteran at writing commercials but a complete novice at directing them. Why would a small production company that had to hump for every little job take a chance on me when there was a whole town of younger, more experienced film people who were barely working themselves?

My last resort was a man I'd had lunch with many times when he was in town selling commercials. After encouraging me to go into film when I was in Chicago, he now had quite a different message.

"So you used to handle some of the biggest companies in the business as a creative director, but you don't know a goddam thing about shooting commercials. And what's worse, by the time you'd be any good at it, you'd be older than most of the creative people you'd be working with. What twenty-five-year-old wants some dried-up ex-executive shooting his commercials?"

As I adjusted to my new life, my nights were filled with dreams. I had become interested in the meaning of dreams during my psychoanalysis years before and had used them to resolve my various conflicts.

Freud's ideas helped me create a new value system, which I needed because the one I was raised with had became unlivable. I found Freud to be a wonderfully permissive authority, and I much preferred his views to the guilts of my religion. For instance, in analysis there was no right or wrong, so there was no God judging me every time I wanted to express myself. If I made love to someone, I wasn't committing a mortal sin—I was being healthy. If I masturbated, it wasn't sin—it probably meant I was lonely. But if I did either when I was younger, I believed all the angels in heaven would draw their swords at me in anger.

In Freud's system, only matter mattered. There was only earth and how I felt about it. The only transcendent thing going on inside of me were my dreams, and they were not messages from a wrathful God, but fumes rising from spent psychic material. Dreams were simply kindly monsters that crept out from the dark center of myself every night hoping to find understanding.

During most of my time in Chicago, dreams were my only spiritual reality. Now with free time to think and feel, I read Carl Jung to better understand my growing sense of a larger reality. His concept of the universal unconscious, of our being part of an immense, living, eternal mind, began to make sense to me, and my dreams took on larger meaning. Rather than dreams as mere visions of a mind searching for adjustment, they became the charts of an evolving mind searching for the eternal. Jung helped me make the leap from wanting to be merely well adjusted, to wanting strongly to transcend. I didn't ask myself toward whom or what because I was still unwilling to reaccept a God-centered universe. Jung gave me an acceptable way of incorporating the "spiritual" without readopting the idea of absolute right and wrong.

When I first came to Los Angeles, I would awaken in the mornings and find my sheets damp from the hazards and risks in my dreams. They were always about climbing down. I dreamed again and again about climbing down, usually from a high mountain. The rocks were sharp, the way was dangerous, and it was bitterly cold. White mountains of ice and snow offered no resting place, and I was always climbing lower and lower.

Finally, these gave way to office dreams. Sometimes I would go out to lunch and when I came back, my office would be gone. Usually some younger man would have it. Work was going on, but I had no real part in it. Often, ranking executives were angry at me for being late or gone. More often than not, I was forgotten. Once I came back and found that my small office had been moved to the basement. Once it had become a flower stall in a subway station with neon lights over it. Another time I had a tiny office at the end of a labyrinth of corridors. Often I opened a conference room door where a meeting was going on, but no one inside knew who I was. My clothes were old. My salary was a pittance.

Each morning I awoke drenched in sweat and was often left with a gnawing feeling that I had made the wrong choice. When I was frightened and missing my old executive status, I would wake up feeling it had been a mistake to give up everything. When I was in touch with my emerging self, I would see the dreams as the expected discomforts of losing an old skin.

Either way, I had to recognize that leaving my past life was causing me tremendous psychic upheaval, and that the past had a deeper hold on me than I consciously knew. My search had taken me outside of not only what society felt was rational, but outside of what I, too, must have thought rational. If I had listened only to my fears in those moments, I would have returned to life in a corporation. Instead, my strong desire for fulfillment put me in touch with an untapped, deeper strength that came with its own rationality. Despite the risks and the persistently fearful dreams, I pushed on, trusting my more supportive inner voices. I had shifted from the accepted traditional values to my own set of unique ones, and by doing so, I uncovered the first traces of my inner path.

SIXTEEN

LOOKING FOR AN OPENING

Finding a way out of advertising and into film was now the only thing on my mind. A friend who was a movie critic in Chicago, Roger Ebert, was in town and invited me to a party he was going to that weekend in Malibu. Our host had written one of the classic books on film, and the evening promised to provide many movie industry people with whom I could talk. I jumped at the chance to go.

The night of the party, Roger introduced me to the host, Arthur Knight. As we talked, I told him why I had come to Los Angeles and asked if there were any people there I might talk to about getting into film. Arthur and I spoke for a while, and then he introduced me to his next-door neighbor, someone he called "a hot young producer." (Two years later he would produce one of the highest grossing films of all time.) The living room was small and filled with people, and before the producer went for a drink, he suggested I meet him on the deck where it would be quieter.

Excitement rose in me as I stepped outside to wait. The house was in Malibu, only a few feet from the surf. It wasn't elaborate, but it had a California grace and simplicity that made the setting magical. The sea was quiet and brightly lit, and I felt like my life was on a roll. I was living in a beautiful part of the country in a wonderful house of my own, and had an exciting life ahead of me.

When the producer came out I asked him if he would suggest a way an advertising person like myself could get into the film business.

"What did you do in advertising?" he asked.

"Well, I'm producing commercials now, but I was vice president and creative director back in Chicago. One of the largest advertising agencies in the world."

I somehow thought it would enhance my chances to bring out all the big agency artillery that usually impressed the smaller production companies. It didn't impress this guy at all. In fact, it might have been better if I had told him I worked for the First National Bank of Chicago.

"Well, I don't know. You could probably work in the advertising department in one of the studios."

I didn't want to go into a large company again. Perhaps that might have been a good idea years before, but now I wanted something simpler and more direct. When he saw disappointment on my face, he continued.

"Or you could get into the business the way I did. Find a book and buy it, and take it around to the studios until you find someone who wants to make it into a picture. Then work on it as an associate producer or something."

It was common in the business to have worked as an agent first, or an attorney, or an executive in one of the studios, and use the exposure to find literary properties. I knew what he was suggesting, but I didn't have the connections to do that.

"I don't know how to do that. I'd like to work directly for a producer and learn the business that way."

He shrugged and glanced back into the roomful of people.

"What if I worked with you, for nothing, for the next year or so, and after I learned the business, you could start paying me something?"

It felt a little outrageous offering to work for nothing—after all, I was not just out of college—but I thought I'd ask.

"Why would I want to train you? You'd just end up being one of my competitors."

The instant he said that, I understood. In one sentence he had communicated the way the business really worked. It was every man for himself, and the name of the game was to find a hot property. I realized he was not going to help me, and that no one could help me as much as I could help myself. Suddenly there was little else I wanted to say.

"If you find something, and you want to talk about it, give me a call."

I thanked him, and after some small talk, he smiled briefly and wandered back into the party.

I stayed out on the deck for a few minutes watching the surf roll in. The producer had helped me, but not in the way I expected. I wanted him to offer me a ready-made position, but it was obvious that I'd have to create one myself. I could suddenly see the disadvantage of having worked in a large company most of my life. It didn't prepare me to develop things on my own.

In a moment the host arrived to find out how the conversation had gone. When I told him what had happened, he shrugged as if that was typical of the way the business worked.

"Maybe you oughta try developing something yourself. Seems to be the way people do it."

He put his hand on my shoulder and led me back inside.

That night I drove home through Malibu Canyon, which I considered one of the most thrilling drives in Southern California. I chose it because it made me feel like everything was going to be all right. I pulled off the road at a scenic view point and looked at the moon-drenched cliffs of the canyon across the creek.

It was becoming clear that I had to find a literary property. The producer told me that he'd paid $50,000 for the book he was then readying for production. I couldn't conceive of doing that, and I didn't want to go into the advertising department of any of the studios. I wanted to go into production directly. The only option that seemed possible, as well as creatively interesting, was to try writing something myself. I was aware that there were lots of people writing screenplays. It seemed that everyone in town— every doorman, every waiter, every delivery person—was working on one. Still, I had spent my life as a creative person, and I really wanted to write. I began to feel the excitement of a new creative challenge before me.

Beneath that, however, I was feeling quite unsettled. I had somehow imagined that getting into film would be as easy as getting to California had been, but now the future felt like it could be a long, hard road. One of the secrets appeared to be earning an income while developing something else, and I felt gratitude for having my job at the agency.

Working in "the business" would have been great, but I sensed that instead of looking for a job in film, I should keep doing what I was doing and begin writing immediately.

SEVENTEEN

BEGINNING TO WRITE

The following day I went into the agency, pulled out a pad and pen and began jotting down some ideas. I had never liked typing and always wrote in longhand, perhaps because it felt more like drawing.

Week after week passed, and between commercials I would close the door to my small office and write. People from Chicago would come and go, executives would appear and disappear, and I would continue writing. I'd stop long enough to check a print at Technicolor, see an editor and cut a scene, or cover a shot, then go right back to my office to write. When I was satisfied with a scene I had written, I would take it to a script typist. Every Wednesday night, I'd go to a screenwriting class on Hollywood Boulevard. My dream was to write a film.

My curiosity about how people searched for meaning in their lives was becoming as important to me as writing, and I found myself reading books that I'd had little time for in Chicago. At lunchtime if I wasn't writing, I would take an apple from our reception desk and go somewhere to read what other people had written about their experiences. One of my favorite places to read was the Hollywood Bowl, where I would park in the shade at the far end of the parking lot.

The first book I got into was *the only dance there is* by Ram Dass. One curious thing was that Joan had wanted me to read it while we were still married. She had obviously tried to open my spiritual side, but I wouldn't listen.

I did, however, become interested in Ram Dass' book when it was suggested to me by an actor I met shooting a commercial in New York. She recommended it when I spoke to her about my fascination with the collective unconscious.

Ram Dass was an ex-professor who left Harvard University to become a spiritual seeker. While in India, he transformed his life and returned to this country as a western-born, eastern guru. The book was a collection of public addresses in which he talked about his discoveries and about how he was attempting to bridge the two different worlds.

I had never done any drugs beyond alcohol (I always thought of tranquilizers as medicine), but from reading the popular press, I was aware of the spiritual trips that LSD and other drugs stimulated. This book was my initiation into the contemporary western search for spirituality, and I found myself being cautious lest I be drawn into another religion. I also had another hesitation —the embarrassment the American corporate male felt toward anything unconventionally "spiritual." I had usually dismissed such things as more of the flakiness of Southern California.

Alone in my car in the Hollywood Bowl parking lot, eating my apple, and reading forbidden books on the inner journey, I felt like a little kid in the basement reading his first book on sex.

There I was reading about mantras, chakras, and karma. Feeling drawn enough to secretly give a mantra a try, I began silently uttering "Om Mani Padme Om" as I sped along the freeway toward a shooting location. After months of such silent utterances I gave them up, but much of the Ram Dass book stuck with me. For me it was a handbook of beginning spirituality. I learned a lot about diet, meditation, and personal consciousness, and it started me thinking about my own experiences in a different light.

The second paragraph of the book got my attention right away.

> The motivation for doing this is most interesting—it's only to work on myself. It's very easy to break attachments to worldly games when you're sitting in a cave in the Himalayas. It's quite a different take you do of sex, power, money, fame, and sensual gratification in the middle of New York City in the United States with television and loving people around and great cooks and advertising and total support for all of the attachments.

I didn't then, and still don't, share the traditional seeker's belief that to become truly fulfilled in life you have to give up the world. When I considered entering the Trappist Monastery I discovered that my path led out into the world, not into seclusion —into life, not out of it. I continued to back away from religious denial of any kind. If there was a God and a path of discovery, it had to lead right through the marketplaces of the world as well as through the deserts. It felt anti-life to deny the earth when it was where I lived.

Now I was beginning to see my passion for freedom a little more clearly. What Ram Dass called the world's "attachments" was, for me, dependency on something that limited my freedom. I had always gravitated to the stability of large organizations, but they in turn had always pushed their values on me. I was comfortable there, but comfortable like living in a luxurious prison cell.

Giving up worldly attachments was often misinterpreted, I thought. Most monastic orders believed in vows of poverty, celibacy, and other acts of self-denial. But I believed that freedom came not from releasing the pleasures of earth but from releasing dependency on them. A life of material pursuits became an attachment only if I sacrificed the integrity of my "self" in the process.

Ram Dass sparked the realization that my attachment to institutions was not only about my need for emotional and financial security, but also my fear of change. I realized that what was uniquely me would have been smothered if I hadn't finally had the courage to break the bonds and set myself free.

It was a proud papa who went to the airport to pick up Sarah. I first spotted her as she emerged from the passage with the stewardess. God, she was getting tall and beautiful! She looked around for a moment, then seeing me, she hurried over. We laughed and hugged and with our embrace tried to dissolve the months since we had last seen each other.

We'd been in touch by phone and letters every week, so there wasn't much catching up to do. We were just two people trying to bridge the space that had come between us. I had planned a trip to Disneyland, of course, and to Universal Studios, and the beach. I also thought a curious nine-year-old would like to see the statues of the mammoths in the La Brea tar pits, and Olvera Street. There were many things I loved around town, and I wanted to share them all with her.

When we drove up Nichols Canyon Road, I pointed out where I had seen the deer, the house in which a rock group lived, and a few other homes where famous people had lived at some time in their careers.

Sarah loved our house and got along easily with Stray. After seeing the pool, she noticed the same thing I did the first time I saw it.

"Can I jump off the roof?" she asked.

"Of course."

We laughed and changed into our bathing suits. I showed her how to climb up to the roof, and then stood below as she jumped out over the blue waters and plunged ten feet toward the bottom. She came up sputtering in her happiness and I knew she felt at home. I needed that from her. I needed her to accept me and my choice to come here.

I took some time off work to be with her, and because she always slept late, I had my mornings to write.

One day soon after Sarah left, I arrived back in the office from my lunchtime reading in the parking lot to find a close friend from the Chicago office waiting for me. Without smiling, he said he wanted to talk.

For years, Kurt had been one of my closest friends. We'd worked together on many different accounts, he as a writer and I as an art director. He had attended a small dinner party for Joan and me when we were engaged and was the person I'd talked with about starting an agency together. But he had gotten a promotion and gone to England to run our office there, and by the time he got back, we had lost touch.

There was something in the blank expression on his face that sent a chill into my stomach as he spoke. I followed him into an empty office and closed the door behind us.

"They want you to come back to Chicago," he said.

There was no preamble, not even a smile. He had chosen to be a corporate executive over being a friend.

"I won't go back. There's nothing I want back there."

My face must have gone ashen as I got the drift of what was actually happening. I sat down, and in an attempt to relax, tossed one leg over the arm of the chair.

"I don't think you have any choice."

That remark shifted my mood from shock to anger and I sat up straight.

"The hell I don't have a choice. What d'ya mean, I don't have a choice?"

"I mean, you don't have a choice if you want to stay with the company."

We just stared at each other for a moment. I tried to remember the two of us years earlier. I saw how much we had changed. In the past I, too, might have chosen duty over friendship, but I could never have done that now. I saw how transparent that kind of power was and how blind and unfeeling it had made me.

"I now have responsibility for production out here, and as I've been hearing it, you aren't quite pulling your weight."

There was a lot to what he said. When I first came to the California office, creative people avoided me by requesting other producers to do their commercials. I'd expected this to change over time but it hadn't. They saw me as a has-been executive on the way out, when what they wanted was a hot young producer on the way up. There seemed little I could do about it, so rather than force the issue, I used my free time to write. But the truth in what he said was painful, especially after so many successful years.

"We talked about it, and we think you should come back to Chicago and take back your old job as creative director. You've been here longer than anyone really wanted, Don. And you're making more money than anyone else out here."

My anger had finally cooled, and I looked out the window for a moment to reflect. When Kurt saw that I was thinking about what he was saying, he softened.

"Well, at least come back and talk about it."

I got up from my chair and moved toward the door without trying to establish any warmth between us. Our old relationship was obviously over, and I didn't want to give him any more leverage than he already had. I preferred to wait and talk to a few other people in Chicago.

"Lemme think about it … but I don't think so."

My car wound up the road in Nichols Canyon, which now felt lonely and hazardous. It was still early afternoon but I opened a bottle of wine and sat on the deck and stared out into the canyon.

Even though the company was offering an alternative, for me there really was no choice. I had fired a few people but nothing like this had ever happened to me. Now I could see how cold I must have been when I handed them back their lives. How unfeeling I was when I told them they had not made it. More than once I had stared into someone's tears while listening to them plead to stay. But I'd said, no, it just wouldn't work. It looked like *what goes around, comes around* was true.

Yet under the pain was a sense of relief. I was happy to be pushed out of the nest. I had grown comfortable having the job while I was writing, but I knew it was time to make a change. As they say in California, "The universe was trying to tell me something."

When the news got back to Chicago that I might be leaving the agency, my home phone began to ring.

The chief creative executive called, and he too asked if I would come back as creative director. I told him I didn't want to do that. Then he asked if I would consider other possibilities or at least come back to talk, which I finally agreed to do. A kind of native superstition of mine said to take a good look at any opportunity because they don't come around that often.

The following day the chief executive officer of the international division called and asked if we could talk when I got there. He wanted me to consider going to Europe for him. It didn't feel right, but I did agree to talk it over.

Then there were a couple of well-meaning lookie-loos asking how I felt and offering their sympathies.

With this sudden threat to the status quo, my interest in reading dream symbols now became an interest in trying to read actual events. As I grew more sensitive, I began to realize that people and events in real life had symbolic meaning for me just as they had when they appeared in my dreams. I was feeling nudged and pushed by my circumstances, and as I began to notice this, I tried to interpret which way they were leading me.

A case in point was what happened when I arrived in Los Angeles and tried to find an opening in film. When nothing materialized, I felt blocked and wondered if I was being "told" by the events in my life that film was not right for me. I kept working and kept waiting for an opportunity because things had always opened up for me in the past, but nothing came. Now when I was about to irrevocably sever my connection with the corporation, my old life suddenly came alive with new opportunities. Was the universe actually urging me back, or was it the pull of old attachments that I had not really broken? Every bone in my body wanted me to stay in California, but before I made a final choice, I resolved to go and get a better feel for what was happening.

A few days later, I was on the plane to Chicago having reached an important decision point—to be free, I had to make a conscious choice to sever the attachment. If I wanted to be free of the dragon, I had to go back and cut off its head.

It felt strange being in the old city that I had left with such finality, but it was good to see Sarah again on her turf. On my way from the airport to the hotel, I picked her up so we could spend the evening together before my schedule got hectic.

The following day, I had meetings with the heads of various divisions within the company. In each meeting it was glaringly clear that I had indeed changed and that nothing remained of the old attractions. I was relieved that I felt no calling to return, but it was different when I met with my old friend who now headed Leo Burnett International.

"I want you to work in the international division with me," he said. "I've wanted to talk to you about it several times since you left here, but I agreed not to try to hire anyone from domestic to go international."

He smiled broadly as he spoke, and I was reminded how much I liked and admired this man.

"But now that you're leaving, I'm free to at least ask you. First thing I'd have you do is go to Europe and try to make our offices over there more like real Burnett offices. You know what I mean?"

It was an attractive offer, and I might have accepted it easily if this had happened a few years before, but now I felt like I had found my own road.

"Ken, I'd rather write. I've started writing and just don't want to take the time to go to Europe. I might as well go back into advertising."

"What's wrong with that?"

"I want to go into the movie business."

He stopped for a moment when he realized what I had said, and just looked at me, perplexed.

"Think about it. Go for a few months, and if you don't like it, come back. You can keep your house in Los Angeles if you like, and troubleshoot for me internationally. You can even work out of the Los Angeles office if it makes you more comfortable. But at least for now, ya' gotta go over to Europe and help me find some good creative people. Stay in Paris and find us a topnotch creative director if you decide not to stay."

"Well, let me think about it."

I smiled at his warmth and manner, and at the gift he was offering me. As I got up to leave, I noticed a warm glow in my gut that suggested I might be going.

In the end I had to force myself to accept the European assignment because I really wanted to write. I decided to give myself Paris as a going-away present from advertising. Karen had convinced me that nothing would happen in Los Angeles while I was gone, and that I really should give myself my first trip to Europe, especially since it was paid for. After mulling it over a few days, I finally asked her if she'd go with me, and when she agreed, I called Ken for instructions.

Karen was painting more and thinking about going to an art school in the south of France. She'd never been to Europe and was aching to see it, especially the Paris museums. I was thrilled that she would be joining me, even though it would be a while before she came over because she wasn't able to get off work for the full time I'd be there.

The company had offices in seven European cities. My assignment was to live in Paris and visit them all, bringing to each the spirit that had made the agency the giant it was in America. The assignment was a plum and I'm sure it needed to be done, but because Ken wanted me to work with him internationally it felt as if he was giving me this first job as an enticement. I liked being courted again after the ego beating I was taking in Los Angeles, and I resolved to have as good a time as possible.

For the next few months, I lived in a furnished apartment in Paris across from the Russian embassy on the Bois de Boulogne. Each week I visited one of our other offices, doing business reviews, having creative meetings, and helping to make ads in all those countries. Karen was over for three weeks, and if I had to be away for a day or so, she'd stay in Paris because it gave her extra time to visit museums. I was still feeling closed off about having a committed relationship, but we had a wonderful time together while she was there.

It was a happy business trip, with fabulous weekends all over Europe, and a great way to say goodbye to advertising. I was almost sad to leave it all behind, but it felt like a trap again and I was hearing a call to return to my writing. Finally, after about three months, I phoned Ken to tell him I'd found a creative director for the Paris office and was coming back. He was disappointed, but as a friend he understood.

During a day of debriefing in Chicago I was offered the opportunity to go to either South America or Japan, but I had to refuse. I was happy to be leaving the world of big business—and to be giving myself the private time I wanted.

The company let me stay a few months beyond what we had originally agreed so I could celebrate my twentieth anniversary with the firm. One of the many wonderful things about the Leo Burnett Company was its generous heart, and I was very grateful for their support.

When it was all over, I returned to Los Angeles and to writing, and to face some of the most profound inner challenges I could have imagined.

EIGHTEEN

WRITING FULL TIME

Of all the difficult choices that led me to the point where I was writing full time, none was as traumatic as leaving the corporate paycheck.

From the time I was a kid, I had drawn a regular paycheck. It was the way life worked, like breathing in and breathing out. A regular paycheck that came even when all else seemed to fail was a narcotic to the part of me that always felt insecure. Living without knowing where the money would come from was like cutting off my own life-support system. Going it alone was cold turkey. Deep in the recesses of my male-provider mind, alarms began to ring and I wondered if I could survive. As a substitute, I would go to the bank twice a month and pulse money from my reserves through my personal checking account as though nothing untoward was happening to me.

When I left the agency, I withdrew my pension and profit sharing, sold my company stock, and put it all in mutual funds. Now I dutifully thanked the universe for the happy accident of providing the resources so I could write.

But I was sure it was more than an "accident." I had the sense that some unknown forces had overseen the accumulation of my reserves and were now watching, and that they would grade me on how well I managed my time. If I handled myself in a reasonable manner, I would be rewarded by earning an income from my efforts, just as I was rewarded for good conduct back in Chicago.

So to express my seriousness, I kept a routine. I would get up at dawn and walk around the mountain with Stray, watching the ball of sunlight blaze up over the San Bernardino Mountains. Back at the house, I would make coffee and then sit down at my writing table. I would write as long as I could and spend the rest of the day doing research for the writing or working around the house. I would go to bed early and repeat the process the following day. The only other rule was not to spend any money unless it was necessary.

I would never let myself forget that my current reserves were not because of work I was doing in California but because of my sense of responsibility in Chicago. It was as though I had been successful back there out of a pact with hidden forces, and I wouldn't know if they were still supporting me until my work out here brought in an income of its own. My house, my car, the way I was living, and even my career, were the result of that pact, and I sometimes wondered if I'd strayed beyond its boundaries by coming out here in the first place.

So I worked hard to keep my part of the bargain, waiting for any success to signal that the forces had accepted my move. Until new income came as a direct result of my writing, I couldn't let myself relax.

Each day, I wrote for as many hours as possible, and wishing not to be distracted, I spent more time alone, got to bed earlier at night, and woke up earlier in the morning. Soon I was getting up so early that I was up in the middle of the night, and going to bed at dusk. The day's axis had shifted, and because it had, I found myself withdrawing from any kind of social life apart from seeing Karen and a few other friends.

My life challenged my sense of security, but it was so satisfying that I couldn't understand what had held me all those years in Chicago. I so loved writing that I often felt guilty about the wonderful life I was having on the mountain. Yet at times I was haunted by the fear that I had strayed beyond my limits. In the back of my mind, I believed that quitting the hard workaday world of business to write movies on a mountain in Southern California was not an acceptable thing to do. If I had asked other people, they would have counseled against it. If I had been in a corporation, the board of directors would have defeated my proposal.

But I hadn't asked for advice, and I didn't submit my choices to a board. I was free to go all the way. And it felt good because I kept hearing that little voice from the deepest part of myself telling me that this was the time in my life to make no compromises.

So each day I would turn out pages of script, counting them as I wrote, as if I were cutting wood to build a house. As the pages gathered and scenes formed, I felt closer to realizing my new life.

There was a second show going on inside me that was beginning to interest me almost as much as the writing. I was using my free time to explore ways to gain a deeper understanding of myself.

Because I had spent my adult life working at such a hectic pace, I never had the time to go inside and see what was there. In my last few years before I left Chicago, I began taking the family for a month's vacation, hoping for more internal time, but there wasn't enough for me to penetrate the surface. I was so wound up by the time we went that it took me a couple of weeks to relax, and by then I began thinking about what I had to do when I got back.

Here on the mountain, time was different. I had more of it than I knew how to use. I was no longer wound up from the pressure, and there was no office to go back to, so I was free to do as I pleased.

What I noticed most was that as my contact with the outside world lessened, I received an increased flow of communication from within. It was as though some inner spirit had taken over my internal photocopy room and had begun sending me memos all day long. Some came from the finance department, some from personnel, some were from the creative department or research, and each one had its own style and its own interests in mind.

But some came from deeper sources, and instead of addressing mundane matters, they carried messages about the meaning of things—of my values, of inspiration, and of goals larger than financial ones.

Soon I began to expect this flow of communications and gradually turned to it to help guide my actions. If I needed an answer that didn't come on its own, I'd ask, and answers would arrive in many different forms. So in the course of time, as the dialogue continued, I was having board meetings inside myself.

As this inner communication developed, there were two clear voices who spoke for the rest. One was cautious and saw problems in their most familiar, material context, and the other was more optimistic and suggested new visions of what could be. The first I called the "chairman of the board," because he always spoke in a pragmatic and slightly preemptive way. The chairman was having a field day with my new life.

"What are you doing?" he would say soon after I started writing. "You have no money coming in, and you're paying alimony and child support. You just bought yourself a house, and a new car, and you're hiding like a recluse on a mountain. You're simply not being responsible. If you were a corporation, you wouldn't be making such a blind gamble. The entire management would be fired."

The chairman's picture of things was generally negative, but logical enough to cause me concern. I rarely debated him directly, because he always had the proof of history on his side, but when he was finished I usually took time to reflect on his point of view.

My inspiration came from the other clear voice, who was the visionary on the board. Some of his ideas sounded outrageous at first and were usually met with silence from the chairman, but he mostly got his way. It was his idea to come out here, and he was the source of most of my optimism. Even when things were roughest, I could depend on his vision to convince me that everything was going perfectly according to plan. He was also the source of my creative inspiration, and I always thought of him as "my little voice."

"Don't listen to the chairman," my little voice would say. "You're not a corporation and your life need not be conducted according to a rational strategy the way a business is. You started writing, but you're discovering the hidden nature of yourself, and that's just as important. What's going on inside can be just as productive as what's going on outside but in ways that might not yet be measured in money. You've worked a very long time for this. You've earned this. And I can tell you that it's no accident that you can afford to give yourself this opportunity, or that you're doing it. Just stay attuned to what's inside and your new life will unfold beautifully."

I always learned a great deal from these meetings and began to look forward to the guidance when things weren't going well.

The story I chose for my first screenplay was quite violent. I had toyed with and rejected a number of other ideas but had become intrigued with this one. I called it *Mojave*, after the small town in the desert that served as a backdrop for the drama.

It was a story about a Vietnam vet returning home and the townspeople failing to see that a trained killer has entered their midst. Once an heroic soldier, he killed many guerrillas in Vietnam. Now home, he carries a hot coal in his gut that's just waiting to ignite. After a number of misunderstandings created by a local sheriff, he explodes and kills more than forty pursuers in a desert chase that goes on for days. In the end, through a deal with the government, he slips back into the military's Special Forces and disappears.

Writing screenplays was a little like making up dreams, except that in writing I had to take responsibility for what I committed to paper. A writer acts like a god over the events and characters in his dramas, deciding who does what, when, and for what reason.

I also saw that every detail in a film was there because it helped communicate a message. It didn't take a great leap of imagination to see that if this was true in film, perhaps it was also true in life. Perhaps everything in my life was there with purpose and meaning. I had already seen a subtle pattern in the events that brought me out here, and also in having the financial reserves that let me write, so I began to look for deeper meaning in other things around me.

My new life was coming at me on two levels. One was the learning to write—the getting-up-and-doing-it-every-day kind of writing—and the other was the education I was getting the rest of the day.

At first, I saw the non-writing time as inactive, empty space, but soon I began to realize that it had volume, depth, and purpose just as the writing did. Because I was living alone and saw few people, I had time to explore things around me that I was becoming aware of, but knew little about. One was the subtle reality that is often best perceived during inactive, receptive times.

No one I've ever read described the difference between the "subtle" and the "everyday" realities the way Lao Tzu did. His writing was the only source I found that successfully described the presence of another realm that can be perceived while living in this one. To the ancient Chinese, the substance and energy that exists in the subtle world actually influences this reality, and only by understanding it and including it in our experience can we learn to bring harmony to our lives.

This is how he introduces the subtle world in the first bigram of the *Tao Te Ching*:

Thus, without expectation,
  One will always perceive the subtlety;
And, with expectation,
  One will always perceive the boundary.

The source of these two is identical,
Yet their names are different.
Together they are called profound,
Profound and mysterious,
The gateway to the Collective Subtlety.

It was true. When I was actively engaged in looking I saw only the boundary of things. When I shifted my perception to sensing and being receptive, I became aware of the subtle patterns in my life and learned to trust them more.

As the cold, hard edge of the corporate world faded, a softness emerged in me that was as healing as the warm California sun. Back in Chicago, when I was feeling so much despair, I had read a novel by a local Greek writer, called *The Odyssey of Kostas Volakis*, about an immigrant who came to this country during the bitterness of the Depression. To this man's despair, he was able to find only a wretched job washing dishes, and a poor windowless room to live in. Over time the man found a suitable wife, and soon she bore them a male child. The boy was born weak and crippled, and was dying in the sunless life of his immigrant father. The man clung to the single belief that if he could get his boy back to Greece, he would be healed by the bright Hellenic sun.

I'd realized that I too could be healed if I could just leave the cold, gray towers of Chicago for a place that had sun and flowers year-round. And now, as the months blazed on in California, I found that my life was indeed healing. The hardness of the past was losing its grip on me, and a softer, wiser, and more loving person was emerging. Before, my feelings of success and well-being had come from marketing reports that measured sales, market shares, and volume. Now I was getting my excitement from the new awarenesses that gently bubbled to the surface of my consciousness.

Beliefs that I had clung to all my life, white knuckled, began to release and slip away. Where my happiness once came from external achievement, now it rose from being in tune with myself. My feelings of personal value were shifting from caring about what was going on down below, in Hollywood, to what was happening inside me.

I had kept a collection of beliefs in my mind the way people keep books on shelves. The more I had, the more sophisticated I felt. But now I was seeing that the opposite was true. They showed only where I had been and tended to be an obstacle to new understandings. So gradually over time, I let my collection of beliefs drift away like smoke in a soft breeze.

My internal chairman was another matter. He was having trouble with my "interests," and it was worrying him more and more.

"What would the people that you used to know think?" he would ask. "How about your more rational friends? What will happen to you if you keep this up? Your interests are making you less valuable in the marketplace."

I listened to him and began to worry about becoming involved with things that were too detached from what I used to consider important. It was a conflict. Was I becoming interested in something valuable, or was it irrelevant?

But when I "sensed" inside, I knew that my deepening awareness was of value. I knew that what I was doing was important to me, and that I really had earned the time to go as far into this as I wanted.

Karen was experiencing her own creative rebirth. The trip to Paris had revealed how important art was for her, and she was eager to quit work and paint more.

We had been seeing each other exclusively for quite a while. I had never been with a more gentle, loving person, but I was feeling unable to commit to a relationship.

She decided it was time that she, too, go for what she wanted. So she quit her job and moved to Santa Barbara to spend her time painting.

When she left, a close friend, a lover, and one of the sweetest people I ever knew, slipped out of my life.

SUBTLE LANGUAGE

When I took power into my own hands and let my little voice direct me, I was immediately led out of my active world into solitude on the mountain. It was as if an invisible, internal bias had pulled me out of the mainstream and was leading me into new territory. Despite an inner critic that kept questioning whether I should let myself be drawn into seclusion, I sensed that I was on the right path.

When I reached my new home, I thought that the tough times were behind me. I assumed that my life, after a short period of adjusting to the transplant, would resume the powerful thrust of growth I'd always known.

But by following my own urges, perhaps for the first time, I found myself in a land with very different natural laws than the one I'd left. I had entered a realm in which methods that led to success before no longer worked, and I was forced to move forward in more subtle ways.

I began to pay close attention to the obstacles on my path and to honor them as if they had something to teach me. As I observed each situation and watched the effects on my life, a language developed that I began to vaguely understand and respond to.

Regardless of how my life appeared on the surface, I caught glimpses of my purest desires being fulfilled, even though my current, more obvious needs appeared threatened. So I let the material necessities take a lesser priority, and continued exploring the world of the subtle, letting its language of inner feelings and outer events guide me toward my ideals.

NINETEEN

THE HERO

While *Mojave* was being typed, I got a list of writers' agents in Hollywood and hired an assistant to type a personal letter to each one. There were about one hundred and forty of them.

Weeks later a close friend who was in production at Fox laughed when I told him what I had done.

"How many replies did you get?" Larry asked.

"Ten. And out of that, two offered to represent the script." I was proud of myself for having found an agent on the first try.

"Who are they?"

When I told him the names he bit his lip. "Never heard of either one of them."

I realized there was an indictment in his not knowing them, but I really didn't want to use my friends to find an agent. I wanted to do it myself.

"Let me read it," he said.

I gave him the script and began the first of many Hollywood-waits. A "Hollywood-wait" is what I called those times when my momentum and my future were suddenly in the hands of someone else, and the only thing I could do was wait.

Part of my introduction to the "subtle" world was the presence of Marissa, a wonderful friend I had met originally in Chicago when I cast her in one of my Pillsbury commercials. When I moved out to the canyon, I saw her one day running near the reservoir at the bottom of the hill and from that time we were like brother and sister. She would often come up during the day to sun herself on the deck, and we'd discuss esoteric things.

One afternoon Marissa was there when I finished writing, and I went outside to join her.

"I think it's time you met Jeffrey," she said out of nowhere.

Her comment had the ring of authority to it, as if I had suddenly come of age and was to be taken into an inner circle.

"Who's Jeffrey?"

"My astrologer. I think it's time you see him and have him turn you on to some of the things he knows."

She got up and began gathering her things.

"Are you kidding?" Astrology had always embarrassed me.

She would chill if I failed to respond openly to her ideas and my response drove her into a thoughtful silence. When she finally spoke, I listened carefully.

"Carl Jung trusted astrology, why not you? Why can't you open that thick skull of yours just once and see for yourself? You trust Jung, don't you? You talk about him all the time. Jung even wrote a foreword for the *I Ching*."

"What's the *I Ching*?" I teased.

"We'll talk about that another time." She slipped on her blouse and began buttoning it. It was an old-fashioned sheer blouse, with tiny colored flowers on it. As I watched her get ready to leave, I realized how much I appreciated the easy quality of our friendship and how nice it was to be with someone who felt like family.

"Okay," I surrendered. "I'll talk to him. How do I reach him?" I trusted her enough to go and at least hear what Jeffrey had to say.

"I'll call for you and set up a time next week." Before she left, she jotted down where I was born and my exact time of birth.

I felt awkward and embarrassed. Here I was, a grown man, ringing the doorbell at a strange house in Hancock Park, waiting for an astrologer. When the door opened, a young man looked at me with a bright smile and clear shining eyes.

"Donald? C'mon in. I'm just finishing your chart."

Soon he had his recorder set up and, flipping a blank tape inside, he got down to business. There was a part of me that wanted to flee before he began. I imagined a few of the guys I knew from business who would have laughed at me sitting there with my hands in my lap waiting to hear what the stars had to say.

"Well, I'd say you went through a major change in marital circumstances a couple of years ago."

My mouth dropped open.

"Did Marissa tell you that?" The doubter in me rose up strongly.

"Oh, we talked when she gave me your birth time, but we didn't discuss any other details about your life. Why, have you gone through something? I would guess you have."

"Well, I did, actually." The color must have drained out of my face from feeling so vulnerable, but I was curious.

"Well, there's a complete rupture here. You might have changed jobs while you were getting out of a marriage. You might even have moved."

He went on about various aspects and the changes he thought were likely. I was astonished at how much he knew about my past and listened raptly as he raced his finger over the symbols he had drawn on the chart. He would chuckle every now and then as he saw the wry side of what had been an obviously distressing situation for me.

By the time I left, my head was dizzy from all the terminology, but I couldn't help being impressed with the synchronicity between the chart and my life. I was also excited to discover yet another system of self-knowledge that was not based on right or wrong. In a way, it was even less judgmental than psychology because astrology didn't consider one's behavior healthy or unhealthy. Every action was life. All experience was valid, desirable, and worthwhile because it could lead to greater awareness.

As I drove home, I smiled. The door to self-knowledge *was* guarded by fierce dragons—and now I saw that they came from my own untrusting mind, created by my fear of anything new or different.

The doubter in me still wondered how effective astrology was, but it offered me another piece of evidence that there really was a subtle, less obvious reality in life, and I resolved to find out more about it.

Sometimes when I got up before sunrise to start writing, I would finish for the day around noon and get into my car and go driving.

Often I would head up to Mulholland, which overlooked both the Los Angeles basin and the San Fernando Valley. I loved driving because it got me out of the house, and I liked Mulholland because of the continuous, snakelike curl and the solitary stretches that were fun to negotiate. At other times I would drive through the orange groves in Ojai or up through the Angeles National Forest. Sometimes I went south and east into the deserts. God, I loved California.

And sometimes I would go to Venice.

As I walked among the crowds at Venice beach, I saw the downside possibility of what I was attempting to do. Had some of these people been hardworking executives at one time? Had everyone just dropped out? Who were these young people with skinny arms and tattooed hips? I would see the junk floating under the pilings at the Santa Monica Pier and wonder if I would end up like one of those empty plastic bottles. Was something beginning in me, or was something ending? Was I building or crashing? My ex-wife had warned me that Los Angeles was the last place people go before they jump into the ocean.

I looked down at the jeans that I now wore every day and saw that they were as faded as all the other jeans on Ocean Front Walk. I wondered if at that moment my former friends were in a Procter & Gamble meeting back in Chicago. What was the market share of the new deodorant we introduced as I was leaving? How was Camay doing? Did they get their new super-lather strategy working? These questions used to mean everything to me, and now they seemed like trivia. My newfound freedom was the most important thing, but was that also an illusion? Was I closer to fulfillment now than when I was working on the Jolly Green Giant? Or was I simply another loser? I nodded at an old man who smiled at me as we passed each other.

In part of my mind I was still an executive, but in another part that image was melting like a warm, wax dummy. The ego structure that held me in the system was dissolving, and I had no new form ready.

I stopped and studied my reflection in a mirror that was leaning against one of the tee-shirt tents. That was no corporate executive looking back. My big toe wiggled at me from the front edge of my sandals, and I looked spent in my jeans and faded, button-down, oxford-blue shirt from Brooks Brothers.

Could anyone see that I was dying to the world? Was I, in fact, dying to the world? Or was I just being born? It was no comfort to look in the mirror. Deep down I felt like I was being born, but I also felt I was dying. I just didn't know which would happen first. Feeling a little disoriented, I decided to walk back to my car.

On a side street, my mood began to lift as I passed a white picket fence covered with bright red bougainvillea. The beach area was getting crowded as I pulled the car out and headed back to Nichols Canyon.

On my way home, I decided to stop at the bookstore.

Reading was one of the ways I kept in touch with my more subtle feelings. I still read the paper every day but found myself feeling less connected to what was going on in the world. From the time I moved to California, I had quit reading bestsellers and preferred books by writers on an internal path. I loved Teilhard de Chardin and read a little by St. John of the Cross, the latter having been translated by a neighbor in the apartment across the hall in Chicago. I read Thomas Merton again and enjoyed a wonderful psychoanalysis of Martin Luther by Erik Erikson. To get back in touch with the roots of Christianity, I reread some of the New Testament, but I finally quit reading any Christian writings until I became interested in the mystics many years later.

I began reading Hindu teachers but never really connected with Indian mysticism. I discovered Bubba Free John and Sai Baba, along with Rajneesh and Muktananda. I read what I could find on yoga but leaned more toward the Buddhists.

One of my favorite books, though perhaps strange for a casual reader like myself, was the *Tibetan Book of the Dead*. I saw it as a metaphor for life as well as for death. I was never a serious student but always loved having an open book ready. I went back to Alice Bailey, Edgar Cayce, and Gurdjieff, and reread much of Jung.

I loved having lunch at the Amrit, a restaurant in Muktananda's local ashram, but rarely went to the meditations. I joined the Transcendental Meditation (TM) movement but quit meditating after a few months and finally forgot the mantra altogether.

My intuitive pull was toward books rather than methods or religions. Systems felt like straightjackets to me—writers' lives were more interesting. Krishnamurti was one of the last teachers I read and the most interesting because he concluded that we each have to find our own way. He emphasized his convictions by resigning as head of the international movement he'd been groomed to lead since his childhood. His point of view was expressed in this final speech to the group.

I maintain that Truth is a pathless land, and you cannot
approach it by any path whatsoever, by any religion, by any
sect...I do not want to belong to any organization of a spiritual
kind...If an organization be created for this purpose, it becomes
a crutch, a weakness, a bondage, and must cripple the
individual, and prevent him from growing, from establishing
his uniqueness, which lies in his discovery for himself of that
absolute, unconditioned Truth...

Krishnamurti's observations struck a truthful note in me. I
became content to continue my investigations alone. The
searcher in me wanted to go all the way, to flee into the desert or
sit in a cave, to do anything just to satisfy my deep longing to
awaken the truth in myself. Yet another me wanted a house in the
hills and a new creative life in film. Whenever I felt the
frustration that arose from this split, I would go a bookstore and
once more try to find some answers. One of the closest and best
stocked was the Bodhi Tree on Melrose.

I parked my car where the door wouldn't get dinged and
paused a moment to look at the antique jewelry in the window
next door. Once inside, I stopped at the table of new releases and
picked up a new book on the life of Gandhi. I wondered, as I had
before, what I was doing writing a script about murdering dozens
of people while at the same time I wanted to read nothing but
spiritual searchers.

Clearly I was still living a split. I thought back to my earlier
years and realized that there had always been a discrepancy
between my ideals and how I actually lived my life. In advertising
I sold sugared breakfast cereals while I wouldn't eat them myself,
but in the end I had to stop. Could I write a script like *Mojave*
that was aimed only at making money and still have my ideals? I
realized I was letting my work override my values again and felt a
knot forming in my stomach.

Sometimes it seemed the whole country was living a split.
Maybe it was everybody's problem, or maybe that was the way we

had to live if we wanted any semblance of a normal life. Reality for this country was whatever appeared in the *New York Times, Wall Street Journal, and other major media.* Nothing much was reported there about the inner search. In fact, they seemed to have difficulty handling anything spiritual besides traditional religions. But I didn't want to think about my own values just then.

I reflected on my commitment to *Mojave*. It was a huge risk. I had spent months working on it, and a lot of money. Even more important, I had put the full force of my creative judgment into it. Yet in another sense, I was like a gambler who had walked up to a gaming table and placed a good portion of his wealth on the next roll.

The degree to which I had committed myself to the success of this screenplay bothered me, but I was thrilled with the risk. One thing was clear—I had put too much into it to walk away now.

I wandered into another room. There in front of me was a book I was familiar with, *The Hero with a Thousand Faces,* by Joseph Campbell. As I browsed through it, I remembered that it was already among my books at home. I suddenly felt a strong urge to go read it.

What attracted me to Campbell's book was that it explored life transitions in myth, and I wondered if it could help explain my own feelings. I had a gnawing sense that I was in a decline—an obvious expression of this was how detached I felt from contemporary life. I used to eat and breathe advertising, but now it had little meaning for me. I could never get enough of politics before, and now I could barely read about it. I was active socially while living in Chicago, but I now cared little for it. At first I thought I had withdrawn out of exhaustion, but on a deeper level there was a part of me that felt I was dying to the world, almost as if from a terminal illness. But I knew I wasn't sick, even though I was slowly losing my attachment to life. I knew it wasn't an emotional depression either, because I was familiar with that from therapy. Most interesting to me were the deep feelings of fulfillment under my sense of dying, as if I was being pulled toward some kind of culmination.

The answer that made most sense to me was something I'd heard about an Eastern way of life. A person's life was thought to unfold in three stages. The first was for becoming educated, the second was dedicated to working and making a contribution to the culture, and the third was reserved for an internal search.

The idea of three stages, or three acts in drama, came up in my screenwriting class. There was a beginning, a middle, and an end, and each part served a particular function in fulfilling the demands of the story. When I reflected on my own life I saw that I'd spent the first part getting an education, the next part working in business, and now I was most definitely on an internal search.

What was exciting about *The Hero with a Thousand Faces* was discovering that myths, too, were often three-act plays, and I thought I had stumbled onto a potentially important structure for successful filmmaking.

There was even more to it than that. I believe that ancient myths are allegories for our real lives, and that they have survived because they still carry important messages. They're like cultural dreams that can be interpreted to reveal unconscious truths.

Bruno Bettleheim wrote a wonderful book called *The Uses of Enchantment* about the meaning and importance of fairy tales in the emotional lives of children. He felt that the real power and attraction of such mythical stories lay in the archetypal figures that children related to in working out their own conflicts.

But it was through Campbell that I first began to see how myths could help me understand my feelings of detachment, and how my need to withdraw from business might be part of a deeper search.

The standard path of mythological adventure ... is a magnification of the formula represented in the rites of passage:

separation—initiation—return: which might be named the
nuclear unit of the monomyth.

A hero ventures forth from the world of the common day into a
region of supernatural wonder: fabulous forces are there
encountered and a decisive victory is won: the hero comes back
from this mysterious adventure with the power to bestow boons
on his fellow man.

Prometheus ascended to the heavens, stole fire from the gods,
and descended. Jason sailed through the Clashing Rocks into a
sea of marvels, circumvented the dragon that guarded the
Golden Fleece, and returned with the fleece and the power to
wrest his rightful throne from an usurper.

A startling realization for me was that even the life of Jesus
followed this theme with the crucifixion, death, and resurrection.
So did the lives of Buddha, Moses, and Arthur, along with
countless other heroes of myth, religion, and drama. I had
discovered a map of human development that could explain my
own growing detachment. Perhaps in its highest expression it
could describe a path to new levels of awareness. It struck me that
both Muktananda and Krishnamurti had experienced a complete
breakdown of their personal realities prior to reaching what they
felt was their "enlightenment."

It appeared that this structure of "separation—initiation—
return" that existed universally in myth was the world's
unconscious speaking to us, revealing the way toward growth
through its "dreams."

I found new evidence that by permitting myself time to
search I had begun living an expression of this universal pattern. I
had separated myself from the attachments of the past when I left
my career. After I withdrew and started writing, I began a period
of searching for new beliefs and ideas. The world of myth was
showing me the psychological challenges encountered in the
death of one identity and the creation of a new one. I read

Campbell's book as if it was a guided journey into the realms of my personal unconscious.

Several days later I got a message on my answering service from Larry. Excited, I called him right back. By this time I had become friendly with his assistant, and she got me through to him easily.

"Don, I like your script," he said, but in such a way that I didn't know if he simply liked it or was willing to do something with it.

"Great!" I said, not knowing quite what a writer says to a film executive who likes his work.

"I've got an idea and want to talk to you about it, but I'll be out of town for the next few weeks. Can you come in then?"

"Of course I can! I'll see you when you get back."

I made an appointment to see him as soon as he returned and began pacing the living room, as had become my habit when I had to wait.

It was during times of challenge that my fears were like dragons creeping up from the dark pit inside of me. Making sure these monsters stayed asleep was largely what kept me in safe routines most of my life.

However, having disturbed my inner landscape by leaving Chicago, I sensed that the dragons were on the prowl more often. It was as if I had released them by leaving the security of the status quo, and now a torrent of the monsters had come rushing into my world.

The dragons I had to deal with in California were mostly survival fears stimulated by issues of money and starting a new career, but they were small torments of the mind next to those that appeared when a huge tropical storm hit my beloved mountain. When I lived in a high-rise, rain was a fairly routine affair, no matter how hard it came or for how long. Now living in a remote house in the hills, rain could melt the earth like hot water over sugar.

After a very wet December and January, February came in for the knockout. Storms that looked like a string of powder puffs on the television weather map were coming in from Hawaii. One after the other, they came until I thought the mountains themselves would dissolve. But it wasn't until the next week that we expected the worst to hit.

I went down to the firehouse to get some burlap sacks. All along the canyon people were busy filling them with dirt to help contain the streams of mud flowing down the mountains. I put piles of empty bags along the driveway and, as a trickle of mud would seep out of the hillside, I would fill a sack and dam the stream on the spot.

It was a Saturday when the worst finally came. Two doctors who shared a house nearby stayed home from their hospital rounds and several of my friends came up to help. In a number of places the hillside would bulge as if suddenly pregnant, and then as we watched, it would give way to a flowing ooze that spilled through the vines and covered the driveway. Several feet deep, the stream of earth made its way across the road and down the other side, gathering more mud as it went.

I piled up a wall of sandbags to protect the house and went to bed that night wondering what the darkness would bring.

My yellow slicker lay in the hallway with the pants rolled down over my tall rubber boots all ready to climb into. Waves of rain beat on the flat roof, and periodically I would go outside and fill more bags if I discovered the hills moving again. Stray wanted to go with me each time but he was terrified by the storm's violence so I left him in the warmth of the house.

The electricity had gone out early in the day, so there were no lights or clocks, and no news from the television or radio. The road below was washed out, and I felt as if my life was under siege. The phones were working only intermittently, so the car radio became my only reliable connection to the world. Every few hours I would go sit in the front seat and listen to the weather reports. On one such trip, well after midnight, as I climbed out of the car I heard a rushing sound from above, and then the screams of several people from the canyon below.

"Hello!" I hollered. "Are you all right? Do you need some help?" I could hear quieter voices in the darkness but could not make out a reply. I guessed that everything was okay, so I went up the driveway toward the rushing sounds above me.

Several trees had fallen across the driveway and I had to climb over them to get to the noise. Suddenly the ground below me gave way and I slipped into a river of mud up to my waist and started sliding down the mountain. I grabbed a small tree and held on tight, terror closing my throat. I clung to its branches and pulled myself to firmer ground, inching up toward the road that had given way. Still the mud flowed from higher up, and I heard the people below calling to one another again.

I managed to claw my way to a secure spot and sat there shivering from nerves and the biting cold until I could compose myself. Then gathering my courage, I made my way to the garage and picked up a shovel and some burlap bags to start damming the flow again.

The following morning the rains subsided, but as I walked down the driveway, I found another large bulge in a vine-covered hillside. It was pushing over a retaining wall the way a fat man's belly hangs over his belt. A neighbor and I stacked bags to help hold the hillside back and then pegged several large tarps on the hill to keep it dry.

My coffee was cold in its muddy cup and I smelled like I had spent the night in a wet sleeping bag. I was exhausted from the week-long ordeal. Stray had been running in the underbrush, and when he returned, he put his cold nose into my hand. I could feel that he was drenched to the skin, so we went inside and I built a fire to warm the both of us.

I had never been so physically threatened as I was that week. Living in a high-rise and raising a family in the middle of a city did nothing to prepare me to stand up to such a storm. I was both exhilarated and threatened by the constant pounding of the storms as they kept coming in. I'd had to defend my right to the house all the way down to my core. When I was sure we couldn't possibly handle any more water on the mountain, we had days and days more rain. It was awful, and at the same time wonderful, to have to stand firm in the face of a torrent that would not stop.

The ordeal struck me as a test of some kind. It forced me to assert my claim to what I owned, as if the forces that brought me out here were making me fight for what I wanted.

Yet it was more than that. At first, I defended the house as if it were life itself, but as the storm wore on, I was somehow released from that illusion and realized I could leave it all behind and start over if I had to. The freedom was exhilarating. My blind attachment to the house was broken, and it left me feeling both more vulnerable and more secure than ever before. The illusion that I was my house was gone, and another layer of my defenses had been stripped away.

TWENTY

THE SUBTLE AGENDA

When I was a kid we played a game called Scavenger Hunt. Teams would find and follow clues that had been hidden around the neighborhood. The course was set up in advance, with each clue leading to the next, and when all of them were properly figured out, they led to a treasure. The team that got there first, won. Success depended on how accurately and quickly we were able to decipher each message, then move to the next, until we had completed them all.

As I looked back at the series of changes I'd made, I was reminded of Scavenger Hunt. I felt blocked when I began, but when I understood the clues my life was offering, I was released and led to a new place. Then I would go along for a while until I reached another block, and when I figured that one out, I would be led to the next place.

The way I got through each obstacle in my life was by trusting the same way of making choices that had always led to my best creative work. This meant choosing not what I thought I "should" do, but what I "desired" to do.

That wasn't easy. I'd been raised with the belief that to follow one's desires was not only selfish and prideful, but sinful. We were taught: "First comes God, then comes everybody else, and then comes me." But reading William Blake struck a note that felt true—that my desire was the universe's desire—and when I first felt that in my gut, doors of understanding began to open.

The way forward came from simply following what excited me, and as I did, I slowly became aware that the clues appeared more and more often. Soon I found them everywhere. What had begun as a single flash of insight continued and slowly revealed a more subtle level of reality.

A pattern emerged that I could trace back to that first clear moment in Lincoln Park. Deciding to leave my marriage uncovered my unhappiness with my career. Following the urge to come to California revealed my desire to write. And following my desire to write penetrated into a deeper realm that fascinated me more than anything.

I thought I was going along, step by step, following the clues and choosing what I wanted, but I became aware that a more subtle agenda was unfolding. I thought I was making career choices based only on my feelings, but now it felt as if I was being led into a deeper experience of life and of myself. My discovery of the "Subtle Agenda" became the most exciting thing, and I resolved to learn more about it.

It reminded me of a time when Sarah and I had gone to an amusement park. I was watching her as she turned the wheel of a little "kiddie ride" car, oblivious to the fact that she wasn't actually steering. But that didn't matter to her. She was having a wonderful time, enjoying turning the wheel all the same.

Remembering this incident made me see my life in a new way. Before I discovered the Subtle Agenda, I made choices thinking I was completely in charge. When things were working well, and I was getting raises and promotions, it made little difference who or what was really steering. But when things stopped working, I was forced to take a closer look, and I began to see the less obvious patterns underneath.

The Subtle Agenda became my new scavenger hunt. Every day I tried to read the clues that were sprinkled in my life to see where they were leading me. Sometimes a clue would come as an idea. At times it was a feeling or an urge that needed attention, or a friend saying something that stood out powerfully. At other times it was an event that seemed to have deeper meaning. But it always included a desire that wanted satisfaction. I'd learned to recognize the clues so if a thing made me feel enthusiastic, I went for it. If something drew me powerfully, I did it. If a book excited me as I flipped through it, I would read it.

I knew that the clues were everywhere in my life, even in my desire to write films. The game was built on several levels. The surface level was what I consciously chose, and the result, which was often different from what I expected, would always lead me to a deeper understanding. The rules were simple—stay alert to the clues and follow yearnings for fulfillment.

Given these rules, I realized that the Subtle Agenda had arranged my life perfectly to play the game. I had no job to report to and could follow it where ever it led. I thrilled at the adventure my life had become.

Each day I became more a student of the Subtle Agenda. Gradually, I developed an understanding of how it communicated with me. It was a harsh teacher at first, giving me hard bumps if I was slow, much the way a mother bear cuffs her cub. One of those "bumps" happened when the corporation wanted me back in Chicago, or gone.

In the weeks before, I had begun to feel that I'd been in the company too long, but I overrode the signals. I also experienced some frustration at not spending enough time writing, but I overrode those feelings too. And when the axe fell, I discovered that I had gotten what I wanted all along but had been too frightened to do for myself. I was like the cub who got scared and stopped at the edge of an icy stream. What I needed to get me to cross was a swift swat on my behind. The ultimatum might have hurt, but its effect and the insight it brought were welcome gifts.

This is when I realized that the rules really had changed for me. I began to evaluate events on two levels. One was the way they appeared on the surface and the other was the subtle learning they brought. So, like the cub, I learned from my misfortune. I stopped learning from the way things worked, and began learning from the way they didn't.

On the day of my meeting with Larry, I arrived at the gate of 20th Century-Fox, gave my name, and was directed to park outside the executive building where his office was. Driving onto a studio lot was as exciting as I thought it would be. I almost ran into another car as I stared at the fake elevated train tracks.

It was almost an hour before Larry finished with the emergencies that plagued his day. Finally we were in a meeting that had to be short because he was late for another appointment.

"I'm going to give *Mojave* to several agents I know to see what they think," he said.

"I really appreciate that," stumbled out of my mouth. "But before I do, I want to think about it over the weekend. I might want to produce it myself. I'm kinda looking for a project."

"Great." In a moment he had his coat on and was gone, and I was left staring at an old set of a New York street outside his window. My life felt like it was beginning to work again. It was like old times. Perhaps I had learned all I needed and now things were going to be okay. Maybe all I had to do was give my whole self over to a project for things to be all right.

Late that night I sat alone in my darkened living room listening to a recording of "The Red Headed Stranger." A friend had given me my first joint a few days before and I decided to try it again. I had called them *reefers* when I first saw the kids smoking them during the civil rights marches, but now I learned that butts were called *roaches*, and that when I had a puff, I was taking a *hit*. So in celebration of selling my first script, I picked up the roach and took a deep hit, then took "The Red Headed Stranger" off the tape deck and put on my astrological tape instead. I dropped a fresh log on the fire, put Stray outside, and sat in the flickering light, listening.

My head was full of satisfaction at Larry's interest in *Mojave*. Even if he didn't want it, which was inconceivable at that moment, at least he thought enough of it to consider it for himself and give it to a few agents.

I took another hit and laid back, listening to the astrologer. Gradually, a second reality seemed to take over. I heard far more on the tape than I had before. The voice of the astrologer became a voice from Olympus, and the ideas were truths from an oracle. I heard that I was about to enter a period of success, but nothing compared to what lay ahead a few years. The success of *Mojave* sounded like it was predicted in the stars from the beginning of time. My life took on huge proportions. Patterns of growth and of learning from my own disappointments were explored and explained, and I heard that new patterns were emerging that would fulfill me beyond my wildest dreams.

I began to see my life as a long braid of many colors leading me to a fulfillment that had lain ahead from the beginning of time. There were events and challenges, some even upon me at this time, but the overall pattern led powerfully onward.

Glancing around the room, I redecorated it with the funds I would receive from the sale of *Mojave*. I would put a skylight over the fireplace, and one in the bedroom so I could look up at the stars at night. And perhaps I would put a hot tub out beyond the pool in a spot that overlooked the canyon. Success was tasting very sweet.

It became clear to me why I had never felt totally fulfilled in advertising—I had never completely given myself over to it. I had never had the courage to risk everything on an idea that was totally mine. Now, that's exactly what I was doing. I was as high as a kite, and couldn't remember the thought that led to the thought that I'd just had. I got up, put Willie Nelson back on, and listened to God riding along on horseback. He and I were riding home.

TWENTY-ONE

RITE OF PASSAGE

Larry called me the following Monday, as he said he would. He told me that after a long and painful introspection, and a discussion with an agent friend of his, he decided that the script would not be good for him to produce. Both he and his friend felt it was too much of an exploitation picture, one that appealed to the violence in an audience with little to redeem it socially. He thought it was well written, though, and should be shown around. He asked if he could give it to a few agents he thought were better than those I had found, and maybe they could do something with it. He was sorry.

During the following month I had meetings with a couple of agents Larry had given the script to. All of them said that I was a commercial writer and that the script, because it was well done, would make a good "calling card" but it would not make a movie. They also thought it was an exploitation picture with too much violence—this was years before *Rambo*—and that there were better Vietnam stories around town. An agent from William Morris, one of the biggest talent agencies in town, said he would represent me as a writer, and that if I wrote any more scripts I should bring them to him.

Not selling *Mojave* was a terrible shock. I had worked more than a year on the script and my creative instincts told me it was good. I had passed up living in Europe to write it and had spent much my reserves to finance it. In all my years in advertising I had never taken such a blow to my creative judgement. It was devastating. I had been overlooked for raises and promotions without feeling much, and even when we lost million dollar accounts, it was only abstract money, and abstract pain.

This was different. I was alone, with no large corporation behind me and no significant financial base underneath me. All I had was my own creative judgment. It had always been my strength before, and I now wondered if it was faulty. Everyone who read the script liked the writing and felt the characters were well developed. It had a strong conflict and the story got more powerful as it unfolded. It felt good to me all the way down to my toes. All the benchmarks I used to judge creative work pointed to a successful outcome.

Were they right? Was it un-produceable because it was too violent? Should I keep trying to sell this one script? I couldn't imagine doing that. I'd be carrying it around like a dead child, looking for someone to give it life.

More frightening to me was the possibility that this was the beginning of a deeper crisis. I had left the safety of the corporation and was unaccustomed to working alone. I wondered, now, if I had stumbled into some kind of disaster.

Or was I supposed to learn something from this? Was the Subtle Agenda trying to tell me to write something more positive? Did it want me to find another place inside myself from which to create?

Reflecting on the screenplay, I was shocked that I, the writer, was so full of anger and violence. The story had not been forced upon me by some producer. I wrote it because it was an action picture that might have strong box office draw. I never once thought about the negative impact it might have on audiences or what contribution it would make to the quality of life. I wrote it because I thought it worked and would launch me into film.

I was still living the split that caused me so much conflict in advertising. My desire for success and money was leading me in one direction while my desire for deeper fulfillment was taking me in another. I saw the irony of my life on the mountain. It was so wonderfully idyllic, and the only violence was coming from my own psyche. I wondered how much of the conflict that I'd experienced throughout the years was the result of my own internal split.

I had never tried giving birth to my own dream before, and even though I now saw its flaws, I was unprepared for the grief of watching it die. No wonder I had spent so many years protected inside a successful corporation—a guy could get himself killed out here.

On the freeway it takes just a minute or two to drive past the city of Mojave, and I felt as if I had done just that. More than a year of work had disappeared in the blink of an eye. All the excitement I had built up collapsed. The money I was thinking about spending on the house evaporated.

The new ways of making choices that I was learning to depend on were not working and that troubled me. I had taken a couple of strong steps into my new life but the results weren't supporting me. There was nothing in my astrological reading about a failure like this. What could have happened? Under the pain, I had a feeling that the Subtle Agenda was leading me, but I couldn't understand where.

I took Stray for a walk around the mountain to do some serious thinking about what to do. I reviewed my chances of starting as a screenwriter, how long my money would last, how much I wanted to continue to write, and what I would do if I stopped. I also asked myself what I really wanted to do, because that might decide everything.

I began to hear murmurs from my inner board of directors, as if real trouble was brewing.

"We need to have a meeting," I said, hoping to bring order to my thoughts. "I want to be sure we're in agreement on what to do now."

The chairman spoke first.

"I'm not sure film writing is the answer. It's a young man's game, and here you are trying to learn a new craft twenty years after your competition has learned theirs. I'd suggest getting a job in management or something like that."

There was always something vaguely defeatist in what my chairman said, and the insecure creative person inside me who needed support never felt encouraged by him.

"I still want to stick it out," I said a little grumpily. "I love writing and I feel like I'm getting closer to selling something, despite how it looks right now. *Mojave* might have failed because it doesn't express how I really feel. I'd like to keep at it, and maybe try to write something on the hero's journey."

In these discussions, the chairman only spoke of my writing or my career or about making money, and never of how much he valued the internal exploration I had begun. It was as if he thought my search was the work of a family idiot, seen but never spoken of.

We waited for Stray to return from chasing a rabbit before we continued.

"I'm inclined to agree with the writer," my little voice finally said. "Purely on a career level, he's gotten a good reception from some respected professionals in the industry. The hero's journey is a wonderful film idea because it works on motivational levels as well, but I'm even more intrigued by his discovery of the Subtle Agenda. It's fulfilling him more, and on a deeper level than screenwriting is. It's an unexplored frontier for him. He discovered it by trusting himself and following his own desires, so I wouldn't suggest he abandon it for a job just yet."

I had long ago learned the importance of subtle motivations in advertising. The "Fly the Friendly Skies" theme was a great example because it spoke to people's fears and anxieties about flying. Calling the frightening sky "friendly" was clever enough, but I always thought that the words held an even stronger promise that a friendly deity was watching over United's passengers.

Understanding the deeper currents of meaning in communication had always been an interest of mine. And the hero's journey seemed like a natural and powerful theme for a film. Audiences had responded to it many times before. Most of Disney's early work was based on it. An excellent example is *Pinocchio*, the wooden puppet that is transformed into a real boy. *Star Wars* is another more recent and more successful example.

When I discovered the hero's journey, I was excited not just because it made a good film structure, but because it shed some light on my own recent experiences. The rite of passage metaphor was popular in myth, and now in film, because it expresses the stages of growth and change we must all pass through on our way to fulfillment. But of increasing importance to me was that it reflected the grandest journey of all—how to awaken the awareness of the eternal within one's self.

"It sounds like it could make a lot of money if you ever got the idea on film," the chairman said.

"Yeah, look how much *Star Wars* made!" I added excitedly.

"But I also think," my little voice reminded us, "that on a deeper level, he wants to combine his newly discovered values with how he earns a living. Perhaps since he's found a parallel between the myth of the hero and his own inner search, a story that combined those elements might be the way to do that."

I felt good that all the members of the board finally agreed on something, and was excited that perhaps this meant my split was being healed.

There had been no choice about whether or not to keep on writing. I loved what I was doing more than anything in the world, despite the risks. I couldn't have stopped and gotten a job, no matter what the consequences. I knew I was heading in the right direction, even if recent events didn't support my feelings.

I was looking for a way to combine my inner values with earning an income—that's what I left Chicago to find. Perhaps the Subtle Agenda was showing me that the flaw in *Mojave* was that it didn't do that. It didn't express my true values. This made sense to me since I was still feeling the split when I wrote it. The story had nothing to do with me. I wrote it to make money and get my career going, with little thought to whether it was an expression of myself. I was beginning to understand how artists struggle to stay true and also earn a living. I was excited and filled with anticipation that perhaps I could find a story that would let me combine everything I wanted into one project.

Nevertheless, an unsettled feeling existed alongside my determination. I had the vague awareness of an approaching winter in my life. There was a slight decline in my natural energy that must be the way a tree feels in early September, when the cold wind delivers its first message that the vitality of summer is passing and an encroaching dormancy will take its place.

Then I began finding evidence that reflected what I was feeling inside. I saw that my financial reserves were indeed running out, and the energy in my body was ebbing too. In my dreams I saw many symbols that expressed my decline, but found no hint of rebirth anywhere. My hopes were as strong as ever, but when I looked closely at the signs in my life, everything seemed to be diminishing and nothing was growing.

An orange gray cloud hung low over the Los Angeles basin, and I realized for the very first time that the city's air was polluted.

When I got back to the house, I found that a messenger had leaned a 20th Century Fox envelope against the front door. There was no note from Larry, just the script inside. I unlocked the door and tossed the script on my writing table that looked out over the canyon. Suddenly I felt as if there was no ground under my feet. The bridge that I thought *Mojave* was had taken me out over the ravine, and had dissolved under me. I took a deep breath, and like the coyote in the cartoons, I decided not to look down, expecting that the next script would be the one that would carry me across.

The financial heat didn't lessen. Joan called to ask if I was willing to spend more money on Sarah's private school. If so, would I pay for her to go to a prep school in the Bay Area? Joan's work on her doctorate in psychology was taking her to San Francisco and she wanted Sarah in school near her. This would allow Sarah to go home to her on weekends and perhaps even during the week, and of course would make it easier for her to come to see me too.

I wanted my daughter to continue having the best education possible, and because Joan couldn't afford the increase, I said I'd pay more than our agreement called for so that she could go to the new school. I was happy about having Sarah here in California, even though it added more financial pressure at a time when I could afford it least.

Making this decision from my heart rather than from a financial strategy felt good. Perhaps if I'd asked my chairman of the board he would have been more hard-nosed, but I swallowed the new financial pill and trusted that things would work out. After all, I'd have my daughter nearby. And things had always worked out before.

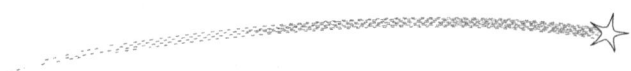

DUAL WORLDS

In this stage I found myself traveling through dual worlds—the physical and the subtle. The outer path was becoming more obscure while the inner one was opening.

By letting myself follow internal guidance, I discovered a connection to life that I'd never before perceived. I found that life was language, and I heard a gentle voice speaking through all things. I began listening for words from my heart and having conversations with the events unfolding in my path. The heretofore elusive subtleties of life ignited with luminous clarity, revealing hidden meanings, quiet truths, and a subtle path forward.

I developed a hunger for knowledge that I could not satiate. There was an urgency to learn as much as I could about the Subtle Agenda. As I digested book after book, I discovered new meaning in works that I had discarded years earlier and brilliance in the ancients I had never fully understood. In my search for clearer glimpses into the subtle realm, I tried every device, amulet, system, process, and belief. Though each had something to offer, I found none that I fully trusted. I kept hearing an admonition that life was my teacher.

By finally accepting that my lonely predicament was its own truth, I realized that the answers must be inside me, and that I would have to find my own way.

TWENTY-TWO

HOT PROPERTY

When the disappointment of *Mojave* subsided, I tried two other script ideas, but after several months of writing, my energy and enthusiasm just ran out. I showed them to the agent who said he'd represent me, but he wasn't excited about them either. Like budding flowers that suddenly wilt and die, the two stories lay stillborn on the shelf.

I began to experience fear gathering in the fringes of my awareness the way a pack of wolves collects around a campfire. Something was wrong. My expenses were increasing and my stock market investments were not returning the money they had in the beginning. I read the signs to mean that the Subtle Agenda might be changing its direction, that it might be on a different course than film writing. The Subtle Agenda had led me out here but was not yet supporting my efforts. Where were the events in my life taking me? I felt I was being bumped to either get busier writing or find some other way of earning an income. Either way, the pressure had been switched to high.

Responding was not going to be easy, because something was definitely happening to my creative power. Where at first my enthusiasm allowed me to work on a script for many hours at a time, now I was barely able to write for even a few hours a day. The words just weren't coming with the same energy they had before.

Thoughts of getting a job again started to resurface, but I felt so committed to the challenge of writing that I didn't want to dissipate my focus in any way.

Pacing over a story one day, I anxiously went to the study to, once again, survey the shelves of books there. It was then that I rediscovered one that Karen had given me months earlier, but that I had put aside. It had been given to her by an agent friend who wanted to see it filmed. I sat down with it and in a few minutes became absorbed.

The story described a young prince who belongs to a race of people who, because they have greater than normal powers, suffer persecution and go underground. The prince, unknown to everyone including himself, has even greater magical forces hidden within him. With the help of an older member of the court, he is taken through an initiation in which his powers become partially available. Then, in a life and death struggle for his throne, he uncovers a potent secret that has been buried in his unconscious throughout his life. In doing so, he discovers his full supernatural powers and defeats his adversary.

A thrill shot through me. Here was a story that was built on the myth of the hero: separation—initiation—return. And although it was published material, it was available to buy. The story appealed to me greatly because it so explicitly described the human struggle to awaken to its supernatural origins. With such fertile roots, the film could have tremendous box office appeal. Maybe I had found my "hot property."

Of additional importance was my feeling that finding this story seemed like it could resolve my split. Perhaps through this project I could finally combine my values with what I was working on in my career. Because needing to resolve this conflict was what had propelled me from advertising in the first place, maybe this was what the Subtle Agenda had been pushing me toward all along.

I located the author, Susan, and met with her and her agent. After brief negotiations, we signed an agreement that we would develop the script together and that my agent would represent it to the film industry. We would split the revenues fifty-fifty, and as part of the deal, we also agreed to develop the other related books that she had in print.

In a few days we were into a wonderful period of writing, in which we began adapting the story to screenplay form.

When I was not writing, I thought more about the rite of passage theme. I knew I was in some kind of death-rebirth drama myself, and although the process was universal enough to be a familiar structure in myth, there was not much written about it. I was aware of the mid-life crisis—the disorientation that comes around age forty—but that answered nothing, because the death and rebirth drama can happen many times throughout our lives.

I went back to Campbell's *Hero with a Thousand Faces* and found that the rites of passage were more than mere celebrations. Their underlying purpose was to help the individual separate from one stage of growth and introduce him to the next.

> The so-called rites of passage, which occupy such a prominent place in the life of primitive society (ceremonials of birth, naming, puberty, marriage, burial, etc.), are distinguished by formal, and usually very severe, exercises of severance, whereby the mind is radically cut away from the attitudes, attachments, and life patterns of the stage left behind. Then follows an interval of more or less extended retirement, during which are enacted rituals designed to introduce the life adventurer to the forms and proper feelings of his new estate, so that when, at last, the time has ripened for the return to the normal world, the initiate will be as good as reborn.

This passage explained my detachment from the life I knew in Chicago. My mind was "radically cut away" from the past just as happens in primitive rituals. And, whether I liked it or not, I was experiencing a "more or less extended retirement," which I hoped was designed to introduce me to my new life. What I had not yet experienced was the "return to the normal world," which I interpreted as beginning a new career.

What was becoming hauntingly clear was that my own experience here on the mountain was mirrored in myth and ritual, and that I was playing out an ancient rite of passage that I had not even known existed.

I was struggling with personal issues, yet the fundamental structure and process seemed to be universal. I could see clearly how my own difficulties were described in myth and how the rituals reflected the stages I was going through. I became astonished at the synchronicity of it all.

Dissatisfaction with the past and desire for renewal seemed to be such a strong imperative for humankind that stories and rituals are devised to guide us every step of the way.

Out of this awareness came new insight into the dimensions of my own difficulty. I had thought I was just changing jobs but now found myself in a mythic struggle of rebirth. The universal appeal of this process fired me with even more desire to incorporate what I was discovering into film. But I was also filled with profound longing to understand more about what was happening to me. I began to see the drama being played out in myth and ritual as an aspect of what I was experiencing as the Subtle Agenda.

Now more than ever, I wanted to find the clue that might end the string of "bad luck" I was encountering. What was it that my Subtle Agenda was trying to bump me into discovering?

The writing experience was exciting and satisfying. Susan was easy to work with and willing to adjust her material to fit the new medium as long as the integrity of the book was maintained. In about six months we had written the final draft of the screenplay and I had given a freshly typed copy to my agent. Then, once again, I waited.

People who go to work every day know nothing about the Hollywood wait. But writers and actors, and almost everyone else in movies, wait for meetings, wait for auditions, wait for an agent's call, wait for a response, and wait for work. So, like everyone else, I waited.

As the months went on, my agent would call and tell me that various directors, producers, or studios had read the script and for one reason or another had passed. The studio that had released an Arthurian picture was very interested, but then decided against it. The director of an extremely successful science fiction movie loved it, told my agent one Friday that he wanted to do it, and on the plane home to England that weekend decided to pass. Finally, a producer that my agent also represented read the script and wanted to make a deal.

We entered into negotiations that took months, and as time wore on my funds continued to diminish. I was on the clock to make something happen, and perhaps it was part of their strategy, but time appeared to mean nothing to them. Furthermore, we were beginning to see that what we were being offered was very good for them, but not for us. Like many script deals, this one gave us no assurance of doing the rewrite, and possibly no real input on the actual production.

It seemed they wanted the script, but wanted us out. The longer the negotiations went on, the less it looked like we were going to get the kind of deal we wanted. When I heard the producer had gone to Egypt on a picture and would be gone the better part of a year, I lost my patience.

Another producer I'd known in Chicago had also read the script and was interested in talking to me about it. Susan and I met with him and his partner several times, and in those meetings came to much the kind of arrangement that we had been unable to obtain before. We would get cash, have our legal expenses from negotiations with the first producer paid, and stay with the project as writers and co-producers. On a handshake, we agreed to the terms, so I called my law firm and stopped the negotiations with the first producer. While the new agreement was being written up, the new producers went to two studios for money, both of which rejected it. Too expensive, too risky, too much fantasy.

Then in a meeting, they abruptly announced that they had lost interest and were going to pass too. I couldn't believe it. They broke our deal. One of them was a friend, and our handshake had meant nothing. I sat in stunned silence. We now had no deal with anyone. They weren't even going to pay the legal expenses they had agreed to.

During the next week, I tried to pick up the pieces. The script had been pretty well shopped around, and my agent said there were few other people to show it to. He did go back to the first producer, but he'd gone on to other things and was no longer interested.

I was devastated like never before. I had raised the stakes higher than ever, and it had come to nothing. I had done everything I felt necessary to finally break through and it hadn't worked. I had bridged the split between the material and myself and had put it all on the line, and it still failed. I was close to losing trust not only in myself as a writer, but in my inner voice as well.

The failure to get the script off the ground sent me into a flurry of reassessment. I knew I was an amateur in the movie business and that much of my difficulty could be laid to that. But despite the truth in this observation, I felt the solution to the problem lay not in the movie business, but inside myself.

My creative success had always come from following inner forces—my intuition, my little voice, my aesthetic desires. But here was an anomaly. Listening to those sources had led nowhere. And because the old rules no longer seemed to work, I felt the growing urge to go even deeper into myself in case there was another, more subtle voice to be heard.

TWENTY-THREE

INNER MERLIN

I walked around the mountain many times in the following weeks, worrying about all the things that were troubling me the way an animal does when he has a thorn in his paw. I was on the fire road when I heard Stray yelp from down below and looked for him over the edge of the slope. He must have jumped a coyote and was now so deep in the underbrush that I could only trace him by his intermittent barking. But I wasn't worried. Stray knew how to take care of himself and was twice the size of the local coyotes.

As I thought about the recent painful series of events, it became obvious that I was on a very slippery slide. If things continued as they were, I would not only be in a very serious financial crisis, but in a pretty serious emotional crisis too. The only thing keeping my ego together was the knowledge that I had been successful before and the belief that whatever inside me had helped me do it then would also help me now.

My chairman of the board had been waiting to speak.

"Look," he said, finally intruding into my thoughts. "You were successful because you were doing your work every day, being a good employee, and earning your paycheck. You got off the track when you decided to go out on your own. Not everyone's an entrepreneur, or even a writer. Look, with all due respect, every kid in the country wants to go to Hollywood and make movies, but fortunately, something stops most of them. But it's not too late for you. Go down there and get a job doing something you know how to do."

I shot a glance down at the city now barely visible through the morning layer of smog and felt my resistance stiffen.

"You're not making any money at this," my chairman continued, "and the little money you have left was earned by responsible effort toward a rational goal. You'd better shape up or there's going to be trouble. Mark my words."

He made a good case, and the fact that I heard echoes of my parents in his last sentence added power to what he said.

"Wait a minute," piped up my little voice—the one who I recalled had led me into all this. "If your chairman was so smart, why were you so unhappy back in Chicago? You left because you had struggled a whole lifetime in your chosen field and once you arrived near enough to see the top, you discovered that nothing was there for you. You were able to see that your life was no longer a reflection of what you felt inside, and that unless you did something more attuned to what you did feel, you weren't going to reach your full potential, or be happy."

Stray came back and I thought he was limping. I watched him for a moment, but whatever it was that was bothering him went away. He shook himself and came over to be petted.

"Also," my little voice continued, trying to regain my attention, "I don't think you've gone far enough yet to even know if it's time to quit. And I don't think you should be measuring yourself by whether or not you've sold a screenplay. You're following a call from inside that is far more important to you than simply earning a living. You earned a good living in Chicago and for a while you were pretty content, but ultimately it will take more than that to fulfill you. You want to find a new way to express yourself, something that's more important to you than making money—you just haven't done that yet."

I was moved by what he said and knew he was right. Just earning a living wasn't the real issue. I was being pulled by a deeper need than that, but felt frustrated that I had chosen such a difficult path. Besides, why couldn't I be happy just making a living the way I was before?

"Yeah, 'following a call,'" I mumbled, mimicking my little voice. "But I thought it was a call to an adventure that included earning a living. I have a daughter to support, and a house and a car. I want a career. I don't want to follow a call into a vacuum. Just following calls doesn't pay very well."

I shut out the cacophony and walked briskly ahead. What had I gotten myself into here? I was lost, sure as hell, and now my little voice had even given up mentioning an income. I was being drawn deeper into a challenge that felt more and more difficult to win.

The only person who I was sure would understand what I was feeling was Campbell. I wondered if there were any clues to what I might do hidden in his book. I went back to the house and pulled the well-worn *Hero with a Thousand Faces* off the shelf and began to read:

> Once having traversed the threshold, the [adventurer] moves in a dream landscape of curiously fluid, ambiguous forms, where he must survive a succession of trials.

"Well, he's got that part right," I murmured.

> The hero is covertly aided by the advice, amulets, and secret agents of the supernatural helper whom he met before his entrance into this region.

I immediately thought of Merlin, the magician who led Arthur through his many trials. And of Obi Wan Kenobi in *Star Wars*. I always felt those magical characters were symbols of the hero's intuition.

And it so happens that if anyone—in whatever society—undertakes for himself the perilous journey into the darkness by descending, either intentionally or unintentionally, into the crooked lanes of his own spiritual labyrinth, he soon finds himself in a landscape of symbolic figures (any of which may swallow him) …. In the vocabulary of the mystics, this is the second stage of the Way, that of the "purification of the self," when the senses are "cleansed and humbled," and the energies and interests "concentrated upon transcendental things"; or in a vocabulary of more modern turn: this is the process of dissolving, transcending, or transmuting the infantile images of our personal past.

As I read Campbell's words, I became even more convinced that I was in some kind of spiritual process of disintegration and refinement, and that I must indeed be in the second stage of whatever process was underway. It felt like the "purification of self" had begun because my senses were definitely being "cleansed and humbled." I had not felt so stripped and raw since I was in kindergarten. I felt like I was part child, laid bare and vulnerable, and part man, worldly and experienced. I was both big and small, and strangely, it felt as if the only way out lay deeper and beyond the horizon of anything I knew. Maybe that's what Campbell meant when he said that interests turn toward "transcendental things."

I noticed that when my external world no longer worked and the process of financial decline ensued, the search for transcendence did indeed emerge. I was even getting the feeling that the external world had destructed on purpose as a prelude to the complete re-creation of myself.

As I experienced the effects of the Subtle Agenda, the world came alive in ways it never had before. Each time something didn't work out, along with the pain, I felt the deeper value in what happened. I became aware of a larger presence within the failure that was unmistakably benevolent, and it made me wonder if it had truly been a "failure" at all.

The spiritual world I was discovering was quite different from religion as I had known it. This was a realm that didn't depend on right or wrong, good or evil, but on sensitivity, trust, courage, and love.

Now, through reading Campbell, I saw that my appreciation for the transcendent might be a sign that a new stage of development was beginning. Perhaps the interest in God that people experience with age is not merely a defense, but a major breakthrough into a new stage of life.

I returned to the pages, looking for clues about what might lie ahead.

> In our dreams the ageless perils, gargoyles, trials, secret helpers, and instructive figures are nightly still encountered; and in their forms we may see reflected not only the whole picture of our present case, but also the clue to what we must do to be saved.

I had often read that a teacher appears when the student is ready. Is this what Campbell meant by "secret helpers" and "instructive figures?" Maybe my instructive figure was my little voice, and what about the Subtle Agenda? No other teachers had appeared. I had encountered no visions and heard no voices from souls beyond. I had met no psychics and wasn't moved to follow a guru. My initial interest in astrology had almost faded, and I consulted no other "divining" system to provide direction. My guidance was all coming from trying to understand the life around me and urgings from inside.

So if my now familiar little voice *was* truly my instructive figure, was the Subtle Agenda my secret helper? If so, I had found my teachers and they were both inside me. Suddenly I realized just how much I was taking charge of my life.

When I looked back, I saw that once I made a commitment to change my life, things around me went into motion as if a stage manager had been given the orders to move scenery in a play. That first choice was a trigger that began what seemed to be an independent movement toward fulfilling my desires.

What I had to do now was understand what I had set in motion and learn how to work with it. This brought to mind a scene from Disney's *Fantasia* in which the sorcerer's apprentice learns to get things going but hasn't yet learned to control or stop them. There was little help on this from Campbell, but one passage did catch my attention: "The ordeal is a deepening of the problem of the first threshold and the question is still in balance: Can the ego put itself to death?"

Was he referring to the sense of vanity I usually associated with the word ego, or the Freudian definition—the conscious self that lies between the unconscious and the external world?

This was most difficult to understand. Obviously I was heading toward a "death" of some kind, but what part of me needed to die? Was it the "me" that had been unhappy in Chicago, the one I had set out to change? I felt in my bones that he *was* dying and thought the process was close to complete. What more needed to go? Did my desire for a career have to die? I had already become more interested in personal fulfillment than in film. Would I now have to choose one over the other? What deeper understanding did I need to put solid ground under me once again?

> The original departure into the lands of trials represented only
> the beginning of the long and really perilous path of initiatory
> conquests and moments of illumination. Dragons have now to
> be slain and surprising barriers passed—again, again, and again.

If I was actually experiencing what Campbell was describing, how far along was I on this "long and really perilous path?" Were the trials I encountered thus far the last, or would there be more "dragons" to slay and more "surprising barriers" to pass "again, again, and again?" I felt ready to face anything but had no real understanding of how or what to do. Maybe my little voice had some clues.

I was reminded of the closing scenes of *Star Wars* when Luke and the other fighter pilots are making their final pass at the Death Star. Obi Wan Kenobi's relationship to Luke is like Merlin's relationship to Arthur—both magicians act as guides and communicate telepathically.

In this scene, all of Luke's comrades have failed at striking their targets and have been defeated using the latest scientific instruments and guidance systems. On Luke's last attempt, Obi Wan Kenobi, now in spirit form, is heard telling Luke to "trust The Force." He tells him that he cannot rely on his instruments to find his way into the vulnerable heart of the giant Death Star, but that he *can* do it if he lets his internal impulses guide him instead. It is only through his deepest resources that Luke is able to connect with and wield the power of "The Force."

This scene symbolized what I was encountering. The ways I usually solved problems were not working, and I, too, had to make the shift and follow my own internal guidance system.

The writer in me was fascinated to see how important the "secret helpers" and "instructive figures" are to heroes in myth. As the challenges become greater, the hero needs a visionary source that can be trusted in even the most confusing times. To do this, the helper must speak from a dispassionate, even transcendent world that lies beyond earth's illusions and conflicts.

Magical characters like Merlin and Obi Wan provided that in stories, but in my ordinary life the inspirations burned brightly from inside me, even when objective evidence clearly told me the opposite.

More and more I trusted my little voice as my guide, my Merlin. It whispered advice to me in those moments when an important choice was about to take me in a new direction. It helped me unlock clues the Subtle Agenda presented, always urging me to make my daily life a reflection of what I felt inside, and asking only that I be more honest, more real than I had been the moment before.

I recalled how the relationship with my little voice had begun in Chicago when it reminded me that I wasn't living my values. When I left the agency, it gave me the courage to follow my desire to write. When *Mojave* failed, it told me that it might be because I wasn't writing what was in my heart. Then when the fantasy script came to nothing, it told me that maybe I needed to write an original story and stop looking outside myself for something to pull me along. Each time something failed it had helped me see that with it came something of value, and this is what kept moving me ahead.

With each step, my little voice had led me further inside myself. With each failure, I was led past what had been my limit before, and it now appeared that all the barriers would have to fall. I felt alone but not lost. And even though I was sure I was heading in the right direction, I still experienced fear about the incessant failure of my old familiar ways not working the way they used to.

I had become so absorbed in writing and in what felt like my life and death process, that it seemed there was no room for a long-term relationship. Karen had been wonderful to me and for me, but I wasn't ready for any kind of commitment. When she moved to Santa Barbara, there were no others for quite some time.

Then when I was taking Sarah around to apply to schools, I met Monica, a poetry teacher at a private school in Los Angeles. We had pretty well decided on the Bay Area school, but Sarah had not been accepted yet, so to be safe we were applying at a few other places.

Monica was both a poet and a playwright. We liked each other from the beginning, though I felt some guilt about hitting on one of Sarah's prospective teachers. We spent a lot of time together, and I grew to care for her and her young daughter a great deal. Still, I was not interested in committing to any relationship until I got my life on solid ground. On one hand, I resisted intimacy, but on the other I longed to once again have the great love that Joan and I had shared in our earlier years.

Memories of our now scattered family came rushing back when Lynn, Joan's daughter, stopped by from Alaska with her boyfriend. They stayed with me a few days, but we barely mentioned the divorce. I guess we were hoping we had healed enough of the pain and wanted the past to stay buried. I was grateful for the time we spent together and glad that she and I had made a new beginning.

THE THRESHOLD

With the continuing signs of decline appearing everywhere, I began to suspect that an epic moment was approaching — one that would require all the knowledge, courage, and wisdom I could muster. I felt that the challenge would happen on my material path, but that to meet it successfully, I'd have to remain as aware as possible of my purest ideals.

As my material losses mounted, I felt continually challenged and tormented. Because I had always measured my worth in money and success, I was unnerved by the lack of progress in my work. With no new financial support developing, I felt the physical part of my world weakening, and I became frustrated and depressed.

It was obvious that a cleansing was under way. Each bright new opportunity was ending in failure as if life were trying to extinguish itself.

With my past ending and the future refusing to begin, my animal instincts sensed a trap. But as my difficulties persisted, my little voice asked that I go deeper. Instead of retreating in fear, I let myself open to my inner impulses and trusted that whatever unfolded, I was being led in the right direction.

TWENTY-FOUR

INTO THE STUDIOS

I was finding it harder to write, and the fact that I was able to spend less time at it worried me. I was interpreting the events in my life as if they were dream symbols, and because there was still no income from writing, I was looking for a clue about what that meant. Perhaps the Subtle Agenda was preparing me for another change.

My little voice kept after me to write what I was experiencing, but I was losing hope of finding material that would interest the major studios. Most moviegoers were in their late teens to early twenties, and the inner journey was a far cry from what the average kid wants to take his date to see on a Saturday night.

I could either try to please an audience or write to satisfy myself. At times I wished I could get interested in something that would simply make money, but I couldn't. Not anymore. As my awareness of the Subtle Agenda increased, the ordinarily obscure world of the eternal so invaded my daily life that only tales of mythic proportion could contain the impact of what I felt.

As time went on it became difficult to believe that I could write for myself and for the movies. But I wasn't ready to give up. I had written six scripts, although only three were complete enough to show around. I decided to try one more.

The story I started working on was about a powerful businessman who is connected to a group of higher beings who watch over earth. He is one of twelve people on the planet who is responsible for doing the work of what I called "The Brotherhood." He has lived a varied life, is tired, and because he never married, has missed the usual warming influences of a family. Fatigued and having lost interest in life, he appeals to the board to let him leave earth. They listen to his request but refuse, reminding him that a requirement for one of The Brotherhood to leave earth is that he find a suitable replacement, which he has not done. When he persists anyway, The Brotherhood agrees, but with the condition that he train an apprentice that they will send. To his dismay, the candidate is a twenty-year-old girl— young, naïve, and totally unaware of anything but material existence. He realizes he has a hard task ahead of him but agrees to take her on.

In working with her as his apprentice, however, he gradually falls in love, and having opened his heart to her, decides he'd rather stay. When he tells The Brotherhood his wishes, they tell him that the girl was not a true apprentice, but an angel sent to help him open his heart—the last thing he was to achieve before his life on earth could be completed.

Several people read *The Apprentice* and found the script too confusing or obscure. It died from lack of interest.

Monica and I had become a comfortable pair, seeing each other almost every weekend. It was easy and non-threatening for me, although she would get upset occasionally because I still considered our relationship a casual one. I needed my privacy and plenty of time alone, and any more of a commitment felt like it would have pulled me off track.

I was getting tired of writing and my money was running low, but I still wanted to find a way to end my streak of difficulties. Since I had made my living moving creative projects through large corporations, I wondered if I would be more successful working in one of the studios. If working from the inside would give me the power to make the kind of films I wanted to, then I would do it, even if it meant going to work for someone else.

As it happened, Larry had been negotiating with Disney about being head of production, but after a while he decided against it. They would not offer him an employment contract, which was unusual in the industry, and because they had a reputation for being troubled recently, he didn't want to make himself that vulnerable. But he was aware of my desire to work in film and of my admiration for the studio's early work. I couldn't believe it when he told me he'd suggested they talk with me!

Larry was a great friend from the beginning. We'd met through a woman friend while he was in the story department at Fox. He'd had a brilliant rise through several other studios on his way to his current position as head of production at United Artists.

Larry combined many unusual qualities for a studio executive. He was sensitive, bright, artistic, and went out of his way to make creative people comfortable in a system that didn't always do that. Beyond these qualities, he also had a much larger dimension than what I was used to seeing in most young executives in this business, or in advertising. He had a world view, and a deep interest and caring for humanity. Feeling these things strongly, he tried to make pictures that reflected his vision, but this was not always possible given a system with kids as its primary market.

He was always much busier than I, and often he would come to the house and sit by the pool, silently reading from a tall stack of scripts. Larry didn't know every detail of what I was going through, but we were together often and were able to communicate in ways I always cherished. Over the years I grew to love him as much as any friend I'd ever had.

When we first became acquainted, he saw me as a pretty salable screenwriter. As we got to know each other, he thought I would make a good studio executive. Then after he read *The Apprentice*, he saw me as a true believer.

This succession of observations might have raised my spirits if I hadn't been trying to break into such a competitive business. When he called me a "true believer," I felt a shot of fear that perhaps my inner journey was taking me out of touch. But my hope was that there were other people in Hollywood besides Larry who shared my vision. When I heard that he'd suggested me to Disney, I felt that I might meet them there.

In a series of lunches, I met with Disney's head of distribution and got along wonderfully with him. After that he organized a lunch at the commissary on the studio lot with the chairman of the board, the president, and the head of marketing.

We talked about a lot of things, but the central issue for the company was the continuing decline of film revenues. Its other ventures were keeping the company healthy, but its movie business was in a long financial doldrum. Since the president had the title of executive producer, the responsibility was clearly his. He had interpreted the studio's historic strengths in his own way and had a rather poor box office record.

Disney had a long reputation for producing powerful films based on traditional mythic themes. Whether management was aware of it or not, these films most often followed the structure of the hero's journey. This was the main reason I was interested in working with them despite Larry's description. By the time this opportunity arose, I had researched many of the films in Hollywood that were based on this classic theme, and had found that Walt had produced more than his share.

I saw the meeting as an opportunity to show them why so many of their earlier films were classics and still valuable. We spoke about the rite of passage and the hero's journey as themes and about the reasons stories based on those structures were so appealing. But they had stopped using this classical material and were making movies without providing any underlying psychic nourishment. I was dying to go into the company and help them make the kind of pictures they had made before—the kind I knew would work for them again.

My moment came when the chairman asked me why I thought one particular space fantasy film hadn't made money, especially given the success of *Star Wars*. In preparation for the meeting, I had reviewed several of their most recent films, and I had screened this one a few times.

"You killed your hero in the second act," I blurted out. "You created a compelling hero, had him up on the edge of heaven in an incredibly visionary space vehicle, but before he could fulfill his quest, you had him killed by some undistinguished minor character."

The chairman was watching me closely and I could see that he was moved by what was being said.

"It would be like killing Luke Skywalker in the middle of *Star Wars* ...."

"But he was a murderer!" the president broke in. "He had to die."

"But why make your hero a murderer?" I asked.

Within a few weeks I was back at Disney for another meeting. I would start as soon as I could, hired probably by the chairman of the board but with a title of assistant to the president. I would have responsibilities for production and marketing, and in three months was to be named a vice president. But I had no contract.

As I left the studio I wondered how important having a contract was, but I dismissed it. I'd never had a contract in all my years in advertising, and I was on too much of a high to worry. It just felt good to be wanted.

On my way home I called Monica and asked her to have dinner with me. I wanted to celebrate, especially with her. She'd been right there for me though so many frustrations, always supportive, never judgmental. When I told her the news, she was delighted, and we decided to go to a fancy Moroccan restaurant in West Hollywood.

The night was wonderful. Larry had somehow found out where we were and sent someone to the restaurant in a gorilla costume to sing "When you wish upon a star ..." I was horrified in the moment but quite touched. We ate what seemed endless courses of food, had too much wine, and savored how good it was that things had finally turned out.

When I drove through the Disney gate the first morning, it was like a dream come true. The dream of working on this lot went all the way back to seeing *Snow White*. My head swam with images as I drove to a parking spot on which my name was freshly painted.

I was proud of myself for landing in a major studio without having had much practical film experience and could not have imagined a better place to begin. I longed to make the kind of films that had always turned me on—films that had sweep and vision, ideas and themes that challenged the mind, and new worlds that stretched far beyond anything I could imagine.

This was a key job, I mused as I entered the executive building, and I would soon be able to do what I had always dreamed. Here I was, assistant to the president, with the assignment of doing pretty much as I pleased. A younger man was acting-head of production, but I was to work in both marketing and film development which, in my mind, was a good use of my abilities and experience.

I stopped and spoke to a few people I had just met and went to my new office, which was in the same wing where Walt had worked. The hallway walls were filled with movie posters, relics from old films, and an historic gallery of production stills. I had finally gotten where I wanted to be, and my head was full of ideas of what was be possible.

Within three months my dreams ended. I had reached the big time in office politics. My experience was in advertising, which in the East, always had the reputation of being one of the most highly competitive businesses possible. But it was nothing compared to the in-fighting I ran into in Hollywood. I was stonewalled by the young, acting-head of production who didn't want me near his department and didn't like that I was reporting around him to the president. He refused my friendship and I was not invited to screenings, story conferences, production meetings, or even into planning sessions. I was not given any new submissions to read and saw no current scripts in production. When I discussed it with the president, he said that I had to learn to work with him because he *was* going to be made head of production. I was a transplant being rejected by its host.

The marketing department was headed up by a man who had been in the company for years and was primarily focused on the company's theme park activities. He was doing a good job and had some responsibilities for the overall company but had assigned film advertising to one of his vice presidents.

He was quite friendly, always available, and gave me a clearer look at my situation. As we talked one day, he expressed his concern about my predicament. He saw that I had no tangible responsibilities and as a consequence, no real power. It became obvious as we spoke that they had no place for me in the chain of command, no day-to-day assignments, and that despite the title, I was getting no support from the president.

My initial feeling that I had been the chairman's idea was probably right, as was my feeling that the president had little interest in me. He gave the appearance of wanting change but had the place locked down tight. The trouble the company was having in the marketplace was merely a reflection of the knots inside. It was now clear to me why they hired without contracts.

I gave the situation a good try, trusting that things would turn around. But as proof of my naïveté, I didn't see the end coming until the week I was fired, which happened to be a couple of weeks before I was to be made a vice president.

When I was cleaning out my office, the phone rang.

"How's it going?"

It was Sally. One of the first and most successful women executives in Hollywood, she was referred to by the media as one of the "baby moguls." Apart from being pretty and quite young, Sally was smart and blessed with tremendous enthusiasm. She was a strong production executive at Fox and was becoming a close personal friend.

"Great. I just got my head handed to me."

"What happened?"

"I'll tell you about it later."

"Well, this might be your lucky day. Come on over and let's talk. A producer friend is looking for someone and I told him about you. He's looking for someone who's interested in fantasy to help him build a company. Are you interested?"

"I'd love it. But would you mind if I called you in a day or so? I'm feeling a little raw and I want to let my head clear awhile."

"No problem, call me on Monday."

I put the phone down and, from a box on the floor, picked up a still of Mickey Mouse from *The Sorcerer's Apprentice*. It had been framed for me only a few weeks before and my eyes got blurry as I stood there looking at it. What was happening to me? When would these disasters end? Feeling suddenly weak, I sat down and buried my face in my hands.

TWENTY-FIVE

A SECOND CHANCE

I
t was a long drive home.

If you've ever felt bad about yourself, it couldn't be worse than on one of those blisteringly hot days in Los Angeles. The heat is scorching and seems to sap the very life force out of you, vacuuming it into the blazing heavens.

When I first came to Southern California it looked like a garden. But on this particular day, as I was driving slowly home, instead of seeing giant bird of paradise bushes around gated mansions, I saw burned-out lawns and rows of rundown stucco bungalows. The broad sweep of Sunset Boulevard was strewn with cans of rotting garbage and cluttered with fast food shops. The blond bodies I saw on the beach in Santa Monica had become poor, spent prostitutes along Hollywood Boulevard. On a hot day in Los Angeles, there are no successful producers and no young starlets, just out-of-work actors, winos, and hopeless ladies of the evening. I couldn't wait to get home to my mountain.

When I arrived, Stray was at the head of the driveway waiting to greet me, and as always, he followed the car down to the house. My body felt heavy as I got out, gave Stray a quick rub on the head, and went inside. I took off my clothes, just as I used to when I got home from school as a child. Soon I was staring at the pool wondering what had happened to me.

Monica was out of town for a few days and even though I could have used some feminine caring, I was glad to have the weekend alone.

I spent the next few days in a stupor. I was stunned and couldn't believe that I had to absorb another disaster. One minute I was as high as a kite and the next, I had crashed to earth. I'd gone in with my heart open and found a street fight.

It appeared that nothing could stop the string of misfortunes I was encountering. I felt like a punch-drunk fighter who was losing the last of his pride in a flurry of slow-motion blows.

There was an awful sluggishness in my body that pulled me down every time I moved, and I was reminded of how tired I'd been feeling. I had no energy to go on, I thought. Life was getting heavier and I couldn't find the strength to stand up and walk into it. I lay as if wounded in the quiet heat, staring at a bold fly that landed on the back of my hand.

Down below, a gray pall of smog was creeping up the canyon, and I wanted it to come and enshroud me in sleep. My lack of energy and will was dissolving all sense of who I was. My exhaustion was erasing any male, "macho" invincibility I had left. Lost was the belief that I would live forever, and in my weakness, I saw myself old and unable to take care of myself.

The fly I had been watching now walked up my arm. I could see that it was green and blue and wondered about all the places it had been.

I thought of Sally and began to question whether I should go speak with her. Maybe no matter what I touched, it was going to go wrong. Everything was decaying and falling apart, and there seemed nothing I could do to change it.

The fly stopped and looked at me. I had never seen one so brave. Then as it started cleaning itself, I brushed it off and got up to call Sally.

The next morning we sat in her office drinking coffee while we caught up with each other. Sally was having a values crisis of her own. She was thinking about leaving and going into independent production, and spoke of several other things she was considering. Then she described the man she wanted me to meet and what she knew about the project.

He was a producer with a number of very successful pictures to his credit. His company was on the lot at Fox, and in his overall deal, he'd gotten approval to develop a multimedia theatrical "event," a full-length feature film with state-of-the-art sound, additional screens, lasers, and other special effects to heighten its dramatic power. This would be a reserved-seat event for one theater in each city and would run for months, and if successful, even years in each location. He was looking for someone to give the project full-time attention, someone who would write the business plan, find the special effects, and develop the story.

I met Irv over lunch at the commissary and we got along well. I told him about the kind of films I wanted to make, about the hero's journey, and that if he wanted a project with wide appeal, we might base it on a known myth. He agreed and offered me a six-month contract. If we both liked what was happening, we would increase the term and conditions.

I then met his partner, a wonderful man who had produced and directed a number of major films and was currently working on a spectacular production over at MGM. Russ was very creative and we got along from the beginning. I agreed to work with them, and as it turned out, one of my pleasures during the next six months was being on the stages where Russ' new picture was being done, and watching him handle some wonderfully lavish dance scenes with large choruses.

On my first day, as I was shown to my new office, I smiled when I learned that it had once been Tyrone Power's office and dressing room. Tyrone Power had always represented something to me beyond being a film idol. He had gone to the same Catholic boys' high school in Cincinnati that I had, and I always identified with him. The school admired him too, speaking of him often and even displaying his autographed picture in the hallway. But when he got a divorce, they took his picture down and never spoke of him again. Later, when I was going through my divorce and struggling with my religion, I often thought of how dramatic it was when Tyrone Power fell from grace.

I had a warm feeling about him as I opened my attaché case on his old desk, looked into his wall of mirrors, and put some of my things away in his bleached oak vanities. It seemed as if I had finally met him, and that we had some things to share, because by this time, I had made some pretty hard choices of my own.

The Subtle Agenda was feeling remote to me, and it slowly faded into the background as I set about getting the company organized. Still, I was aware of how each step I had taken in the past had prepared me for the next, and I began to feel as though something really wonderful was lying ahead. I wondered if my initiation was over and if all the difficulties had been refining fires in preparation for this new project. I knew exactly what I wanted and felt I could no longer be thrown off by anything. Now working with some of the most successful film people in the business, I knew exactly what kind of picture to make, and how to recognize it when I found it. The job required marketing, production, and story experience, all of which I had, to one degree or another.

Sensing that this was the moment I'd been waiting for, I felt a strong upsurge of enthusiasm and joy. As I fell into the excitement of my new creative venture, my troubles finally seemed to be over. I even applied for a second mortgage on the house so I could add the skylights and the hot tub I'd been wanting. Life was suddenly fun again as I quickly became familiar with all the special effects possibilities in town. I met with professionals of all trades and talents and filed reports on what I was finding. Soon I had a rough business plan and began looking around for a story.

Before we made a choice, we wanted to make a brief survey of world myth. We hired a mutual woman friend of both Irv's and mine, an anthropologist who had worked with Joseph Campbell on his *Atlas of World Myth*. I was hoping to find a story to base our project on, the way George Lucas appeared to have done with the Arthurian legends in *Star Wars*.

My interest was not just in making a film. I wanted to make one that could become a classic as well as a major box office draw. To do this, I felt that the story's underlying theme had to be deeply rooted in the unconscious of world audiences. I wanted it to somehow express the human search for the eternal, the search that lay at the root of all classic stories, regardless of how it was disguised.

Despite all the earlier assurances, I was soon confronted with a split between what I wanted to do and what I was asked to deliver. The quest for the eternal was an essential element in my vision of the project, but it turned out to be unimportant to them. In conference after conference, the stories I liked were put aside, and those I thought of as shallow were pursued. Their ideas would have made good pictures, I was sure, but they were not the kinds of films I wanted to make. Over the months, I found stories that I loved and thought would satisfy them too, but I was never able to get approval. I was getting discouraged and could see that things were not likely to change.

One story possibility that I liked was *The Earthsea Trilogy* by Ursula LeGuin, a classic story about a young man in training as a magician. I felt that learning magic, if used properly in a story, was a metaphor for the pursuit of the eternal power residing within the self. Other expressions of it included the power of the Holy Grail in the Arthurian legends and The Force in *Star Wars*.

The young man in this story, while playing with other apprentices one day, gives way to a moment of arrogance and conjures up a forbidden image the students had vowed never to create. Upon his doing so, the image suddenly escapes his control and runs free in the world. As the story unfolds, the reader realizes that the image is his own shadow, and as it stalks him, the young man becomes terrified. In an important scene, the horrible force approaches him, getting closer and closer until it's just inches away. Suddenly, it leaps and is absorbed into the young man's body. Rather than being killed by the dark figure, the lad is instantly empowered as a magician when he finally accepts this refused and frightening part of himself.

The story was wonderful and had enough characters and images to make full use of the special effects. Plus it possessed the dramatic structure I had been looking for. But the others didn't like it, and I couldn't get them to see its power the way I did. Again, I seemed to be in a split situation. It looked as if we would get a successful film off the ground, but if it didn't reflect the theme that had become so important to me, what had I gained?

One of the many special effects suppliers we were considering was Quantum Leap, a multimedia company in Venice, a few blocks from the ocean. They were developing a project much like ours and were familiar with *The Earthsea Trilogy*. The company was being financed by a group of wealthy, young investors who had become socially conscious during the sixties. Now they wanted to make what they called "conscious" films, although no one could define just what that meant. Still, something about them made me want to use them for our project at Fox.

As the months wore on, I met with them a number of times to fuel their interest in working with us. We spoke about the types of stories we might use, and the more we got to know each other, the more I began to feel that, given the opportunity, I could do with them what I was unable to do on the studio project. At one point, they even offered me a top position in their group, one that would give me the freedom I ached for. But the salary would be about half.

My chairman of the board objected as he watched what was happening.

"I know you don't listen to my advice any more, but you're working with a very successful producer and director who can write their own tickets anywhere in town. Maybe you don't like what's happening to the project, but for you, it's a beginning in film, and if you stay, you'll make some money and earn yourself a credit on the picture. Then you'll have something to sell, and you'll be in a better position to do your kind of pictures next time."

His advice made sense, but it also made me uncomfortable. Everything he said was true, but I couldn't conceive of having come all this way toward fulfilling a dream, and at the last minute settling for something less.

Fortunately, my little voice leaned toward going to Quantum Leap.

"You are slowly learning to go for what you really want," it said. "No matter what lies in store, you will not have failed because you will have chosen what you desired. That's been hard for you to learn, but notice that each time you had what you called a "failure," you were taken closer to your dream. Yes, it vanished in front of you, but it led you deeper into yourself, and something better has always come along to take its place. Once you really know that there's never failure, only growth and change, from that moment on, you will always go for precisely what you want. If right now working with this new company is what you want more than anything else, how can you not go for it?"

The chairman grumbled about my taking such a substantial cut in income, but I wasn't listening. I was trying to understand what my little voice was telling me. Was it true that there was no such thing as failure, only growth and change? Or was he trying to prepare me for another disaster? I, too, was concerned about the huge drop in income, but how could I not do it? I felt a hot flood of desire in my chest every time I thought about making the move.

To make a long story short, when my contract was up for renewal, I gave Russ and Irv my notice and moved to my office near the beach.

TWENTY-SIX

QUANTUM LEAP

A pattern was broken. Rather than watching a dream slowly die, or working on a project that had become a compromise, I made a move to do what I really wanted. I remembered how split I had felt at the agency and the years of frustration spent waiting for things to change. I had come a long way.

I wondered if this single act—learning to consciously take control and choose what I desired—was the goal that the Subtle Agenda had been leading me to all along. Would listening to my little voice and responding honestly to how I felt be enough to stop this disintegration? I was soon to find out.

Monica had been watching me go through each of these shocks, and although she was always there for me, our relationship wasn't going anywhere. I just didn't feel enough of a spark to make a real commitment, and with my busier schedule I began drifting away.

I had left people behind as I went through these failures, thinking they wouldn't understand what I was trying to do, although that was not the case with Monica. One friend from the past kept trying to persuade me to go back into advertising, but I wasn't secure enough about what I was doing myself to feel comfortable defending it to others. So I gravitated toward new people who didn't need explanations. It reminded me of the struggle it had been telling friends why I lost faith in the Church, and why I was leaving my marriage, and why I was leaving the agency. I wanted total freedom to go all the way, and even if I didn't rationally understand it myself, I didn't want anyone or anything in my life that might compromise it.

Unfortunately, the process of continuous change was causing me to feel alone. I was reminded of how alienated I felt when I saw old friends from Chicago. The motivations in our lives were so totally different that we had little to share. Their struggles went on in familiar ways, which meant being intensely involved in making it in the corporation, in won and lost accounts, more or fewer stock options, new houses, promotions, and more and more success. But the most important thing in my life was a solitary trek into the center of myself and I didn't know how to talk about it. Success and failure had a whole new meaning to me. What mattered most was staying true to my deepest impulses. I had given myself over completely to following my heart, and how would I explain that to someone who wanted a rational strategy?

At Quantum Leap, I met and worked with a different kind of person. In addition to their multimedia focus, they were attempting to express their spiritual ideals in film making. Some had been with the TM movement, some had worked at *est*, others were following Muktananda, and still others were doing their own versions of many different things.

I was now head of production and marketing so there was little chance that I would be unable to do the kind of project I wanted. In my first weeks, I trotted out all the stories I had found and fallen in love with on the last project but couldn't get done. Everyone was excited about the material and I was in heaven working with people who felt the same way I did.

We had a few meetings, one with the author of *The Earthsea Trilogy* and another with the well-known English director who had made *The Red Shoes* and who wanted to direct our project. But as I pushed for making deals for the material, I found out that while there was plenty of heart in this new company, there were no funds available for production.

Each time I raised the question of finances I was told "money was no problem" because the board was composed of wealthy people who would write a check if necessary. But they preferred to raise outside capital for production costs, so I was asked to put all my efforts into the business plan that would attract investors.

Despite the growing tightness of money and the quickly escalating interest rates, everything looked good for the company and I was enjoying my new relationships. After several months work, we were finalizing the business plan when we heard there had been an emergency meeting of the board. The sudden scramble behind closed doors made everyone on the staff edgy.

My daughter Sarah was coming to town for Thanksgiving. Unable to get away myself, I sent someone from the office to pick her up at the airport. She arrived just as a hastily called meeting was announced, and since we were all a tight little family, I invited her to join us.

The staff had been called together for the announcement that there would be no employee paychecks that day. As concern raced around the room, everyone was told not to worry because money was being transferred from one bank to another and we would all be paid the following week. Given the tight money and the recent search for outside capital, all of which had been publicly discussed, the news was not that surprising or upsetting for most.

Yet, it was not that simple for me. I had never been in a small company before and had no experience with running out of money. I was a little embarrassed that Sarah was there to hear the bad news, but the board was so reassuring, I thought the trouble would soon pass. I was comforted that my contract guaranteed me a large bonus just after the first of the year, which was only about six weeks away.

But the tight money in November proved to be just the first trickle through the dike. By Christmas, management was forced to lay off all the employees but two of us. Investment capital, which at first appeared so easy to raise, was slowed by 18 percent interest rates and fear of committing funds to uncertain ventures. The board members panicked at the shaky investment climate and hesitated to put any more of their own money into the company.

The offices, which were once so full of spirit and excitement, now fell silent. New desks, new carpeting, new chairs, all now empty and unused, looked still and lifeless in that final week. The only other person who stayed behind was Kinnear, the legal counsel and now acting manager. I was there to plot a marketing strategy, in case any money became available, and Kinnear shuttled back and forth between our offices and the board's temporary space in another part of town. Each time he returned, I met with him, eager to hear the news, and each time it was worse.

All during this dark period I believed that we would get the company back up and running again. We were working on negotiations for new money, and another company, a special effects company that had done two of the most successful science fiction films of all time, looked like it would join us as a partner.

Then one day, Kinnear returned from one of his shuttles and asked me to come to his office. He had a slight smile on his face when I sat down, and for a moment I thought things had finally turned around. But then came the awful news. The company was going to be closed at the end of the day.

The force of his words smashed into my stomach, and heat exploded all over my body. I could only half listen as his litany of words continued. The offices were to be padlocked for nonpayment of rent at the end of the week. There would be no bonus for me, despite my contract, but there would be a small severance check. I could sue if I wanted, but since they were filing for bankruptcy, it could take years to collect even a small portion of was I was owed. The board was sorry about everything, but that's the way it was.

My mind went blank. Then it began a clamor of confusing ideas, looking for answers that might put everything back together again. I was horrified. As I thought more about it, a sharp pain that felt like a dagger in my head moved down through my chest, then sank deep into my stomach. I started to get up but I got dizzy, and as I sat back, I felt myself hurtling down into the black pit that lay hidden inside the center of myself.

If there was one moment that could be called the final straw, this was it. It was as if a bomb had just exploded in my gut, and the force of it slowly transfixed each cell of my body as if on slow motion film. I was completely unprepared for an internal event of such destructive magnitude.

I had been sure it was my destiny to pull this project off, and now, in this one moment, all my dreams finally collapsed. I was financially devastated. I was empty and emotionally vulnerable more than I had ever been. I looked into my heart and was sure there was no God in the universe.

My mind raced. I had no future. There was nothing I wanted to do. There was no job I wanted to find and no energy to work even if there had been one. There was no city to which I wanted to move. There was no story I wanted to write. How could I keep the house in the mountains, or Sarah in private school? Where would I go? And for what? I had no interest in anything. I only wanted to go into a deep, everlasting sleep. It was the darkest moment in a long, treacherous night.

I looked at Kinnear who now had a big smile on his face.

"What are you smiling about?" I muttered.

"I was thinking about what Muktananda would do in a situation like this."

I just sat there, bewildered, unable to ask what he meant. Kinnear had met Muktananda in India years before and, working closely with him, had helped develop the Siddha Foundation in this country.

"He'd laugh," Kinnear finally said.

"How could he laugh?" I asked incredulously.

"He'd say, 'This, too, is God.'"

I just looked at him blankly.

"One day we were trying to get to the airport," he recalled, "and our car ran off the road. Now we were obviously going to miss a very important plane. Many people were waiting for us in another city. When I looked at Muktananda, he was giggling as he walked around looking at the damage to the car. I asked him why he was giggling and thought it was such a joke. Then he said what I just said to you, 'This, too, is God.'"

I had definitely not gotten to the stage of inner development where I could instantly disengage from a disaster and see that it was just as much an expression of God's love as a bouquet of flowers. I couldn't, because in that moment the disaster was ending my life.

As I thought about it later, I was glad that Kinnear had been there with his little story, because it let me know that a light was shining even in that darkest of moments.

We embraced, and I went to my office to put a few final things in my attaché case. As I was leaving, I paused for a moment and looked down the empty hall toward where Kinnear sat working, then turned away heavily. I walked out and soon found myself heading east on the Santa Monica Freeway.

I was driving in a tunnel of darkness with only a peephole through which to see traffic. My life had ended. Not because a dream was extinguished—it was deeper than that. In my marrow, something had finally gone out. Every future I had ever imagined was now dark and lifeless. I was no longer being pulled by my desire for life. I was just existing, my hands on the wheel, falling forward into each new moment because there was no other way. Suicide? I was too tired. I was just trying to steer my car.

TWENTY-SEVEN

THE NADIR

I returned to my house in the mountains like a wounded bear seeking a place to heal itself. Stray greeted me as lovingly as always. He was excited to see me and didn't know that I had, once again, come home with my guts in my hands. Thank God for this dog who wasn't judging me as mercilessly as I was. His innocence helped me be gentle with myself.

He watched as I picked up my attaché case from the front seat, and then became particularly alert as he heard me gather the supermarket bag from the car floor.

With his head high, Stray seemed almost to prance as he led me to the front door. There I found a notice from the animal control officer stating that I must keep my dog on a leash or face a fine. I couldn't do that. Stray would have died on a leash. He never left the property except with me. And he never got into trouble except for a couple of minor incidents. He needed to feel free to run as he wished. We both did.

On the way home, not wanting to leave the mountain for a few days, I had stopped and picked up some of my favorite foods. It was all deli food—cold potato salad, salami, cheese, a turkey leg, and of course, a good bottle of French Chardonnay. Whenever I felt really lonely or had a bad day at work, I always treated myself to whatever foods I was craving. This time, as I unpacked them, I realized they were the same foods that were special to me when I was younger.

As a child, I'd go across the street to my grandparents' house after breakfast and look in their refrigerator. I'd always find various kinds of sausages and cheese, all of which they loved when they were growing up in Europe. There was usually a wide range to choose from, since my grandmother was from the Alsace region of France and my grandfather had come from Bavaria. I also remembered that when I traveled back home to Cincinnati during my first few years in advertising, my mother would always have my favorite foods waiting for me in the refrigerator. Now, taking care of myself, I felt a little lonely.

The sun was low and a foggy chill rose up from the canyon and rolled into the pool. I slipped on a light jacket, poured a glass of wine, and went out to the deck to watch the sunset. The trees were tinged in pink, and looking for the source of the color, I found crimson clouds burning from the sun setting beyond the mountains. It felt good to be home, but as I thought about the future, a chill ran through my body. I pulled my jacket tighter around myself.

The full force of loss arrived during my sleep, and I spent a harsh, lonely night wrestling with it. My dreams were disturbed by a tumbling series of threatening images, and the terrible hurt of failure ached in my stomach and crawled across my shoulders. I heard cries from the darkness, the hideous screams of hunting coyotes, and the haunting calls of owls. It was colder than usual with the wind blowing through the trees, so I kept the heat on high and blankets pulled up around me all night.

In the first light of morning, I rolled awake and found that I had a headache which I thought was only partly from my several glasses of wine. The dull hurt throbbing in my head and my heart was more from what had happened the day before.

The bomb that had gone off in my chest in Kinnear's office still reverberated through me. In that dark moment, I felt the final surrender of my life to forces beyond my control. A soft "pop" in my chest became a death-bringing silent explosion that burned hotly for a moment, then left everything black.

Stray and I walked up the driveway for the newspaper. The violence on the front page reinforced the images of dying things that I had been seeing everywhere over the last few months. I had read *Countdown to Armageddon* and it reflected what I was feeling inside. I believed the author's prophecy of doom and his interpretations of the Bible because they reflected the endings in my own life.

Several pines near the mailbox were turning brown and dying, and a tree surgeon had told me there was little I could do. One of the bonsai trees near the pool, the largest one, turned brown and died within a week of my noticing it. My energy was running out, and my mood was being perfectly reflected in the things around me.

Back at the house, I made coffee and took a hot cup outside as I went to check the remaining bonsai trees. They were some of my favorite things and seeing them all healthy helped my mood lighten.

I had always loved the mornings here. It was the time of day when I could best smell the orange and lemon blossoms. Four citrus trees stood on the hillside beyond the pool, their varieties chosen so that at least two would be blossoming throughout the year. No matter how bad I felt, their sweet aroma always made me feel grateful for my home in a sunny climate.

I was feeling as though the forces I'd set in motion had gotten out of control and were stripping me of all my dreams. Suddenly, the entire string of failures went off in my head as if I had stumbled across a minefield strung with tripwires. I felt a little sick to my stomach.

The cup now felt cold in my hand, so I tossed the coffee over the hill and put the cup down near one of the tiny trees. A phone rang several times in the house below, and Stray looked up as if it might be for him.

Everything that had excited me when I first arrived in Los Angeles felt like it had happened in another lifetime, and now I was in some after-death state reviewing all that had gone before. Where were all the people I had encountered, and what were they thinking? Was there anything I might have done differently? Why had this felt so inevitable? Why had this happened to me? Each of my steps became vivid, and I could feel the losses all over again. Even the far-off fiasco at Pillsbury came back to torment me.

After a few weeks, I began experiencing a calm around the mountain that felt almost unearthly. My life was in suspended animation. Everything had come to a standstill. The silence was like a warm blanket wrapped gently around me.

From the time I'd moved into the house, a process of stripping away had begun. It had persisted doggedly through all my experiences, and I was sure that the forces pursuing me would see me finally annihilated.

A power source that had been turned on during the early part of my life had suddenly turned off when I moved here. I felt I was being worked on and remade by subtle forces that were at heart benign, yet unrelenting.

Clearly the purpose in all this was that I slough off the past like old skin. I realized that I'd moved here and bought my house on the mountain for precisely that reason, as if the Subtle Agenda had paved the way. Then under the constant pressure created by the changes and failures, all my old ideas vanished—my values, even my reason for coming out here in the first place. Everything that I thought was me, everything that defined who I was, had been slowly stripped away, leaving me bare and exposed.

I hadn't chosen the failures, at least not consciously. I was following my heart. But now it seemed that in making my choices, I had selected pathways that would eventually dissolve, stripping away all the attachments that once held me. It felt as if the quiet force of the Subtle Agenda was supporting me by blocking avenues that would not in the end have given me the fulfillment I desired. Each choice had been a teacher, each disaster a release. I had unwittingly trapped myself into learning exactly what I needed to learn so I could ultimately have what I really wanted.

I had spent most of my life running from my fears to keep them from overtaking me. But in the course of starting over, I had triggered each one, and in doing so, I learned to heal them instead. The cocoon on the mountain had been my crucible of learning and the process had completely changed my life. An old part of me had died, leaving room for a new one to be born.

In the weeks following, when I had the energy, I tried to put together ideas for multimedia events and movies, but they all turned out to be empty phantoms of desire with no real substance. Shadow projects would appear from the past and seem real enough to have meetings about, even with some powerful people, but nothing came from any of them. Nothing was growing. It was as if I had moved into an alternative world, a parallel earth that had the appearances of the old, but was ghostlike and had none of the meaning or content from before.

I took Stray with me to the end of the driveway to check the mailbox. He delighted in everything we did together, even the simplest of things like collecting the mail. Getting a notice from the fire department to clear weeds from the hillsides gave me a momentary shot of fear, but I let the worry drift away. A runner dodged Stray as he came down our driveway, unaware that this dog would never hurt anyone.

From the mailbox I could see the whole Los Angeles basin, and as I stopped for a moment and stared at the view, I wondered what was going on down there in the city.

Everything on the mountain was unfolding slowly, frame by frame, as though my life were a film and I'd been given the opportunity to study each cell. I saw each event coming and as a scene unfolded, each moment would stop, grow large and specific, then after I had a chance to carefully view every detail, it would finally pass. It reminded me of the way time stopped in a near-death experience I once had in Hawaii.

I was producing a pool of American Dairy Association commercials, and we were shooting a scene with an underwater camera. We had been using snorkel gear for several days, spending most of the time in shallow water just inside the reefs.

After a while I got bored with the long delays between takes and wandered out beyond the reefs. I was watching the sea's bottom, which at its deepest was no more than about four to six feet below me, and was admiring the many colors and varieties of fish.

I surfaced, treading water for a moment, and looked for the crew. Seeing that everything was okay, I put my mask back on and swam out a few more yards. Without realizing it, I had swum out beyond the shelf and when I looked down, I discovered that the bottom had dropped off fifty feet or more. It was like accidentally stepping off a building. I involuntarily gasped for air and a shot of water suddenly filled my throat and I was caught in a spasm of coughing. As I choked, I noticed a number of large dark shapes moving along the bottom, which sent my heart into an immediate and primal struggle for survival. My arms and legs began a panicky flailing to get back to the reef, and my breath was halted by the gulps of water I now had in my lungs.

Yet it all took place in slow motion as if I was both struggling and watching what was happening. I became separate from my body and could see myself dispassionately while at the same moment, I was fighting for my survival. Somehow I'd stepped out of time and saw clearly that I was different from my life.

Now I was experiencing everything on the mountain distanced in the same way, but this time the feelings went on and on. I was standing apart from my life while everything familiar was falling slowly and irreversibly away.

Gazing down at the city, I became aware that I had separated from my dreams and had become a detached observer who could see the larger picture and know that everything was moving toward fulfillment.

I went to bed early but I couldn't sleep.

My shoulders ached whenever I thought about what had happened to me. One thought after another floated through my brain and I stretched my neck and backbone, but the aches wouldn't go away. I realized just how stiff I was as I slowly got out of the bed for aspirin.

The moon was high and full as I walked through the house. The resounding climax of events forced me to sit and reflect on everything that had happened. The warm evening drew me outside by the pool where, for the longest time, I just watched the clouds in the surface of the water. I knew I had to find work, but there was nothing I wanted to do. I'd heard that Kinnear and the others were building a new company, but I wasn't interested in working with them. I was in too much pain to try anything right now.

If these last years had been my cocoon, then this was the moment after the caterpillar's pupal body dies. As it is with the caterpillar, no one else could see what was happening to me, except the witness deep within my soul.

Throughout all this, there was a spirit that stayed alive, watching—a place within that did not give way through even the worst of it. But it was no longer in my head, or my ideas, or my thoughts. My life was now in my chest, a feeling of warmth down near my heart.

THE AWAKENING

It was a peaceful passing, although not like that of someone crossing over in the quiet of sleep. Instead, I was awake and transfixed, watching myself being consumed. It was a long, conscious transformation. The dying ego held on and on, and while struggling to save itself, saw all things darken through its closing eyes. Everything that once held it together had pathetically given way bit by bit, and when finally forced to the limit, it released and let everything go.

The unthinkable had occurred. I had reached the end of my emotional resources, my desire to resist was gone, I surrendered to the overpowering forces of the Subtle Agenda.

To the observer, I had come to anonymous ruin, my dreams shattered and my ideals lying scattered on the mountainside. Yet beneath this collapse, another life was in its nativity. What now lay discarded was the previous self, grown obsolete and useless, no longer appropriate for the journey ahead. A spark of aliveness had been ignited within the corpse, and it burned, though hesitantly at first, with new fire, new form, and new vision.

Love had given birth to itself in my heart and was felt in my body as a new presence, an awareness larger than my own, but within me. This new presence inspired me to find unity in my work, in unity with love, all as a sacred becoming.

THE RETURN

After a time of decay comes the turning point. The powerful light that has been banished returns. There is movement, but it is not brought about by force. The upper trigram K'un is characterized by devotion; thus the movement is natural, arising spontaneously. For this reason the transformation of the old becomes easy. The old is discarded and the new is introduced.

Wilhelm/Baynes
The I Ching, Return (The Turning Point)

The structural reorganization completed and the adult fully formed, the pupal shell splits and the adult emerges. It spreads its wings and flies away.

Alexander Klots
A Field Guide to Butterflies

The return and reintegration with society, which is indispensable to the continuous circulation of spiritual energy into the world, and which, from the standpoint of the community, is the justification of the long retreat, the hero himself may find the most difficult requirement of all.

Joseph Campbell
The Hero With a Thousand Faces

TWENTY-EIGHT

THE BRIDGE

I arose before dawn from what had been a miserable night, and after making coffee to take with us, Stray and I headed around the mountain to watch the sunrise. In the predawn light and morning haze, the city lay hidden, leaving only the mountain ranges and broad valleys barely visible. I liked to imagine that the earth was still in its prehistoric stages, and at the moment of dawn when the red-orange globe rose, I would see it ascend over an ancient, primal world. By stepping out of time and viewing everything fresh again, I felt gratitude for my life and love for the species that lay asleep below me.

Even though I was still removed from the things around me, on this particular morning, I noticed a new, warm feeling beginning to replace the pain and anguish from the Quantum Leap disaster. It was a sensation of quiet well-being, and it felt so good that I stretched my arms above my head and breathed deeply, sucking in the crisp morning air.

I was surprised at how good I felt. Having my life dissolve in front of me had not been like falling into the black pit after all.

When I had first become aware of the black pit, I saw it as the place inside me where my fears would hide. I imagined them as dragons sleeping in the pit, their presence creeping into my dreams at night. I lived cautiously so as not to awaken them, because they so often humbled me. And if I ever felt one climbing from its dark repose, I would immediately stop what I was doing to let the turmoil subside. In time, my dragons held me hostage, my fears kept me from doing anything that might arouse them.

Now having survived worse than I could imagine, somehow the pit and its monsters became somewhat transparent and lost power over me.

This new perception came through as a tentative glimpse, one that I was just barely able to recognize. It was like discovering a new clue in a scavenger hunt that would take me to a new place.

As I drew in deep breaths, my mind and heart expanded. If I could live the rest of my days without the dragons, without the fears to restrain me, then the future would be unlimited and I would be free to move toward whatever I genuinely desired.

Stray and I stopped and sat down on a crest where I could see lights coming on and activity beginning. The city was teeming, but my interest in it had faded. Instead, I felt a new life springing up from within me. In the past, what was happening in the world was always more important than what was happening inside me. But these days, there was an entirely new aspect—what I was sensing inside was the only thing, and what was going on in the city no longer mattered.

This was a remarkable shift. It was as though all the world's activities had leapt inside me, and nothing vital remained outside. The potential that I always thought was waiting for me out there, was now a fertile place within, and I was carrying all that was possible in the center of myself.

As wondrous as it was, with this new perspective came new conflicts. The feeling that nothing external really mattered was so subtle and so new that it was difficult to trust. The chairman was quick to tell me that I was wrong to believe it, and I felt a fight brewing.

As I watched this conflict rise, I noticed that a pattern. A similar lack of trust had accompanied the initial stages of all my new perceptions. They arose from such a quiet, tentative place, it always took considerable time and effort to offset crushing objections from my rational mind.

This time there was a different twist. I noticed that when I let myself feel that nothing outside mattered and consciously shifted my trust inside, the internal feelings gathered so much strength that my rationality was unable to object. It was like a bridge across a chasm that got stronger and sturdier the more I trusted my weight to it. Perhaps I could build my future from the inside out.

I looked around from where I was sitting and saw Stray eyeing me, his chin laying flat on his paws. I got up, swatted the dust from my jeans and started toward home. Soon I became aware that a meeting was about to begin. The chairman, unable to contain his nervousness, spoke first.

"This is looney-tunes! Of course what's happening out in the world is more important than what's happening inside. One is objective reality and the other is only your impression of it. An example that you might understand … you need money and you're not going to get it by just thinking about it."

Stray heard me muttering to myself and thought it was directed at him. He trotted over, and after I gave him a couple of deep massages around his ears, he went on his way.

"You've come full circle," my little voice interrupted, "You've discovered again, this time in an entirely new way, that if you can trust what you want, the very act of trusting it will help bring it to you. You might not fully understand the importance of this yet. That will come with time."

He was right. I didn't fully understand. I thought I had trusted before, only to be disappointed, especially recently.

"But as you've noticed," my little voice continued, "each new so-called failure brought a new level of understanding. And each time you moved forward again you were able to bring more of

195

yourself to the next venture. Things haven't worked as you anticipated because you were being led to deeper realizations necessary for you to ultimately have all you desire."

That struck home. I had long believed that the Subtle Agenda was leading me somewhere and that the adventure itself was the most important thing, even more important than my success in film.

"One thing the Subtle Agenda has been guiding you toward is knowing that your desires hold the key to the fulfillment you want You must trust that, and trust the appropriateness of whatever the Subtle Agenda brings. When you do that, every result, even failure, is an expansion toward your true goals."

The chairman had been listening patiently and was even moved by what he heard, but he was waiting for his moment.

"Right now, trusting my desires feels like the hardest thing of all," I said, "because all I want to do is be quiet and let some time pass. When it's time to go back to work, I want to feel inspired about it, like it's really the right thing. I've worked hard to make contact with myself, and I don't want to lose that. I want to find a way to make a living and stay true to what I feel."

Stray started toward me again, but when he saw that I was ignoring him, he trotted away. I watched him stop near an abandoned car on the fire road, and it bothered me that people used the mountains as a dump.

"You're encouraging me to trust my desires and I want to, but if I do I'll be gambling everything I own."

"Follow your desires, not your fears. You must learn to first trust what you want, allowing it to take root and grow inside you, and then take it out into the world."

I was touched by what I heard. For the first time since I began this journey, I could feel my future right inside myself.

"Look," the chairman finally interrupted, "What you're saying might sound great, but where's all this talk ever led him? Everything he owns came out of past rational efforts, and since he began following your directions, nothing has worked. This has gotten us nowhere. It's time to come back to earth and do what he knows."

I shared the chairman's concerns but was more eager to understand and experiment with what my little voice had told me.

"Tell me exactly what I should do," I said aloud. Stray's ears perked, and he looked at me for a moment then turned away.

"That's not how it works," my little voice replied. "You have to find your way by yourself, just as before. All I can tell you is what you already know. Trust how you feel. Follow what's true for you even if it appears irrational."

My deepest urge was to let time pass and not go looking for work right away, but the chairman was reaching the point of exasperation. He was more worried than ever about the money situation.

"I'm sure you can use some time off," my chairman shot back. "That's probably okay for a little while to restore yourself, but you'll have to find an income soon. I think you should get a job with an advertising agency just to get some money coming in."

With just the mention of going back into an ad agency, I felt a sudden weight in my chest and across my shoulders. I'd grown accustomed to being led by guidance from my little voice, but this physical reaction to the chairman's proposal was new. I couldn't remember ever being able to know when something was wrong by how it felt in my body. I was excited by my discovery and wondered if this was what my little voice was hinting at when it said to "trust how you feel."

To test how my body responded to options, I imagined several kinds of work—going into a film studio, writing scripts, and going into an ad agency. All three felt heavy and binding, but I was surprised to find that going into an ad agency felt lighter than the other two. Did that mean that I should go back into an agency again?

"Don't think," cautioned my little voice, "feel."

An agency? I was too shocked to even consider it.

"It doesn't have to be a big agency," the chairman hastened, smelling a victory. "It doesn't even have to be an ad agency at all. I think that you need to get your feet on the ground, and you know advertising a lot better than film production. Maybe you could go to work for a smaller manufacturing company as a marketing executive or something."

I'd handled advertising for some very large accounts, but that was a far cry from being a marketing executive. Furthermore, I'd come to think of myself as more of an artist than a businessman, even though I hadn't made any money at it. Thinking about finances sent thoughts tumbling around in my head, and getting nowhere, I waited for help from my little voice.

"Relax. Don't think about it. Learn to sense with your body. What is it telling you?" My little voice was as clear as I had ever heard it. "At first the feelings will be subtle, almost too subtle to detect above the fears. But be patient, and you'll feel yourself slowly being drawn in a new direction. Things won't begin as ideas anymore, but as new stirrings inside you."

It was strange that I could listen to my little voice and still trust it after all that had happened. But I was already feeling that resting for a while was more important than finding work. I could feel the chairman bristling.

"This kind of talk gives me the creeps," he said. "It's too 'feely-feely' and not enough hard planning. Following your feelings hasn't led you anywhere yet. In fact, I'd say that following your feelings has drawn you into some real disasters. But that's all finished. So you had a failure or two. People make and lose fortunes all the time. It's probably even a good thing that you took the shot you did. Maybe you'll be better for it in the long run. Right now I think the best thing you can do is find yourself a job. When you're thrown from a horse you have to climb right back on. You need to get out there and get involved in life again, that's all."

I had a little extra money because in the final weeks before Quantum Leap defaulted, the second mortgage I had applied for came through. At the time, I'd thought I was finally going to be able to add the skylight to my bedroom and over the fireplace and a hot tub too, but fortunately I'd held off until things clarified. I had money to live on, but my mortgage payments had suddenly doubled because of the high interest rates on the new loan.

My chairman usually made sense, especially about money, but as I imagined letting his ideas leading me, I found myself losing touch with the subtle feelings in my body. So after a moment of indecision, I decided to ignore the chairman, as I had done so often before. I would not look for work right away. I had to take time for myself.

Stray and I got home just as the automatic sprinklers were coming on, so he stayed at the end of the driveway. They always frightened him, and I knew I wouldn't see him back at the house until the water stopped.

I walked quickly through the spray, and as I opened the door, I realized that I was no longer the same person who had first stepped foot inside this house. I had been full of visions of what the world and this city held in store for me. Now everything I wanted was inside.

TWENTY-NINE

THE CHILD

The next morning, as Stray and I went out to the street for the newspaper, we startled a deer on the driveway. It was barely light, and when the deer noticed us, it trotted up the drive and disappeared past the wooden guardrail at the street. Stray started after it, but I lost sight of them in billows of fog that rose like huge cotton clouds from the canyon below. Nothing else was moving, not even the birds.

It was magical. The mountain had many wonderful moods, but this was the one I loved the most. It was like a Japanese painting. The blemishes of the city and the coarse brashness of the land were subdued and made hallowed by this misty landscape from heaven. Stray had given up his chase and emerged with a light film of moisture on his coat as he climbed back to the road. His paws made a track of wet prints on the asphalt as he came over to shake near me.

I was between worlds, and the landscape reflected my mood. I felt so much at home that it gave me a burst of enthusiasm to go back down to the city and find work. For a moment I wanted to pick up my scripts and try to sell them, but in the next instant I knew there was no place for me down there. What I wanted to do was up here.

The newspaper was slightly wet as I picked it up and glanced at the front page. The headlines about terrorism were a blow to my stomach, but as I stayed anchored inside myself, the torment was as if from another world. I felt guilty about being so removed from everything, but that was the truth of it. I folded the paper over, tucked it under my arm, and walked back down the long driveway to the house. At the front door, the faintest traces of the coffee I'd left brewing greeted me in the damp morning air.

The wiser part of me realized that the stage manager who had been changing the scenes was still not ready for the next act to begin. The old set was struck, but the furniture was still being arranged for the new one. I was able to wait. My financial condition remained a constant pressure, but I felt that on some level, even a long, frustrating nothingness was active, creative time. Soon I would jolt into motion again, and a new life would begin as it had before.

Days later, I was sitting at the white table at the far end of the pool, thinking about the meeting I'd just had that morning. A friend I met while working at Quantum Leap had come up to the house to let me hear some new songs he'd recorded. He was a talented musician and had written a musical that he presented to us before the business collapsed. His new work excited me, and at first I felt that this was a project I could get involved in. He offered me the kind of financial participation that would make it interesting, and I remembered how much I'd enjoyed working with him before.

Now in the quiet of my backyard, I realized I would not work with him again. I liked the score and the story and everything about the guy, but I got a resounding "no" in my body. The music "felt" comfortable enough, and the story did too, but each time I opened myself to the idea, I felt a heavy weight across my shoulders. As I played with this feeling more, I noticed it happened every time I considered working on someone else's project—not just *his* project, but any project that belonged to someone else.

What a powerful revelation this was! It came as just a feeling, not an idea at all. Suddenly I knew that whatever I would do to earn a living had to come from me. I could never follow other people's dreams again. It was time to fulfill my own.

This was what my little voice meant when it told me to listen more to my body. As I thought about it, I realized that when I first sensed the black pit had become less solid and real, I was also sensing a new kind of communication. It was as if I could now detect signals that before were too faint to recognize amid the static of my inner turmoil. I saw how far I had come since I first grew uncomfortable about my work at Burnett. At that time, I was increasingly aware of conflicts between my life and my values. Now I was feeling a *potential* conflict even before it began.

As I turned in my chair, I noticed a squirrel had come to drink from the pool. When I looked over at Stray, he raised his head and sniffed the air, but he didn't move. He merely watched the squirrel stretch hard to reach the water. The small animal was totally vulnerable while it drank. Stray's body tensed, and he made a slight move as if to rise. Then after hesitating, his mood softened and he relaxed. When the squirrel finished drinking, it pulled itself back from the water, paused a moment to check on Stray and me, then with several jumps, leaped to the pepper tree and was gone.

The experience filled me with childlike wonder. Watching the squirrel thrilled me, and I actually felt love moving from me toward it. I felt love for Stray as he watched without chasing. I also felt love for myself for embracing something so simple. The perfection of it all suddenly overwhelmed me with joy.

In that single moment, Stray was a gentle dog, the squirrel was in a trusting world, and I not only loved everything I saw, I was exhilarated by being able to feel it. The loving dream that unfolded before me was not about how life *could* be, but about how life truly *was*—*if* I could trust my vision and stay open to it. The impact of this simple scene was so great that I could not ignore the message. I had glimpsed life without disharmony.

Suddenly feeling the intense heat of the afternoon sun, I rose from the table and headed toward the shade on the other side of the pool. I sat down heavily onto a cushion by the water and let myself sink into it. Stray had been watching me as I moved, and now that I'd chosen my new spot, he got up, stretched a moment, then started toward me. I assumed he wanted to be closer, as he so often did, but I wanted to stay in my inner space.

My eyelids grew heavy, and I let them close for meditation. In moments, I felt Stray beside me. He laid his muzzle across my hand, but I gently pulled it away. I wanted to abandon myself into a fully quiet state.

In this inner darkness, I was overcome by the ominous and unrelenting specter that was swallowing my life, and I surrendered into it. Within seconds a powerful, falling force pulled me out of myself. I was precipitously hurtling down a tube into a climactic blackness, not merely into total darkness but into a final and ultimately fatal abyss. My string of failures had led to this resounding end.

My life was over.

In another instant, I exploded past the bottom of the darkness and landed into what felt like an enveloping bed of flowers. This may sound strange in the telling, but the utter alienation and terror I felt over the months had abruptly delivered me into boundless, limitless love. I had fallen not into oblivion, but into fullness. I was eternally safe and entirely within love.

I became love. I was saturated in love so complete I felt absorbed into my own soul. My chest opened. Tears flowed down my cheeks. Intense joy overwhelmed me.

This was more than a feeling. I was out of my body and in an experience of knowing beneath all knowing. I did not hear a voice. There were no thoughts. The message was more than sounds, images, and feelings. It was a dimensional vision without seeing, a delivery into a new reality, the sudden understanding that all life—all physical objects, all beings—are, in their purest core, radiant manifestations of love. I knew beyond knowing that everything that exists, in essence and fiber, is at its purest center, a reality that we experience in our bodies as love. Everything that ever existed, or will exist in the future, is a manifestation of that love.

The brilliance of this new awareness brought instant understanding of my life to this point. All my earlier beliefs, hopes, concepts—even my ideals—instantly withered in the simplicity of this perception.

The scene changed and I was a visitor as my past life re-experienced itself, not in discrete scenes or images, but in a rapid sequence of impressions that revealed the invisible nature of each event. Starting with early infancy, each of these moments were made transparent to reveal the persistent presence of fear that was motivating me.

I saw fear again and again, starting with my effort to survive surgery early in my second year of life, to the fear that drove my desire for success, money, and even who to love. My fear of separation from my parents, fear of darkness, fear of school, fear of not being popular, fear of failing in my grades, fear of hell, fear of losing my soul, fear of not finding a career, fear of not being successful, fear of not making a mark on the world, fear of not making enough money, fear of not making it in advertising, fear of loving, fear of not loving, fear of running out of money, fear of losing my house, fear of what would happen to me, fear of life, fear of illness, fear of death.

The fear that had so often dulled my life also muted my ability to be loving. It had also squeezed my capacity to give love the preeminent place in my life that it already possessed beyond my knowing. This experience completely transformed my understanding of what the true energy in my life actually was and is. It also transformed what I wanted my life to be in the future.

In that transfixing experience by the pool, love became the base of understanding beyond all knowledge.

Sometime later, perhaps minutes or an hour—I really didn't know—I finally managed a slight move to feel my body again. I heard a bird in the trees above me, then the sound of a child in the canyon. I was so swept away in love and by love that I wanted to remain disengaged from my surroundings. I stayed still for another bit of unmeasurable time, then with feeble movements, I tested my fingers and then my hand. My eyes still did not want to open.

This was not an experience of my physical death, which is what I expected when it first began. Instead, it was a journey into the clear light of absolute goodness. The experience burned with such bliss, I knew it would become my beacon for a new way of being.

And it has.

But something did die that day—my old understanding of my life. The startling awareness that fear is a temporary illusion, an artifact of perceptual ignorance, so impressed me that I vowed to be vigilant about its presence in every moment. Even more than that, I felt an ardent desire to dedicate myself to love in the creation of my new work and in how I would re-conceive my life.

In the days following, I returned again and again to the cushion by the pool in hopes of tasting once more that amazing event.

I had gotten below the surface garbage I'd lived with most of my life and had my first experience of true rapture. My center of understanding shifted to my heart, and I could experience the wonderment of things instead of simply observing them. My center of gravity was now lower, as if I was sitting more comfortably in my life, and I was filled with warmth and happiness because of it.

I really had reached the bottom of that horrible black pit inside myself to find only deep comfort and harmony. My whole body had settled into it, and I experienced a new sense of love for myself and everything around me.

This was what I'd been struggling so hard to find. I had come to the end of the road in myself and there I was, able to feel the love that was the source and security of everything. There was no dark pit, only an upwelling of tenderness and safety.

This was the place I imagined existed when I was having conflicts about writing commercials for products I wouldn't use myself. This was the place I was trying to reach as I struggled years to find fulfillment in my work. This was the place I ached for when I lived in loneliness, unable to find joy through anything I did.

I could see why I had to go through so much to reach what I was now feeling. There were so many layers in me that needed to be stripped away first. There were countless fears that I had to live through and disarm. I had to give up the safety of trying to live like everyone else in order to become exactly who I was. I had to release the ideologies that sought God but kept me living in fear. I had to surrender the protection and the values of large corporations in order to establish my own.

For the first time in my memory, I was me. I was the person I saw in the mirror, unadorned and simple, without titles and position, without any kind of success—and I could love that man, even without those things. I was seeing him completely for the very first time, and I was proud of who he had become. I was proud that he'd had the guts to give it all up in search of something deeper. And I was glad that he'd had the courage to put his whole life on the line.

I began to cry for the years of struggle it had taken to get here. I cried for the lonely man who had given up so much along the way. I cried for how empty he had been all those years.

Through my tears, I saw Stray get up and walk over toward me. In a moment his head was buried in my chest and I was hugging him close.

What had I been so afraid of in my life? How could I have mistrusted it so? Sobbing in both joy and sadness, I realized that the very thing I'd been most frightened of turned out to be the entrance to my own heart.

Deep inside me something had been born. It must have been what a woman feels when she first senses a child within her. There was new life where before there was emptiness, and the sudden awareness of it changed me. I felt more protective, more fatherly toward myself, and more caring. Having stripped away the years of crust that had separated me from myself, I had found the child inside me again.

The next few days I kept feeling this new life, and it was very exciting. Once, I looked up from my place near the pool, wishing to tell someone what I was feeling, and found Stray watching me from the deck.

"This may seem strange to you, old boy," I said, "but I feel like I'm pregnant." He got up thinking I had called him, and when he arrived, his cold nose searched my face and neck. "You're gonna be an uncle, laddie," I teased, feeling somewhat awkward.

I was embarrassed at having these feelings, but my awareness of the child was unmistakable. It was the presence of a small, vulnerable part of myself that was so real it felt like a separate living thing. And when I'd discovered this presence, I felt transformed into being my own parent. Now I had the enormous opportunity to re-raise myself, to live the kind of life I had always longed for but had never had the courage to create.

A few weeks later, while clearing brush from the hillside, I was startled by a flock of crows flying madly about and wondered if another mating season was upon us. Their calls reminded me of growing up in Ohio where a friend and I spent much of our time in the woods.

After a few hunting seasons, we had become adept at discovering and reading the signs of wildlife. We would slip quietly down the creek beds, looking for any trace of movement, checking each sandbar for tracks. We got so good at reading the clues that we could not only tell what kind of animal had been there, but how much it weighed and whether it was likely to be a female or male. We would listen to the crows calling to one another about an owl or a fox who'd been caught out in broad daylight. We would smell the distinctive odors of each kind of animal and learned to read even the most obscure signs left by the hidden creatures around us. To do this, we had gradually learned to shift from seeing to sensing, from just looking to absorbing. It was my first experience of opening all my senses and perceiving the ordinarily hidden activity around me.

A similar shifting was necessary to detect the new life inside me. I had to switch from my usual perception of myself as a person to something more like the sensing I had done in the woods. If I just looked at things normally, I couldn't see any evidence of what I already knew, which was that something larger was unfolding in and around me. To experience this, I had to disconnect from the environment, then after going inside and momentarily centering myself, I'd shift from thinking to feeling, from seeing to sensing, from analyzing to absorbing. When I did this, a new optimism filled my chest that I couldn't experience any other way. I'd feel the weight of uncertainty lift and know that beyond the range of my everyday vision, my life was becoming creative again. Despite my money worries I felt secure, and I was filled with a deep sense of gratitude for that.

The hectic whirl of the city seemed distant, and once again I was as calm and peaceful as when I was growing up in the country. I would sit for hours, just like I did as a kid, listening to the crows that nested nearby, watching house cats stalk birds on the weed-covered hill below me, and hearing the coyotes that ranged over the mountain. I knew that everything was happening in its own time and in the way it was supposed to. I knew that there was a larger plan, a Subtle Agenda unfolding, and I could feel the fresh stirrings of something new.

I was starting with a freshly plowed field. The old ground was clear. All the past ventures and career worries were gone and no longer relevant. Success no longer meant what it had before. Now it was about living in harmony with the subtle new life growing inside me.

I looked around and saw that the street lights in the canyon had come on with the settling darkness. Stray was impatient to move, to go somewhere with me, but there wasn't enough light to walk around the mountain.

So I remained in the darkness a moment longer and fell into the softness of this new inner peace. I could sense a future emerging from inside me, moving under its own power, and in its own time. I couldn't plan it or force it. I could only open myself to it. And by having to wait for it and feel its worth grow, I was learning patience.

THIRTY

SUNSHINE

A dragonfly swept into the pool area, hesitated, then darted away. My eyes chased it for a moment until caught by the sight of a hummingbird feeding among the pink and red geranium pots hanging from the beams of the house. When the phone rang inside, it startled me. Stray watched as I got up to answer it.

A friend wanted to come up, and I was happy to have her company. A few years before, Jennifer had a bout with a serious illness and had explored several alternative healing methods. During that time, she looked at me and said, "You know, one day, we will all learn to live without fear."

What a strange thing to say, I'd thought at the time. Why would we ever want to do that? Wasn't fear part of a healthy defense? And even if we wanted to and could live safely without fear, how would we ever achieve that? Wasn't it healthy to be fearful at least half the time?

Now I understood what she meant. After having plummeted through my own worst fears and discovering that lying beneath them was a realm of loving security, I found a wholeness I'd never known existed. The only time I lost touch with these feelings was when I let myself be drawn into believing in my fears again.

Where before, my dragons were important motivators, now I saw them as a dissolvable barrier to a much greater source of power—love. Just as Jennifer had predicted, my daily exercise was learning to live without fear.

A car stopped in the driveway outside, and in moments, Jennifer and Stray had come through the house and were settling in next to me by the pool. She lit a joint, and as she handed it to me, we began talking about my discoveries since the bomb went off in my gut. She listened carefully and thoughtfully and grew excited at the changes she saw.

During the conversation, I asked her if she knew anyone who could help me with the tiredness I'd been experiencing. It had begun just as I was finishing my last script and had gotten slowly worse, and lately I was experiencing such exhaustion that I could barely do more than a few simple things each day. At first I fought it, but now I felt the possibility of it having a larger purpose. I thought it was the Subtle Agenda putting up a physical obstacle so I would stay still and pay attention to all the inner openings. If that was the purpose, it was working. I was spending hours and hours staring at the pool, basking in newfound feelings of joy and in such contentment that I could barely move. Despite my inner calm, I was regularly visited by terrible fears because nothing that might bring me an income was falling into place, and I didn't have the energy to make something happen.

"You ought to go see Ellen," she said after listening to me a few moments.

"You said that last time you were here," I said as I squirmed and looked away. Ellen was an acupuncturist, and I didn't want to see a doctor for what I was feeling. I had expected her to suggest some kind of spiritual healer who would be more experienced with what was happening to me.

"I think you'd be surprised at what she could do," Jennifer persisted. But when she saw my continued reluctance, she let the matter go.

The hours passed and we spoke about many things. We got a little high, laughed a lot, and solved a few of the world's problems. Then soon she was gone and I was alone again, watching another dragonfly sweep across the water.

Surprisingly, I was left with a feeling in my body that I should see the acupuncturist. As I wondered about this change of heart, I realized I was responding not to any of the logical reasons Jennifer had offered, but to a hint of desire in my body. She had twice suggested that I see Ellen. The first time, which had been months before, the suggestion had sounded irrelevant, and I had a vague negative reaction to it. But thinking about it this time, I felt a subtle tug pulling me to see her, despite the fact that I had never been to an acupuncturist and was afraid of needles.

I started to move somewhat sluggishly and Stray saw me. He got up and came over, and I had to lift his wet paw off Ellen's phone number. Jennifer had left it behind, just in case.

I had first become familiar with the writings of the ancient Chinese while reading as a teenager. I remembered feeling great respect for them and their ideas, which seemed so fresh and alive even five thousand years later. In my recent searching I had rediscovered these writers, especially Lao Tzu, and found pleasure in reading their descriptions of the subtle world. The difference between now and the first time I read them was that now I could experience the subtle world of the Tao (The Way), where before I had only an intellectual appreciation of the concept. So when I ran across the *Tao Te Ching* in a local bookstore and browsed through it again, it came alive in my hands. I loved Lao Tsu's expression of what I called the Subtle Agenda, and of how to live in harmony with the real and unreal worlds. As a writer, I was thrilled by how beautifully he had written about that which is so difficult to perceive, let alone explain.

Something else that was beginning to interest me, now that I was considering an appointment with Ellen, was that the Chinese had created a medicine—acupuncture. The medicine was an expression of their appreciation of the subtle plane and how it could be used to attune the body to natural forces that keep it healthy and in balance. I remembered reading somewhere that one measure of their medicine's success was that practitioners were paid only when their patients were well and not when they were sick.

But what really fascinated me was what I saw as the biggest difference between traditional Chinese medicine and ours. Acupuncture treats the body as though it is part of a reality larger than merely the physical. This time the idea of going to an acupuncturist felt right to me, probably because I was experiencing an expanded reality in my own life. Also, the belief that illness results from an imbalance of physical and nonphysical energies made me think that this ancient method might be useful in treating my tiredness and might even help me understand my inner experiences better.

There was a new lightness in my step as Stray and I took our early morning stroll around the mountain. I still found myself getting up at dawn, just as I had when I first moved out here, and I loved it. The air was clear, there were few sounds, and the landscape was highlighted brilliant pink and orange as the sun peeked over the San Gabriel Mountains. I was feeling a deep sense of appreciation for everything around me, and even gratitude for the struggles that had led me to what I was experiencing now.

It was becoming glaringly obvious that I could not have reached the awareness that I had without going through the "failures" first. The failures served to shatter my confidence in the things I had always believed. Each time a disaster occurred, it forced me to give up what until then had been a successful way of operating. And each time, I had to replace my long-held beliefs—which were often based in fear of some kind—with ones that I chose consciously and were true for me now. I knew in my heart that I would never have had the courage to trust my own ideas if following popular wisdom had been successful, and because of this, I was even more thankful for all my "misfortunes."

How strange to walk around these mountains without a career or even an income, without knowing what was going to happen, and to feel only gratitude for having been led to such an exquisite place in myself. Who would have thought it?

I had been staying close to the house for months now, tired but in a kind of quiet euphoria. On the outside I had the tentative slowness of an exhausted man, but on the inside I was sharp and very much alive.

Many times I found myself crying. Not because I had lost so much, but because I had finally broken through to myself. Sometimes I would sit holding myself and lovingly rock back and forth as I watched the clouds pass in the pool. I felt as though I had come home. And even though I had reached what seemed like the source of well-being, I was still pestered by the everyday worries of how I would make ends meet.

I didn't know how important it was at the time, but my growing need for money was good, because it was pushing me back into the world. I saw it as the Subtle Agenda bumping me along again, so I trusted that that was what I should do. I felt like a patient who, after surgery, wishes continued rest but would heal more quickly by leaving the hospital and becoming active again.

My little voice was now speaking to me mostly as feelings. It originally communicated through words and thoughts, probably because I used to live mostly in my head. But now that my awareness had become centered in my chest, I would get feelings in my body rather than ideas in my brain. As I made my choices, I'd weigh them inside, as if there was a scale in my chest. If they felt "good" or expansive, I took it as a signal to act. If there was a heaviness or a tightness, I would not.

When I weighed calling the acupuncturist, I felt a slight expansion in my chest, so I overrode my hesitation about needles and finally decided to call her. When the receptionist answered, I explained that I wasn't sure whether I wanted to come in for an appointment or not, but that I would like to talk to Ellen to help me decide. She told me I couldn't because she was busy with a patient. The receptionist then tried to make an appointment for me, but I insisted on talking with Ellen first.

In a moment she was on the phone.

"Jennifer said that I should call you. I'm not sick, but I got the feeling when she said to call you that I should. Could you … she said you practice acupuncture."

"That's true. It's body, mind, and spirit medicine. It works on all levels."

She was not Asian. Her accent was more Midwestern, perhaps even … I couldn't tell.

"Well, I don't think there's a whole lot wrong with me, although I am feeling tired a lot of the time. I don't think I have an illness or anything. It feels like it's more to do with my … changes going on in my awareness. Does that mean anything to you?" I couldn't believe I had said that. Suddenly everything I wanted to say sounded so "California," but it felt true so I stuck by it.

"Acupuncture can be very good for things like that. In fact, since it's an energy medicine, you're my favorite kind of patient. Many people call who want to quit smoking or something like that, but that's not what I do."

I thanked her appreciatively and was turned back over to the receptionist to make an appointment.

When the day arrived, I drove down to her medical building a little early so I could find a place to park without having to pay dearly for it.

Upstairs, as I got off the elevator and heard a baby crying, I realized that somewhere inside of me a baby was crying too—the baby that was afraid of doctors. Once I got to the door of her office the crying stopped, which calmed me a little. I nodded to the receptionist and sat down and looked at the old magazines. I didn't know if I could trust anyone who kept such old magazines on their waiting room table.

After a while I saw a figure in a white coat move behind the reception window. I will never forget how she looked in that moment—totally familiar, absolutely receiving, and very female. God, I thought, what a beautiful, brown-eyed, racy woman. And look how the sun has just risen in her face. I was not prepared for such a sudden and powerful impact. How could all of that be communicated in an instant? She smiled and went to open the door for me.

In her office she did a work-up, interviewing me for more than an hour, as she did with all her new patients. All I could think about was how wonderful she made me feel. There was almost an explosion in my chest.

We discovered that we knew some of the same people and that we had lived in Chicago about the same time for a few years, although she was away in college about the time Sarah was born.

Hovering above this delightful conversation were the forbidden thoughts of needles, which I suspected she had hiding somewhere. Were they in one of those drawers of hers? Where else would she keep them? How long were they? How deep did they go in? How long were they left in? How long did it hurt? Did it hurt? Of course it hurt, but would I live?

I wondered if I would pass out. I remember almost passing out in the army getting my shots. I'm in a very delicate condition right now, I thought. I'm not my normal self.

"Take off your watch, your shoes and socks, and climb up on the table."

"I'm not very comfortable with ... needles." I tried to bring it up as though the thought had just jumped into my head.

"Many people are bothered the first time. But don't worry, it won't hurt. And anyway, I only do one or two needles and they're quite small."

As I leaned back, her smile was like the sun. Once lying down, I noticed how vulnerable I was and how sensitive I felt to any kind of intrusion. I'd been spending many raw and introspective months alone, and now it was difficult to open myself to the treatment.

"Just relax."

Then one at a time, she took each of my hands in hers, and closing her eyes she felt the pulses on both my left and right wrists. It took several long minutes, but I was comforted by her warm hands.

"I didn't realize there's more than one pulse."

"Hmmm, they tell me what's going on with each of the organs."

"Really? That's incredible."

"The ancient Chinese thought of the body as a kind of kingdom, an inner empire, and each of the organs help it function in an orderly way. I think of organs as little people, and by listening to the pulses I can tell if they are having trouble doing their job."

"Like, what's the heart?"

"The heart is the supreme controller, the one in charge of the others. The speaker of wisdom. It keeps the peace."

Somehow I already knew the heart was the speaker of wisdom. I wanted to tell her I had just discovered that myself, but I felt awkward.

"And the liver is the planner, the architect, if you will, and the gall bladder is the judge."

"What kinds of problems are my people having?" I wondered, seeing myself as a child in a ravaged kingdom.

"Well," she said hesitantly, "I would say that your energy is depleted. Your people are all in hiding. I'd say you've been having a real hard time, a siege of sorts."

I closed my eyes and let her do her work. A thrill ran over my body. She seemed to know what she was doing and I smiled to find behind the name Ellen was hiding such a wonderful creature.

That afternoon I kept thinking about her and couldn't confine myself to the house. I felt like walking somewhere other than our usual path, but since we might come across dogs that Stray wasn't familiar with, I took the leash out of the drawer and clipped it to his collar. Once at the end of the driveway, I took a deep breath. I wanted a long, long walk.

I looked down on Los Angeles. The haze that usually screened the city seemed a little lighter that day. I felt good. My body felt young and strong, and I had an optimism that I hadn't felt in ages. I couldn't tell if my sudden surge of energy was from the acupuncture treatment or from meeting the acupuncturist. From below in the canyon I could smell the sweet aroma of orange blossoms.

Since we hadn't encountered any people or dogs, I let Stray off his leash. It was dry for April, and the rabbits spilled dust out behind them as they tried to stay ahead of Stray. I felt more relaxed with the city than usual and wondered about Ellen. It was exciting and comfortable to think about her, as if we were old, old friends.

I heard an ambulance in the distance and saw it snaking down Nichols Canyon Road far below me. I watched it until it disappeared behind a curve then drifted back into my own thoughts.

Ellen was having a strong impact on me, and it felt like I could fall in love if I let myself. The tug in my heart reminded me of when I first met Joan. There had been a distinct difference between what I felt for her as compared to the other women I'd dated. In a very short time, I knew that that relationship was going to be important to me.

Now I was experiencing something similar about Ellen. It was an old and a new feeling all at once. The excitement was new but the importance it held for me seemed familiar. All this time of not being able to really connect with someone had been bothering me. I was waiting, I guess, for this kind of feeling again. My chest was expanding so much I thought it would burst, and I assumed it was my little voice who obviously didn't want me to ignore what I was feeling. I couldn't believe this was actually happening to me while everything else was falling apart. Then I wondered if it really was happening or whether I was just going off into fantasy. Maybe she was involved with someone. I didn't even know her. And besides, how could she be interested in me?

My stepdaughter, Lynn, and her friend Joe, decided that they were going to make their relationship "official." They had built a house together in Alaska but wanted to be married in Los Angeles with me, and in Chicago with her mother and natal father. I was pleased she considered me a father again, and I was happy to be giving her a wedding.

It was unusually cold for May and slightly rainy when we arrived for the wedding at the Self Realization Fellowship Lake Shrine near the ocean. The ceremony was performed by a woman minister, and had a humanness and warmth about it that pleased everyone. Afterward, the drizzle followed us back to the house for a catered lunch.

Sarah had come in from school, and Lynn had several of her own friends in town. My friend Marissa was there, and so were Monica and her daughter. Monica and I still dated once and a while, but mostly we were just friends. I was being the polite host and happy dad, but all the while I was thinking about Ellen and how much I wished that she was there.

A few days later I heard fire engines across the mountain and cringed as I imagined another brush fire. There had been a small blaze in the canyon the previous year but nothing serious, nothing like the Agoura fire that had swept from the San Fernando Valley down to the ocean in Malibu a few years before.

The engines screamed as they coiled around the canyon road, and I saw them coming, several of them, from the fire station at

Laurel Canyon. Their sirens terrified Stray, but they passed my drive as if an angel had marked our stoop but stopped when they reached the houses just above us. Since there were so many trucks and I could smell the smoke, I hurried to check it out. I put Stray in Sarah's room, and by the time I got outside, the house above me was already an inferno.

When I arrived, there were more than a half-dozen fire trucks, and I could see the firefighters frantically trying to reach someone who was trapped inside. A man lived there alone, a runner whom I knew because he often ran down my driveway. He was always friendly, and Stray, after getting used to seeing him on our property, would wag his tail and trot alongside him until he got out to the street.

Several firefighters managed to fight their way inside, but it was too late. They soon returned carrying the man in a body bag. They had found him lying in the hallway between the kitchen and the bedroom. He had his robe half on, they said, and was still alive when they first entered the blaze because they'd heard his shouting.

I'd watched several people die in accidents, but in the past, I had always been too guarded to let myself open to the full impact of the pain. Part of my withholding was probably from my superstition that if I let myself get too close, the next one could be me.

This time was different. I didn't shrink from it. Instead, a part of me opened to the man, and the feelings were so young and innocent that I realized it was the new child in me. He wasn't afraid the way the adult was. He didn't run as if the horror would come after him. The child kept clear eyes and let me feel love for the man who had just died. And for the first time in my life I let myself experience the suffering of someone dying alone. I let myself feel the loss of a neighbor, a friendly man who had also enjoyed the freshness of our morning air on the mountain. I even let myself take him inside where I held him next to my heart. As I stood there, I was for all appearances the same man I had always been, but as I watched this scene, I knew I was different. I felt death in a new way. It was sad and sweet and natural, and I even felt a quiet sense of joy that I had been there to hold him in my heart when he died.

THIRTY-ONE

EMBRACING THE DRAGONS

When I met Elliot for lunch, I wondered how I would describe what had been happening in my life over the past few years. I had purposely shied away from people I'd known in advertising because I felt unable to communicate the depth of the change I was experiencing. The few times I did try, they focused on how awful the difficulties were and couldn't seem to see the larger scope of what was taking place, or appreciate the benefits.

Elliot was a commercial film director whom I'd known for many years. When I was still in Chicago, he'd visit from California and we'd spend time talking about making a film together one day. Then after I moved here, he and I often played tennis but never spoke much about film. Now it was almost five years since we had seen each other.

When I entered the small pasta restaurant on Melrose, he was already at the table sipping a drink and reading the paper. We hugged as we met and got quickly into conversations about the past. He listened with intense interest as I told him about the high risks I had taken, about how I had always been successful in the past, but then how things suddenly began to change. Finally, I spoke cautiously of my recent experience of having come in contact with what felt like my own infant self.

"This may sound a little strange, but I'm actually aware of feeling something small and fragile alive in me. It feels like my own child, or myself as a child."

He just sat there, slowly spinning his pasta onto his fork, while I watched for what seemed an interminable time, wondering if he understood. I had the urge to jump into the silence with more words, but I tried to relax and let him have his time.

"Do you have any idea how lucky you are?"

I smiled in surprise and disbelief.

"I mean, how many people ever get, or take, the chance to totally reconstruct their lives? I make good money, I've made good money for as long as I can remember … you've been to my house. And now I'm buying another one, probably twice as expensive as the one I have."

He was thinking as he turned more pasta onto his fork.

"But I'm a painter. I started in art school and painting is all I ever wanted to do. At this point, I'll never find out if I'm a real painter or not, and I know very well that I am. I was terrific at it when I was younger. And now, all my life is about is keeping up with the bills."

We smiled at each other for a moment. My life was definitely not just about keeping up with my bills, though I had many of the same anxieties that he had. The difference was that I had stopped letting mine make choices for me. I wouldn't want it any other way, but I did long for the day that I could again pay my bills easily and have my values too.

"You've taken the time and effort to find out what your life is all about. You might not believe this, but I'd trade places with you in a minute. Would you with me?"

I thought about it for a moment—of the infinite list of commercials he would have to shoot every year whether he believed in the products or not, whether he wanted to or not, and of always having to execute other people's ideas. And then I thought of the years and years of not taking the opportunity to find out what he was made of, whether he really was a painter or not, and I knew I wouldn't trade.

I thought of my hunger to keep in contact with the child I had found, and of my tremendous commitment to pursuing what my heart was crying out for. Then in a flash, I knew there was a book I wanted to write. I wanted to describe the journey I was on, and the excitement of it filled me. Instantly, I was flooded with a longing to write again.

"No, I wouldn't trade anything. And what's maybe strange is that I have almost no financial resources left. I might even have to sell my house so I'll have the money to write about some ideas I've been having."

"Who better to invest in than yourself?" Elliot shot back. He was a good father and had financed his children's educations, but as frequently happens he had surrendered his own dreams in the process.

"That's right, who better?" My mind was now spinning with the impulse to begin the book right away.

As we left the restaurant we embraced again, and I watched him climb into his new, four-door black Mercedes and wave as he drove away. Then I let myself feel the child inside myself and my new passion to write, and I realized that I truly was one of the lucky ones.

I had been back to see Ellen for treatments several times, and since she didn't discourage my interest in her, I finally got up enough courage to ask her out to dinner.

As I prepared to pick her up, I had all kinds of second thoughts, mostly about how little I had told her about my deteriorating financial situation. For all appearances, I was doing pretty well. I had a house in the mountains, drove a Mercedes (albeit an aging one), and had a look of dependability that people respected. But it only hid the truth. When she questioned me during her initial work-up, I didn't volunteer that I had fallen on hard times. The male in me would not let me do that.

I had made reservations at a wonderful basement French restaurant that I thought would appeal to her. As I parked the car near her place, I felt a pulse of excitement in my stomach.

She lived in a small French chateau-style building near the bottom of the canyon, and her apartment was in the kind of taste that I liked. It was simple, with high ceilings, antique bleached pine pieces, ancient Oriental things, and white chairs and sofas. Plants were everywhere.

She seemed a bit timid now, away from her office, and the more I became aware of her shyness, the more confidence I felt rising in myself.

She didn't like Hollywood very much, which is where the restaurant was, because it had become too rundown. But as we drove, there were many other things to talk about. We both loved France and good food, though she was more interested in health food than I was, and I was more interested in wine.

I thought our dinner was wonderful, and I could feel that she thought so too. I tried to share the depth of my inner search with her, but hid the full burden of the financial crisis. When she asked about my work or what my plans were, I told her about all the reasons I had left Chicago and of my interest in film and myth, but I didn't reveal that my career had ground to almost a complete halt. She seemed to accept that I had no job, maybe because to her not having a job was a sign of wealth. It was a tightrope at first, but we relaxed with each other as the evening passed.

When your life has come to a complete stop, and you have no idea how you're going to rebuild it again, even though you know things will be all right, how can you tell all this to the woman you think you love on the very first date?

I learned that she had been raised in what I would consider a privileged way, partly because of Texas oil money, and partly out of her father's business activities in Chicago. Much of this ended for her family, however, when her father died and little original money remained. She grew up hearing her father, whom she dearly loved, speak to her brother about becoming a doctor. So all of her life she had been drawn toward the health profession but could not find it in herself to go into "Western medicine," as she called it.

While living in New York she met a physician who was on his way to study ancient Chinese medicine from a master in England. It was through him that she experienced a profound, life-changing urge to study it too. She had found an answer to her lifelong dream of becoming a doctor, and she could treat people in ways that western medicine could not.

"You mean people with my kind of problem?" flirting a little as I said it.

"Just like you," she answered, in a way that I could tell she cared—I hoped as much as I cared about her.

One night, a few weeks later, Ellen and I attended a dinner party that was arranged so she could meet a therapist who was a friend of the host. This therapist knew Ellen by reputation but they had never met before that evening. Much of the discussion was about alternative medicine and other forms of therapy, and finally about enlightened ways of handling illness.

Marie, the therapist, spoke of her interest in terminal illness and how it often stimulates the stricken individual to finally make choices that have been too difficult to make before. And how frequently, just making these choices transforms his or her life and often leads to remission.

The subject was of great interest to me, of course, because I saw a parallel between how my life had disintegrated and terminal illness. Both difficulties were served on the individual seemingly against their will, both could mean the end of life as it was, and both could be used to completely transform the individual's inner, as well as outer, life.

What fascinated me most was how to define a "transformation" and what about it could change the course of a disease. My interest was not simply academic. My chairman was frantically urging me to do something about my own terminal finances.

Having first discovered the pattern of birth, death, and rebirth in mythology, I said that perhaps the transformation came when the patient could see the illness as part of a larger process and as a potentially good thing. And that if we followed the trail through myth, death was always followed by a new and higher form of life. I offered that if the patient could see himself in that light and be willing to make the necessary changes, the illness might be the doorway to a more advanced stage. I was even willing to bet that the individual's own higher wisdom, or Subtle Agenda, might have caused the illness as a way to force giving up past attachments and making overdue changes. It was another expression of how the Subtle Agenda worked for the higher good of the individual, even against that person's apparent will.

Later, as we were leaving, Marie came over and told me she wanted to meet again and speak further about all these things. I sparked to the idea and we agreed she would come up to the house later that week.

On the morning Marie was to come over, I was excited about being able to speak openly about the series of disasters I'd been encountering. Maybe she would have insight into where I was in the process and maybe even some ideas about how to rebuild. When I heard Stray barking outside, I put the tea kettle on and went to let Marie in.

Marie loved to laugh, and many of her thoughts and ideas were punctuated, fore and aft, with giggles. Not inane giggles, but innocent giggles that tinkled like little Tibetan bells. We sat down and quickly got to laughing about how life's disasters are so wonderful for growth, and about how if we are able to survive, we grow just like everything else in nature.

After we laughed a while I began to feel uncomfortable about all the levity in the face of my own dragons and wanted to get down to business.

"Why did you pick me out the other night? Why did you want to talk more about these things?" While Marie was contemplating her response, I continued. "I'm glad you did, because it'd be fun to have a friend who's a therapist—I'm just trying to figure out where to begin."

"Well I just had this incredible feeling that you knew something about archetypal images—that you were trying to understand something deeper about yourself through them. And I found that very interesting. I feel I know the search but not the images. I don't know much about myth."

"I don't either, actually. I just feel drawn to this particular aspect—the death and rebirth thing. Mostly I've used the images to find my own way. I'm very familiar with the death thing," I laughed. "Now I've got to find out about the rebirth part."

She inquired about what was happening to me, and the months of suffering that I had never shared with anyone came pouring forth. After I pulled myself together I stood up and began to pace.

"It's a bitch. I don't know how to stop the disintegration. It's continuing right now, even as we speak. I've learned to trust and even appreciate the process, and I know it's leading me to what I really want. But it seems like there's something I need to discover or realize or something ... to get the financial problems to stop. But I don't know what that might be or how to find it."

I managed a smile and sat back down. Marie smiled back and took a sip of her tea.

"I mean, even though I know everything is going to be okay, sometimes I feel like I'm losing my mind."

"Maybe that's what you need to do—lose your mind, your linear view of things. Lose your "old mind" so to speak. Maybe it's about getting out of your head entirely and opening your heart more."

"I feel like I've been doing that. I've made contact with myself in a way that I never have before. I know, because I feel more connected than any time in my life. I feel brand new inside, almost as if there's a child inside of me. And all I really care about is living in complete harmony with it."

"The child probably represents what's emerging in you. I got the feeling the other night when you were talking about myth and the challenge of the dragons in the underworld, that it was just a metaphor for the fear we have of giving up the old way of life. The child might mean that you have done that, and now you're rebuilding."

I was thrilled that she could see these things so clearly, and it was a relief to finally talk candidly to someone who understood the images. But I felt that the abiding presence in my heart area was more than metaphor. It was like a child, a separate consciousness living inside me.

"What's worrying me now is how to translate all this into bread and butter. My financial life is in terrible shape and getting worse, but somehow going out and getting a job feels wrong—it's like going back to work just to save the past. And I'm still fighting this exhaustion that Ellen's working on with me. What I'm trying to find is a way to rebuild, but in such a way that I don't have to surrender my values—in a way that's in harmony with this sense of wholeness I have worked so hard for. Does that make sense to you?"

"Yes, it does. But it might not happen as quickly as you'd like. It feels like what's emerging will have to continue growing from inside you, and that doesn't always happen as quickly as we would like. If it doesn't happen soon, what's the worst it can get?"

"I'd have to sell the house. Sarah might have to leave her private school, and I'd have to go back into a small apartment somewhere until I could see a direction. I guess I'd live off the money I made on the house."

"So what's wrong with that?"

"Well, I'd rather not do that." I smiled wryly. "I want to continue living here. I love it here." I looked through the wall of windows at the profusion of pink geraniums hanging from the eves and at the black pool beyond.

"But that might be the key. You're the one who talks about the wisdom of the Subtle Agenda. Your life is forcing you to change. You might be resisting it."

"But then ... Okay, so I go along with it, sell everything and start over again. Say I do all of that. Then what? What would I do that I'm not doing now?"

"My feeling is that whatever it is for you will have to come out of your own inner plane."

"I know that. But I don't know how to make that happen."

"I'm sure it's connected to your heart, some new way of expressing yourself. Some new kind of being, doing, creating, that comes from your heart rather than from an external need for money. I don't know."

"I'd want to keep writing but not for films. There's a book I'd like to do. It feels a little irresponsible, but it's the only thing that excites me. Should I be willing to trade my house for it? But I can't just go get a job and quit all I've been working so hard for."

"What does your child want to do?"

I had to laugh at the way that sounded. She was happy to join me in my fantasy, and I began laughing too.

"The kid wants to write. But his dad has to earn a living."

She looked at me with a wide grin on her face.

"I hope the kid wins."

On my morning walk around the mountain with Stray, I found myself struggling with issues about how to earn an income without compromising what I'd learned—and I had to come up with something soon. Furthermore, I wanted to get my feet back on the ground. The years of working on film ideas with their long developmental periods would no longer do. I wanted to do simple work, something that I enjoyed, and get money in return. I needed what the farmers back in Ohio called a "cash crop." I wanted to plant and sell in the same season, but whatever I did, it had to be creative because I needed that. Most of all, I wanted to keep my freedom. I didn't want to ever again submit my values or what I believed to someone else.

A young rabbit slipped off the path ahead of us, and Stray tore after it. I paused a moment to wait for him.

Giving up film was a dream dying hard, but once I saw that it would no longer serve me, I was able to walk away without regrets. Now I knew I wanted to build something that was mine —something that I could build using my own muscle, my own experience, my own talents and my own know-how—and make money in return. I didn't know any other way to earn a living and still be true to my inner child.

Although my conversation with Marie did nothing to relieve my anxieties about where my next dollar was coming from, it felt good to share the load with someone who really understood. She was a good friend in a way I'd never experienced before. She not only understood with her head, she felt the values in her gut and was trying to live them in her life too.

The only unsettling thing about the meeting was the realization that my wanting to keep the house might be on a collision course with the deeper purpose of the Subtle Agenda. I wanted to keep it almost more than anything in the world, but was the Subtle Agenda asking me to give it up?

"It doesn't have to mean that," my chairman offered. "I think it would be easier if you just went into the right organization. That way you wouldn't run the risk of having to sell the house. This is an incredible house and Southern California real estate is a great investment. You wouldn't want to sell it, would you?"

I found myself aligning with my chairman. For the first time in as long as I could remember, I begrudgingly agreed with what he said.

"But if you go into a big organization, you'd lose your freedom right away," my little voice said, sounding weak and unconvincing. "You'd find yourself back doing things you don't really like, and then where would you be? Look, I know it's hard going your own way, but the rewards will be worth it. Start something of your own, and once you've created a foundation for yourself you'll probably never have to do it again. If you want to write, you could make time for it if you had your own business."

My own business? I wanted to build something that was mine, but I'd never seriously thought of starting a business myself. Having a business seemed overwhelming and more time consuming than working for someone else. But I couldn't think about it now—it was the first of the month again and I had to pay my bills.

I had gone through all the money from selling my company stock, my other investments were gone, and I had cashed in my life insurance. All I had left in reserve were my IRAs, and they were dwindling fast. It was embarrassing, but every month I would sit down, center myself, and write a little note to the bank. I would call it my monthly yoga because I would have to go to the deepest part of myself, recommit to my dream, and trust that everything would turn out okay.

Dear Mr. Banker:

I am not of retirement age, and I am aware of the tax penalty involved in this transaction; however, please wire the following to my account in California as listed below ....

Sincerely ...

The tension from the monthly financial draws got more difficult to bear as my funds got lower. Where would I live if I had to leave the house? After living in such a wonderful place it would be difficult to be in a small apartment somewhere.

But of equal importance to where I would live, was the question of *how* I would live. I had found an inner peace, a loving centeredness that meant everything to me. No job, no career, was more important than that. How could I keep my inner values, write a book, and still earn enough money to keep the house?

The unrelenting economic pressures were taking me to the end of my resources. I felt like a tiny sailboat in the path of a hurricane, needing to find port immediately if I wanted to survive.

I began to think back to my naïve vision of the monastery in Kentucky. How wonderful it had appeared to me as a young man —the peace and quiet, doing nothing more than tending cows, making simple cheeses and breads, praising the universe each day, and never having to worry about the realities of earning a living. I could write in a place like that.

If the financial erosion continued, and I did have to sell the house, where would I go? I wanted something simple where I could begin all over again.

One morning, about a month later, I found myself putting my sleeping bag in the trunk of my car, and after getting a friend to stay in the house and take care of Stray, I headed out the driveway for Ojai. I had become acquainted with a spiritual community there and decided to take a closer look.

The traffic was still heavy on the Ventura Freeway as I slipped up the Laurel Canyon ramp and threaded my way in. The months in the house had slowed me down. Everyone appeared to be going too fast. Cars were cutting back and forth, competing for space, edging in, darting over, slamming on the brakes, speeding up, grabbing the spot that barely opened in the next lane.

As the traffic thinned out beyond Thousand Oaks, I released my imagination in hopes of seeing the future. Where would I be living on this day next year? How would I feel by then? I had a small vision of a simple place—I couldn't see the where of it, but I felt the what of it, and it was as peaceful as I had hoped it would be.

Krishnamurti had been given wonderful land in the upper Ojai Valley by Ann Bessant and the Theosophical Society. He had returned it, however, when he refused to be the world leader they had trained him to be, and kept a smaller house in the lower valley where he visited all throughout his life.

The community of people lived in the upper valley, working together and offering weekend retreats to visitors from the city.

I had been there several times before and felt a rush of nostalgia as I entered the mouth of the Ojai Valley. As I wound my way east, my eyes were caught by Topa Topa, the huge peak at the end of the valley that was said to be the background for Shangri-la in the film *Lost Horizon*. At times you could see one of the few remaining condors soar over the Topa from their refuge just beyond, but all I saw now were several redtail hawks circling overhead.

Beyond the village center, the land gave way to miles of orange and lemon groves lined by low, rock walls skillfully built many years before by local Chumash Indians who had mastered the craft. As the slope rose from the valley floor, avocado groves replaced citrus and climbed the rough rock into the foothills.

The upper valley was on a high table which rose up to the southeast, and as I switched back and forth along the curling narrow road, I stopped at a viewing spot for a moment and looked back over the long way I had come.

This was one of the few remaining glimpses of the Southern California of my imagination. I first discovered this kind of scene on the orange crates in the supermarkets where I worked in high school. And it still looked just as the artists had depicted. Below me lay rows of citrus trees, flanked by lavender mountains, and above were the clear blue skies.

The entrance to the land where the community was situated, was a simply marked driveway that disappeared into a walnut grove. I took a deep breath and let myself be drawn in.

The next few days were a montage of scenes of what life on the land might be like. My temporary home was under the "guest oak," a sprawling old tree whose arms of branches touched the ground and sheltered my sleeping bag and the few other things I had brought with me. In the early morning haze, the white canvas tents that dotted the hillsides looked desert lavender and pink, and in the evenings they appeared bright orange from the inner lantern lights. A group of us went nude in a cold stream that trickled down from high in the mountains, but even that was no relief from the oven-like heat. I watched the group's rituals, which had been formed out of America's affection for the Indians and the Buddhists, rituals both new and old that were performed with deep sacredness.

I imagined myself buying one of their small trailers, cashing my small monthly checks in town, and beginning to write, here on the land. I would live simply on the earth's soft skin that I'd loved so much as a child, and begin again in the simplest of ways. Whenever I asked myself what I wanted, the feeling communicated back to me was that I live simply and let each day create itself. This place, I thought, could provide me room to do just that.

But late on the fourth afternoon I was finished. Just before the group gathered at the end of the day, I found myself rolling up my sleeping bag and getting my things together. I could hardly breathe as I pushed them into the trunk of the car. The same suffocating feeling I'd had at the monastery years before was choking me now. This had been a possible dream, but I couldn't do it. I was feeling the same pull toward the city I had felt when I left the monastery in Kentucky. In another lifetime this might have worked, but not in this one.

I had to go duke it out in the city. I had to go back into the chaos, back into the traffic. I had to learn how to grab my space in line again, and how to make my own way. Something strong inside was pushing me to leave the pastoral and fling myself back into the marketplace.

Glimpsing a vague recollection of myself deep in a corner of my ancient memory, I suspected that I had come this way many times before and that I had often sought the refuge of a spiritual preserve, looking for a simple life of dedication. But not now. Not this time. Not in this life. I was drawn to participate in the tumult of things, and it had always been that way. My way, my own truth, even my peace, lay down in the city, in the midst of the bustling chaos.

I decided that the next time I had dinner with Ellen, I would bite the bullet and tell her what was happening to me. If we were going to have any kind of relationship, I had to let her in.

In my effort to protect what was developing between us, I had fallen on past practices of not communicating the full truth while a relationship was still in the beginning stages. There was something that had come down through male myths that had always counseled me to serve the good stuff up front, and save the work for later. The male ego liked to look powerful, but it was fragile when it came to erections and incomes. I was having to find new ways to be as honest as I could, and what I felt for Ellen was too precious to risk playing games. This feeling was supported by a growing trust that if whatever I had to tell her was the truth, then it would work for both of us. As much as it scared me, in my new life there was no other way.

When the time was right that evening and she seemed open to me, I began speaking about what was on my mind. The words came first in a trickle, then finally in a torrent. I told her about the values crisis that had pulled me out of my old life and of the difficulties that had led me to spend practically all my money. I shared my feeling that it was all happening for some purpose and that, even though it might look bad from the outside, I felt a new beginning taking place from inside. I told her that I loved her and that staying true in this process was very important to me, and that I hoped she would see it that way too.

Her face changed as I spoke. It was not easy for her. She was, at first meeting, very attracted to me because I was an "adult," as she called it. I had a family, a long and successful career in advertising, a house, and a certain daring to try new things. It looked as if I had it all together and even good enough to move right into.

Her fear, her dragon, was that, once again, here was a man she cared about, a man who appeared to have everything, but under it all, was barely able to take care of himself.

As a teenager, losing her father had broken her heart, and with him she had lost a secure and stable way of life. Later, her husband whom she loved dearly, was not able to put his life together while they were married. Then several lovers who were very important to her, were not able to carry their own weight. Life had never served her a complete, mature, building relationship with a man. And now, when she seemed to have finally met one who appeared to be what she always wanted, someone she could really love and who could give her the stability she longed for, he, too, was in trouble.

"I don't understand why this happens to me," she said softly. "Why can't I have the kind of life I want? I want a man that I can be proud of and a way of life that is secure and growing so we can build and do things together, and travel ..." Her sentence stopped short as her eyes filled with tears.

There was little I could say. From her point of view she would be starting all over again. What was even worse was the possibility that this guy might not simply be taking a series of pretty bad tumbles—it might be this way from now on. Maybe he had spent the best part of his life back in Chicago.

I couldn't blame her for her reaction. A part of me felt the same thing. I was indeed afraid that whatever it was that was happening to me might never stop and could spill over into her life, just as she feared.

How ironic this was. I had almost totally transformed my inner life. I was more whole, more able to love, and more available than ever before. But to the one I loved, it didn't appear to be so. How could I communicate it? Either she felt the potential or she didn't. Even though my life was a shambles to the casual observer and I hadn't gotten it all back together yet, I knew I had finally turned the corner inside myself. And I was very disappointed that she couldn't feel it.

When the evening ended, it was on a quiet, undigested note.

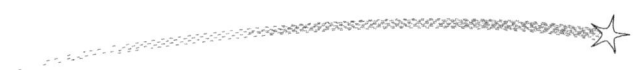

THE OTHERWORLD

I was, in the depths of myself, at peace knowing that I could not have gotten to this stage without first moving through a form of death. As if by consciously passing into an afterlife, I found myself about to choose my next incarnation.

It was a period of suspended time in which I had intense bouts with love and pain. In my heart I felt a wellspring of peace, but vivid memories of death continued to torture me. For a long time there were three "me's" — the dying man, the newborn infant, and the observer untrained to handle either. Perhaps this is what a caterpillar feels while going through its metamorphosis — sitting in a death vigil, only barely conscious of the birthing new form.

This phase was like walking a tightrope, balancing on the thin line of light that illuminates the separation between the past and the future. When I reflected on the past and what I had lost, I became frightened. When I imagined the future and my meager resources, I panicked. So to create my stability, I learned to stay in the present.

This balancing act became my daily meditation — and by working each day to stay in that space, I began the slow process of rebuilding my life, creating each day from my trust of the Subtle Agenda and the wisdom of my choices.

THIRTY-TWO

THE DANCE BEGINS

My money had dwindled to the point where I had only enough for a few months when I was suddenly faced with severe car problems. On the way down the mountain one morning, I noticed a billowing cloud of exhaust behind me, so I took the car to the German mechanic who had been taking care of it. I left it overnight, and after he had done some tests, he called to say that I needed a new engine. Apparently, I had let the car overheat at some point, which had damaged the block, and since the old engine had so many miles on it, it could not be repaired. The estimated cost, compared to the rate I was going through my savings, amounted to about a month's income. I shuddered at the thought of getting so low.

"Let me think about it for a day or so, and I'll call you back. What would you do?"

"I'd do enough so it would drive and then dump it. With 94,000 miles on it, the car isn't worth the investment."

"Well, okay, I'll call you in a day or so."

I wanted to give myself a chance to think and maybe to look around at some other cars. That evening, as Stray and I were walking around the mountain, there was a meeting of the board.

"Get rid of the car," my chairman began. "It's not worth putting any more money into it. Invest just enough to put the thing back together and sell it, then use the money as a down payment on a new car. Let someone else deal with the headaches."

That sounded smart but didn't feel right.

"This is just another dragon," said my little voice, "giving you a chance to test your values under pressure. It's easy to have values when things are going well, but it's more difficult when things are tough. It's no accident it's happened right now when your money is tightest."

There was a part of me, one that I wasn't proud of, that was pushing me to simply put a new head gasket on the car and sell it. The mechanic had told me that a quick fix like that would make it last long enough to sell. A car auctioneer would buy it and probably take it to another state, so who'd know or even care?

"Selling a car with a blown engine to some poor unsuspecting buyer is not a very kind thing to do," my little voice offered, "no matter which state he lives in. The car will have to be fixed by someone, and since it's your car, it's your responsibility. This is an opportunity, once again, to override your fears and trust that if you do what you feel in your heart, the result will be more satisfying in the long run."

What my little voice was saying sounded right to me. How I responded was the big issue, not the money. I was trying to create a new life by being true to my inner wholeness without falling prey to my old split.

After sleeping on it and much thinking, and after feeling how my body was responding, I realized I had no choice but to fix the car properly. I would have to absorb the expense no matter what the effect on my finances. The only reason I would dump it on somebody else would be out of a fear of having less money. And following my fear, I knew, would lead me back the way I'd come. I had to follow my heart.

Of more importance was what this situation symbolized. What was interesting was not simply which choice I would make, but that the situation had developed at all. The Subtle Agenda had presented me with a symbol of my entire struggle right then and was letting me see that I preferred my values to money. This was one of the clearest signals yet that the Subtle Agenda was indeed providing a refinement process, and if this one small incident was a reflection of the whole, I would let my values lead me even at the expense of my material attachments.

Several days later I drove my rented car to the repair shop. The businessman in me felt a little awkward about taking such a severe economic jolt without trying to find a way to lay it off somewhere else, but I let those feelings pass through me. As I walked up to the mechanic who'd given me the bad news, I felt young and naïve.

"What've you decided to do?" he asked me.

"Well, it's a hard choice. There's no way but a new block, huh?" He took me over to look at my pulled engine block sitting on a bench in the garage. It was painful to see what had once been the heart of a wonderful car reduced to a small hunk of steel. It was like going to the hospital to see a friend, and instead, being presented with one of his organs.

"See those pits?" He showed me some erosion of metal around the top of the block near the cylinder holes. "That's from overheating, and they're too deep to machine. I could put it back together so it'd last until you sell it. I could do that for a lot less than putting in a new engine."

Suddenly tired of hearing about it, I turned away and headed back to the car.

"Put the new engine in," I called back to him. "I just can't stick somebody else with it. When it's done, I might sell it."

"If you put a new engine in it," he yelled, "you might as well keep it for another 50 or 100,000 miles."

I nodded as I crossed the lot. I spotted my car, getting dusty in the back corner, with its hood up exposing the gaping hole where the engine had been. It seemed like a perfect symbol for my own life, and I hoped that by getting a new engine for my car, I might be doing the same for myself.

Marie and I met for tea soon after, and when I told her about the blown engine, she laughed at the irony and then so did I.

"What do you think it means?" she asked.

She was aware that I was finding symbolic meaning in everything and that I liked interpreting life's events as if I was analyzing a dream. While studying screenwriting, I had discovered that in a high-quality script every element has meaning. In a film, and I suppose in all story telling, every scene, every character, every event, every word, is chosen for its ability to deliver some kind of ultimate message to an audience. This is what had helped me discover the Subtle Agenda and become aware that it, too, communicated by using the elements in life as language. I was finding meaning, intelligence, and presence in every situation, although I was not always able to understand the communication with complete satisfaction.

"Well, I think my car is obviously me, and having to get a new engine is my need to find a new way to earn a living. I need to find a new economic engine, so to speak. That's one of the reasons I wanted to deal with the situation with complete integrity."

"But what does that tell you that you don't already know?"

"Not much. But I think the real issue is about ending the dominance that fear has had over my life and reconstructing it on a more solid base. And I think the significance of the whole incident is that it provides me with a small, but scary opportunity to feel what it's like to make no compromises—to go through the eye of the needle, so to speak, and whatever survives is alchemical gold."

"What do you mean by alchemical gold?" Marie asked.

"Well, I think of it as a metaphor for what's left after a refinement process. Ancient alchemists were thought to have the ability to transform lead into gold. It's like searching for the Holy Grail or any other symbol of the quest for truth. You don't just stumble upon it one day—it's what you have and who you are after the struggle."

"What a great metaphor! This process is about going through the refining fires and coming out the other side with gold. This also means that you believe life is a school!" She laughed and so did I. Marie's ability to get me to laugh in even the most difficult of times was one of her most precious qualities.

"Well, I would not have thought so in my old life, but I don't know any other explanation for what I'm going through. The Subtle Agenda feels like it has wisdom behind it, and once you begin finding messages in everything, life is one long learning process. I know how it might sound to the average person, but if a screenwriter can manipulate an audience's education for an hour and a half, don't you think a God, or the Tao, our own Souls, or whatever forces there are, can manage it for a lifetime? For myself, I know that I'm being led kicking and screaming through the refining fires into deeper awareness, and seeing life as a metaphor has been a big part of it."

I picked up our cups and went to the kitchen to make more tea. When I returned I continued.

"What I still don't know is how to put a new engine in my life. I understand that the old one is finished. That's abundantly clear. But I don't know what it will take yet to pull myself through."

I developed a huge frown, and a moment later we both began to laugh again.

"What I'm not getting is what the big screenwriter in the sky is trying to get across to me now."

I held my arms up in mock supplication.

"Tell me what I'm supposed to do now. What's the next scene? At least give me a clue. I know I have to do something, but I'm not getting what it is yet."

"You obviously have more changes in store."

"I'm sure of that, but I've changed almost everything in the past few years. The only thing left is the house. And my dog."

Stray looked up when he realized we were talking about him, and Marie and I both laughed.

"Don't worry, old boy. Nothing's going to happen to you."

"But the house might be part of it," Marie added.

"The way it looks, it'll be the last part," I laughed. "After that there'd be nothing left."

"Well, at least you're learning to laugh about it."

"Gallows humor," I replied, tightening my lips.

"How's Ellen taking all this?"

"She wants to understand, but how can she when I'm not sure I do? She'd prefer I get a job but knows I need to do whatever I feel I have to. This is a very hard time for her, starting a new relationship and having to face this kind of thing. I'm not sure I'd take myself on right now if I didn't have to."

We laughed again and then I reflected a moment. I really was concerned about what was happening with Ellen.

"I've been thinking about this," Marie offered finally. "You were born into a family where money was always limited and probably grew up feeling that having lots of it would solve everything. So you focused all your efforts on 'making it' in the world and were willing to give up a big part of yourself to do it because it was better than being poor. So you always did a good job, tried to please a lot of people, and fearfully held on to whatever you could. But ultimately that wasn't enough to satisfy you. There's a lot more depth to life than that, as you've since discovered."

"Yeah, that's true. And I'll always be thankful for having given myself the opportunity to find that out.

"You said yourself that what you have to learn now is to build without fear, and doing that requires a new way of building. I don't know anything about this, but it's an impression I have. Maybe what you have to learn is how to let things pass through you, instead of trying to control them. You might still be forcing things, trying to keep them fixed, trying to manipulate them out there in the world, rather than letting them flow into you and working with them from inside. It might be more difficult for a man, because all his life he learns to push outward and is rewarded by how well he controls the external world."

"I hear what you're saying and it seems right, but I feel like I'm already working inside, and I keep wanting to find a more practical way to solve my problems. I'd like to keep the house, and that's still the number one issue. I'm not sure I can see an immediate financial benefit in letting things pass through."

"Well, you might have to go deeper than whether to save the house or not. When you're living in fear that things will be taken away from you, which is what you were doing in the past, it prevents you from shifting the focus inside and fully releasing. The fear of losing what you have might be keeping you from freeing what wants to come forth."

"But I feel like I have learned how to let go. I've spent months sitting around, feeling my feelings, and waiting for some kind of direction, while a more sane man would have been out looking for work."

"But there might be more to it than that. Maybe it's about trusting that there is a natural—even magical—flow to things, and that if our fear doesn't block it, the flow comes through our lives unimpeded. Maybe when we begin to move and create with those natural forces instead of fear, they become our new source of power."

I suddenly had a picture of what she was talking about. I saw myself on a horse that had come to a stop, lost in the middle of a vast forest. Instead of fighting it to go forward as I always had, I relaxed the reins, trusting that the horse knew its way back to the stable. When I gave it its head, it began moving on its own, and I let it direct me until we were in familiar territory again.

When I told Marie about it, she laughed and agreed. After a moment, I continued.

"I suppose that the horse could be a symbol for the Subtle Agenda … that it stopped in the forest to show me that if I gave my life its head, I could tap into an unused source of power that I couldn't see when struggling so hard to control it. I'm beginning to realize that I've always tried to control things out of a fear that they wouldn't work otherwise.

"What I'm wondering about now is whether the horse is leading me back to the barn, or into a darker part of the forest. I guess I've just got to learn to trust."

I breathed a deep sigh and slid down in my chair. "But whatever it means, I still have to find a way to earn an income."

"You might have to let the income go for awhile, and give yourself time to explore what wants to come through. There might be no money at first."

"You mean I might need to start over again completely?"

"Maybe."

My mind and body suddenly got heavy. "God, I thought I did that when I came out here."

Marie checked her watch and got up to go. It was clear the conversation was over, and although I would have liked to talk more, I always felt obliged to let her go when she felt it was time. I thought I should be paying her because this is what she did professionally, but she always refused. Even though we were becoming the best of friends, I was embarrassed that we spent so much time on my problems and felt indebted to her because she was so willing to give so much. It was hard for me to understand her not wanting anything from me, but I was pleased to discover a new kind of friend.

"I do appreciate knowing you right now," I said. "This conversation has been very valuable to me. Again."

"Well, don't think about it. I'm your friend. I think I know what you're going through, and I'll go through it with you, if you like. I mean, I'll bond with you, and go right through it with you, no matter what happens. It's the least I can do," she laughed.

After Marie left I decided to take Stray for a walk around the mountain. When I got out on the driveway, I checked on the tiny pine trees I had planted on the hillside. They looked dry, so I decided to stop and water them. There were no automatic sprinklers this far from the house, so I had to pull the hose all the way out to them. As the cold stream of water flowed into the dry earth, I reflected on how detached I had become from everything that was happening, but yet how clearly etched each step seemed to be.

Here I was, caring for a dozen small trees that I had lovingly and tenderly planted on the hill, while at the same time, I felt little or no connection to them. It was as if the axis of my life had shifted. I lived here, just as before, but something inside me had moved away.

The house, in a strange way, didn't matter anymore. My sense of security was no longer rooted here, and this gave me the freedom to care more about practicing a kind of modern alchemy —about refining my life—instead of protecting my possessions.

As I watered each tree, I wondered if I would ever see them grown. Or was I just keeping them alive for a future owner?

On one level, the thought of giving up the house was like giving up an important part of myself. On another level, the act was already done, and I was merely tending to things for someone else. To be facing what felt like termination, but with such detachment, was a unique experience. I thought of how people with terminal illnesses must feel as the end creeps toward them. Here I was, staring into the eyes of a devouring dragon, but instead of fleeing in terror, I was studying it to determine whether to fight it, try to understand it, invite it in, or even love it. I was trying to accept the impending change with a kind of loving openness that I had once reserved for only small things.

Jung, I felt, was describing this sensation in a little book by Richard Wilhelm, called *The Secret of the Golden Flower*. In it was a commentary by Jung on the ancient texts on awareness:

> In a certain sense, the thing we are trying to express is the feeling of having been "replaced," but without the connotation of having been "deposed." It is as if the direction of the affairs of life had gone over to an invisible center. Nietzsche's metaphor, "in most loving bondage, free," would be appropriate here. Religious speech is full of imagery picturing this feeling of free dependence, of calm and devotion.

> In this remarkable experience I see a phenomenon resulting from the detachment of consciousness, through which the subjective "I live" becomes the objective, "it lives me." This state is felt to be higher than the earlier one; it is really as if it were a sort of release from compulsion and impossible responsibility which are the inevitable results of *participation mystique.*

The phrase "replaced without the connotation of having been deposed," reflected my feeling that I wasn't really the owner of the house anymore. And Nietzsche's phrase, "in most loving bondage, free," reflected my sense of being liberated by my commitment to this often harrowing refinement process.

But what struck me most was the sentence about "release from compulsion and impossible responsibility ..." being the "inevitable results of *participation mystique.*" When I read this, I suddenly remembered the sense of release when I left the corporation and severed all the usual attachments. I felt an exhilarating sense of freedom from the intolerable weight of having to support values that were no longer my own.

Detachment from my fear of losing the house set the stage for a deeper kind of freedom. I saw that making choices out of a fear of losing something carried with it an enormous weight of effort, and also a serious lack of faith in life and myself. As I had accumulated more things, more power, more position, and more money, there was more to protect and life itself became an adversary. In my moment of clarity, however, the tables suddenly turned—instead of an adversary, my life was now a trusted friend.

To get to this new relationship with my life I had to cross a huge barrier. It was as if nature had said, "So you want to change your life? Well, the laws of ultimate reality will let you, but you have to be willing to move into uncharted territory for awhile. When you step out of the old, you erase the ironclad laws that once governed you, and for a period of time, you will go without perceivable directions. So here is a warning: in between the time you erase the old laws, and before you discover the new, you will experience a void. People fear a void, as nature abhors a vacuum, but you must have the courage to cross the unknown anyway. It will seem like a vast desert, and you will have only your inner star to guide you. But if you persist, and are willing to face any challenge, you will find that it is through the very act of overcoming the challenges and melting the fears that you will replace the old rules with the wisdom needed to create the new life you're looking for."

Ellen had gone away to Tecate, Mexico, to cool out and rest for the weekend. She was going to do some thinking about us and was hoping to come to some kind of resolution.

I was becoming uncertain now about the relationship, also. If she could not understand what was happening, or at the very least accept that I was having trouble and care about me anyway, then we probably didn't have much to build on.

That was the strange part of our relationship. We were falling in love, but at times, fears from both our pasts would rise up stronger than our bond.

We each felt that we were able to love the other more deeply than we ever loved anyone before, but this was a cataclysmic time. We were living on several different levels. In the deepest place we loved each other, but on the surface, she was going in one direction and I was going in another.

While we were together she would feel the financial disintegration I was facing and then return to her healthy practice and otherwise successful life. Her career was growing and expanding, while mine was contracting and withering. She was fulfilled in her work, while I was still trying to find what mine was.

The result was that when we were together, a part of each of us still lived in loneliness. In our freest moments we loved each other as we had never loved before, but we couldn't enter the private life in which the other lived alone.

We met every day as lovers, and in bed our cares dissolved. When we made love we put our loneliness on the side table like a set of keys in the candlelight.

My body felt heavy as I sat by the pool and was a constant reminder of my sense of dying. I desperately wanted to feel the bliss I'd experienced here before, but it did not come. Although my extreme tiredness was lessening because of the acupuncture treatments, I was depressed about Ellen and fretted a great deal about us while she was gone.

I heard Stray give a slight sigh, almost a moan behind me, and I turned to see him barely able to lift himself to his front legs. For some reason his back legs appeared unable to help him. When he saw me looking, he made his usual effort to come to me, but he swayed a moment then almost lunged forward. He finally righted himself and tentatively walked over to me.

When he put his nuzzle under my arm, I petted him softly and asked what was troubling him. I switched my position and checked his hindquarters, probing gently with my fingers. It was then I discovered a large tumor in his abdomen. A shot of fear ran through me, and I sat there for a moment, stunned and unable to move. Finally, I took a deep breath and got up to call the vet. He agreed to meet us at the animal hospital early the next morning.

Stray was sitting with me in the front seat while we waited for the doors to the animal hospital to open. He always panted heavily when in the car, and even heavier when we were going to the vet's. I wondered in that moment what Stray's earlier life had been like and what had caused his fear of cars. I rustled his neck and ears and he breathed normally for a few seconds, then started panting again.

In a few minutes we were inside and I was standing at the examining table, petting him slowly. Then, in a swirl of my own emotions, I heard the words *surgery* and *biopsy*. Then I heard, "But more than likely, the dog has cancer and it's only a matter of time." I didn't know what to say. The vet looked at me, waiting for an answer about whether to operate or not.

I looked at Stray and touched the swelling in his belly. I looked into the dog's eyes, and he looked back at me helplessly. All the times he had been there for me came back in a flash. How he would meet me at the end of the driveway and run alongside the car until I parked. How when I would go out, he would follow me to the street and watch until the car turned the bend. It had been he and I over the years. We were constant even when everything else was changing.

"Operate," I said quietly, too choked up to say more. I knew in that moment that Stray would be leaving me. He had come just a few months after I found the house, and he was leaving now that I was in my death struggle to keep it. I wondered if this told me that the house would be going soon as well. I kissed him and held him tight. Then with tears in my eyes, I backed out of the room still looking at him on the examining table, his head cocked slightly, watching me leave.

On the way home I thought about how much of a guardian angel that dog had been to me. How totally loving he was, how forgiving of my many irritations with him, and how always ready he was to begin with me again. He came when my heart was hurt and without love for other things, and he stayed right through the lonely months to warm me again. I remembered how I refused to buy him a license for so long because he was not truly my dog, and how many nights he would stay up watching me as I agonized over one thing or another. He was truly an angel, and like an angel, he was bringing me a message that everything was completing now. Everything was changing just as Marie had said it would. And with that thought, I released and let him go.

I pulled in under the carport, climbed out, and without thinking, shot a glance behind me looking for Stray. Then, seeing only the empty driveway, I leaned against the car and cried.

When Ellen got back I told her about Stray, and as I spoke, I felt myself give way once again to the awful sense that he'd be going soon. I simply couldn't hold myself together. I had lost too much. Tears filled my eyes as I talked about what had happened and how afraid I was about his leaving me.

Perhaps she had a realization in Tecate, or maybe we connected through our love for Stray, but in those moments we embraced and cried and held each other, and felt the barriers between us dissolve.

She told me that she had done nothing but think about us all the while she was gone. She felt it was time to commit herself to this relationship no matter what it looked like on the surface.

My heart lifted like a bird and I could feel my chest open. The deep silent stream of love that I felt for her now erupted and rushed powerfully up into my lungs and heart. I couldn't believe it was happening.

"But it is," whispered my little voice, "it is."

We, each of us, must act as bearers of gifts into each other's lives, as if we might have made an agreement before entering this life to meet in this hour, at this place, and to offer our own particular kind of being. And in our giving we help the other find love.

❧

In the coming months it took courage again and again for Ellen and me to trust what we had found. The culmination of my financial struggle felt like it wasn't far off, and the prospects ignited both of our fears. But we learned from it too. If we had an argument, we would commit again. If we got frightened that one of us would leave, we talked about it and found a new trust in what we felt for each other.

In this way she was able to love me, despite the fact that my life was falling apart in front of her. And in this way I was able to find courage to love her even though I felt I had less and less to offer.

I recalled part of a poem that Monica had given me to read at a time when she was frustrated and needing to find the strength to continue loving me. It was from *Flying Home* by Galway Kinnell.

> ... while many good things are easy, true love is not,
> because love is first of all a power,
> its own power,
> which must continually make its way forward, from night into day,
> from transcending union always forward into difficult day.

> ... once the lover
> recognizes the other, knows for the first time
> what is most to be valued in another,
> from then on, love is very much like courage,
> perhaps it *is* courage, and even
> perhaps only courage.

As the weeks passed, Ellen and I slowly came together and seemed to reenter a love that we had known before.

Her skin, when I touched her, felt familiar, and so did mine to her. It was as if she was me, and I her, and our bodies each belonged to the other. I was totally taken outside myself by the intimacy of just touching her.

When we made love, even the bed was familiar. I would release and find myself glimpsing fragments of experiences between the two of us, not from the past, but as if happening in this moment in another place. I'd feel that we had gone somewhere else, and when I spoke of it later, find that she had been there too. The images grew in color and abundance, as if we were opening to ourselves in other lives. I would slip into an experience of walking a dockside, and she would be a woman that I had met there. Often I saw scenes in which I was a painter and she was my model.

There was an Oriental scene I remember so clearly. It was of an old man with a very young woman, and in the background was a large farm with vast open lands. There was a house, busy with people, and we were alone together in a room. She was my concubine and I was her master, and we were both students and teachers for each other.

These visits were oddly comforting, because each time it was us, but not the two people we were now. And through these momentary flights into another realm of my psyche, I found more evidence of the rich subtle world into which my heart was leading me.

THIRTY-THREE

DIAMONDS IN THE ASHES

tray got though the surgery all right and was home a week before I let him roam from the house. The tumor was removed and found malignant as expected, so I put him on a diet of the best dog foods I could find. After reading about the effects of foods on health, I was growing wheatgrass for juice for myself and had a great desire to give him some too. I wanted him on a pure juice fast, or even vegetables, rice, or top grade beef, but the vet said meat was too rich and kept him confined to quality dog foods. Feeding Stray dog food always bothered me. How awful it must have been to receive the same dull offering every day.

After his dinner one night several weeks after he'd been home, I took him around the mountain for his first long walk. As I watched him move slower than ever, I wondered how long he would be with me. The vet thought he would have a few months, but I secretly believed that my love would help him beat the thing completely.

The city looked gray behind the evening smog, and headlights were dim on the streams of cars as they moved along the freeway from the city. An owl sat and watched us from the top of a power pole that carried wires from Hollywood to the Valley. As we drew near, the large bird dropped and flapped heavily away like a huge black moth.

I thought about the film studios lost in the haze below. They had drawn me to California, but now I was hardly aware of them. When I felt inside for a response, the pull from the studios was gone—just a vague tingle as if maybe in the future I would find myself involved again. But now they held nothing for me. I was tired of waiting for other people to act.

As we rounded the front side of the mountain, all of Los Angeles spread out in front of us as a carpet of lights. Unlike the studios, the city still tugged on me. I loved it as much as before and couldn't imagine living in any other place. The south of France held a gentle attraction too, I mused, but nowhere else. Stray was not wandering far from me, and I cringed a little at the tenderness he must have felt in his abdomen.

What a roller coaster ride my life had been these past few years. The crisis in my marriage was like that first steep, upward slope. It peaked when I came out here and started a broad turn as I began to write. Then almost imperceptibly, my life began another turn and suddenly went faster and faster, crashing down to earth. For moments, it even went under the earth before it finally lifted, setting me free.

It was a ride that completely changed my perception of life. It changed the way I felt about myself and inside myself. It changed the way I felt about the world and how I perceived it. And it completely altered what I wanted to do and how I wanted to live.

Now I was observing yet another subtle change. I was no longer driven solely by what I wanted to accumulate, but also by a desire to be of some service. Maybe this was the big difference— maybe even the key I needed to begin my new life.

My chairman had been listening and was impatient to speak.

"I hate to bring you back to reality, but you're out of funds and what you should be thinking about is going back to work."

A dull ache hit my gut at the mere thought of it. It's not that I didn't want to work. I was eager to get something going. The ache was from not wanting to be buried in a large company again, not wanting to get lost in an organization. I wanted to build my own thing and have time to write. But that seemed almost secondary now—I needed to generate some cash right away.

"Since you're feeling ready to work, you might do what you already know," my little voice suggested. I tried to ignore him because it sounded like he was referring to advertising, and I didn't want to do that anymore. Doing what I already knew would take me back where I came from, so it seemed like the wrong direction.

"These last few years have not taken you into a different world. Everything is the same as it was, though you might not think so, given your new way of perceiving. Think of this experience as a journey and the present moment as the beginning of a hairpin turn. You've dismantled everything you thought you were, and now you've gotten to the very center of yourself. The difficulty comes because the experience is so powerful and satisfying that you want to stay in it. You want to stay here on the mountain, so that you can protect what feels so precious inside of you. But you can't. What's happened to you is not a destination. It's a hairpin turn, and the road heads back into life."

My mouth fell open. It was true that a large part of me just wanted to sit and watch the clouds pass in the surface of the pool. Part of it was my feeling so protective and fatherly about my inner child.

"Nothing down there feels right yet. I don't want to stumble carelessly around doing just anything."

"Nothing is ever going to feel right if you believe your fear and attempt to stay up here. You have to go down there and get some experience with what feels good and what doesn't. It's harder to launch a boat than it is to guide one. Get into motion and you'll find it easier to discover the right direction."

The thought of going back and fighting it out in the big-numbers machines made me go limp. I kicked at a rock on the path and as I looked down, noticed that my feet and sandals and even the frayed bottoms of my jeans were yellow with dust. I stomped the ground, sending a tiny lizard furiously up a wall of rock into the scrub. I opened my heart to it, but it did not get my message and hid anyway.

Over the next week, I could feel myself holding back from going out and finding work, but my fear of losing the house finally drove me to it. My little voice had almost daily conversations with me in an effort to lead me from the labyrinth.

"Use what you've learned," it kept telling me, but all I could think about were large advertising agencies and giant corporations, and it stopped me cold. Sometimes my little voice would speak to me in rhymes and sometimes in Zen koans. At other times it spoke as a Sufi. This time it uttered one of its own creations.

"Since what happened in the past is the trail forward, then the future is under your feet, don't you think?"

I could never understand these things by thinking about them, but it was hard not to. Instead, I tried to lower my awareness into my heart and respond by how the idea felt. I sensed that my first "job" was close and that it would be familiar, but that was all. I guessed that it was already "under my feet," because the Subtle Agenda had always prepared me well for each new stage before I entered it. And I hoped that desiring an income again would in itself give rise to an opportunity.

"But nothing appears right yet," I would say.

"That's because you're still thinking too much. It's right under your feet. You already know how to do it," my little voice would reply.

"The only thing I know is ..." The advertising part of the sentence always went unspoken.

"Recall the things in your life that you've loved doing. Since the next stage is about a much deeper kind of fulfillment than the last, it would be wise to build from what you love."

The first thing that came into my head was drawing and writing. I loved designing things. I loved writing. I loved photography. I loved type. I loved broadcast and film. And I could do all of those things pretty well.

"Advertising ...?" I asked, not believing what was happening.

"Think of it as your cash crop," suggested an impish little voice.

Since I had undergone a complete overhaul, I was sure the Subtle Agenda had something really different in store for me, otherwise why bother? So part of my difficulty in starting to work again was always imagining something brand new. It made no rational sense that my next step might include where I began. I was feeling a little betrayed by the thought of it.

"But I thought you'd suggest something new and wonderful for me to do. A dream fulfilled, so to speak."

"You keep talking as if you've arrived somewhere new when what you've done is open your heart and learn the difference between love and fear. You must create new dreams from what you love, and you can begin with what you know. What you've discovered is not a new world, but a way to transform this one. Imagine yourself as one poking through the ashes of yesterday's fire. What appears to you now as merely glass must be first picked up and dusted off, and only then will you discover that you're holding diamonds."

My first return step into the world was to be an interview at an employment agency. A certain nervousness awakened me that morning and followed me into the shower. If my little voice wanted experiences, I was going to start him at the very bottom. It also pleased my chairman, who wanted me to check in with the flesh peddlers to see what my stock was currently worth. He wanted to know if my graying hair made me worth more or less in the marketplace.

I trembled slightly as I looked into the bathroom mirror and tightened my necktie to my throat. It felt like the first day of school after a long summer, and I had a nose-memory of freshly varnished desks. Even Stray was looking at me like a farm dog losing a schoolboy after summer vacation.

Picking up my old familiar attaché case made me feel like I was indeed going back to work. I actually had an appointment waiting. But as I opened the front door, I had to go back inside for a moment—the father had to take the child to the bathroom one last time before we descended the mountain.

Stray disappeared in the rear view mirror as I turned the bend in the road, and my hand trembled slightly searching for the news station on the radio. It was as if I was leaving the mountain forever.

Downtown, I parked my car just off Wilshire, and as I tried to find the address, I looked at all the people going to work. Finally, I pushed open the door to the employment agency. The reception room was empty except for one other man who appeared fairly successful. I assumed his suit was chosen to look that way, just as my blue blazer had been. We glanced at each other as if we were frightened patients in a doctor's office. I approached the empty reception desk, and a young woman came out from the back with some papers and spoke without looking at me.

"Yes?"

"I have an appointment."

"Please fill these out first. Do you have a pencil?"

I didn't answer out of annoyance at her not really greeting me.

I hated filling out my name and address, where I last worked, and my mother's maiden name. It felt like there was no way I could put on paper who I was, what I knew, what I could do, or what I had to offer. As I filled out the form, I wondered what kind of company I would even consider working for. Big companies made no sense because I knew I'd have little control over my life. Small companies made more sense, but they might not be able to pay enough. I remembered that I didn't want to be there and wouldn't have been if I wasn't faced with the prospect of losing the house. I finished the questionnaire with a few simple answers and walked over to the empty reception desk and stood there waiting. Presently an older woman came out, greeted me, and took the paper from my hand.

"Would you mind following me?"

"Not at all," I said, as we went down the hall to her office. Once seated, I found myself studying her and her office as she quickly read through my papers.

"Not many jobs around at your level."

"Oh?" I suddenly felt embarrassed for being over qualified and out of work.

"Well, usually people with your experience get their own jobs. We don't often see them."

"I've been out of the business for awhile and I don't really know too many people out here."

Her eyes scanned the paper again.

"You're from Chicago?"

"Yes, a long time ago."

"Are you interested in doing marketing for a theme park?"

"Is it Disney?"

"No. It's an eastern company. Part of a big conglomerate."

"What's the salary level?" I asked, but it didn't really make any difference because I wasn't interested.

"About the same as when you were working in Chicago."

It would get me out of trouble immediately, I thought. I could keep the house and maybe write in the evenings and on weekends. I imagined the pleasure of installing the skylight over the fireplace, but that's as far as I got.

"Do you have anything with a smaller company?"

"Not at your salary level."

Suddenly I wanted to stop this nonsense and start working on my book. I loved the thought of it more than either a job or the house.

"Anything in the marketing department of small a manufacturing company? One with consumer brands? I have a lot of experience with consumer brands."

"No. Given the condition of the economy, this is not a good time to be looking for that type of position."

"Well, if you hear of anything …" As I rose I noticed that she had already put my application on a tall stack behind her desk.

"You should probably start your own company."

"Yeah, I probably should," I answered without thinking as I walked out her door.

THIRTY-FOUR

EMERGING FROM WITHIN

On the way home I took Mulholland because the curvy drive always helped me relax. The experience at the employment agency had been difficult, and the weightiness in my body showed me again that I had little desire for business-as-usual. I had to find a way to draw my future from my heart.

As soon as I arrived home, I changed clothes and found myself pacing the living room, pondering what to do next.

"You should probably start your own company," I said, mocking the interviewer. The whole thing made me feel tight and condensed, as if I'd been crammed into a small, dark closet.

"If you went after the theme park job you could earn enough money to save the house," my chairman protested. "And then if you didn't like it, you could always change jobs. I think you need to have the experience of working after being off so long."

He was right. It would be a quick fix, but it felt completely wrong to me. My chairman appeared unable to grasp what I was feeling, which put us both at a disadvantage when we tried to communicate with each other. I started out looking for work just to try to save the house, but I realized again that I didn't want money to be the deciding factor.

In my search for an income, I was trying to let my desires lead me, so I kept scanning my feelings for a strong urge to follow. But the only pull I could detect was a slight interest in working for a small company. I hoped this would somehow lead me out of my predicament. There were no other clues to follow.

Hungry after a rough morning, I went to the refrigerator and grabbed a couple slices of Swiss cheese. Then I noticed Stray watching me from around the door and tossed him a piece too.

Thinking about working in a small company made me realize how the Subtle Agenda had trained me. Each move I made was to a smaller business, and each brought with it more management experience and more control. It was a series of leaps, from working with some of the largest corporations in the world, to smaller and smaller ones, but the Subtle Agenda had clearly given me the experience.

I had written marketing plans and business plans, had raised capital, and had observed many of the mistakes that can cause trouble for small ventures. The only thing the Subtle Agenda had not provided me was a list of prospects.

When I thought more of working inside a small business, I realized that it would probably not leave me time to write. Working on my book idea was my first priority, but an employer might not agree. Suddenly I was confused again.

"Look in the ashes," my little voice whispered.

So I went back and looked at everything again, and when I thought about starting my own company, my heart leapt a bit. But at the same time it frightened me. Even so, I kept playing with the idea from different points of view and realized that this, too, had been an unfulfilled dream of mine. I remembered wanting to start my own agency back in Chicago, but I had lost the courage.

"It's your cash crop," offered my little voice.

As I thought about it more, I realized that if I was a young father, and my children were starving, and there was no money or food in the house, I could always make ads. I could always earn money that way. Of course, making ads was my cash crop! The thought sent a tingle down my spine.

Then I immediately thought of every reason why I shouldn't do it. I had burned every bridge, used every expletive, intoned every vow, and swore to everyone I ever knew, that I would never, never, never, ever go back into advertising as long as I lived.

"It would be too embarrassing. It would be absolutely humiliating after all this. People would think that I had failed. I can't do that."

I got up from my desk and began pacing the length of the living room.

"Take a closer look," my little voice said gently, as if I was missing something. I stopped and looked out toward the pool.

I saw the shiny green head of a new dragon looking back at me through the window. I had spent years learning to trust my desires and enthusiasm rather than being motivated by my fears, yet I now found myself resisting doing what excited me because I was afraid of how it would look to others. I had refused to build my life out of fear again, but here I was letting it decide my first step back into the world.

I stopped and let the idea of having my own company enter my chest and then waited for my body's reaction. I was immediately filled with excitement. I couldn't ignore it. The only thing stopping me was my concern over what other people might think. In that instant, I saw how often I'd made choices based on what others might think. Just who were all these "others" anyway, and where were they now?

I could not close my eyes to it or run. I had to let myself see that another dragon had come to visit, but as I looked into its scaly face, I heard my little voice.

"Here's a way for you to begin building your new life if you can just release your fear. If you trust what makes you enthusiastic, you will find that just beyond this dragon is the door to what you have always wanted. And once you see that, all it takes is the courage to pass through."

As this gentle message resounded through my body, I opened my heart to the frightening creature still before me and noticed that it was beginning to disappear.

There was no question that I knew the business. And the idea of building my own company sent tiny thrills up my spine. Behind the fear was an opportunity for me. The signs were all clear. I couldn't accept it at first, but once I made the shift, once I moved through the fear, I found that there was in fact a door. The Subtle Agenda had prepared me beautifully for this. I might even earn an immediate income this way, and it would give me the freedom to write.

I felt the beginning possibility of a financial platform developing under me in a way that I hadn't experienced since leaving the agency. Actually, this felt more secure than that had because now I was in control. I couldn't help but see, now more clearly than ever, that what seemed like past failures were instead building blocks to my new awareness, my potential, and my current sense of well-being. I also saw that judging anything a failure was faulty, because to the Subtle Agenda there was only development, change, and progress. Each step, whether a "failure" or "success" in my eyes, joined together to create a structure that could now begin to support me.

During the week, I found myself at the Pickwick Bookstore in Hollywood buying a manual on how to incorporate my own company. The following week I was downtown at the Secretary of State's office, my application in hand, filing for incorporation. The next week I was designing and setting type for my letterhead. I wanted to offer small companies more than just ads, something more like an emotional partnership. So when the name

Marketing Partners was suggested by my little voice and the chairman of the board nodded his approval, I went with it.

How ironic it seemed that advertising, the vessel that I had deliberately broken, would return to help me become whole. I had come full circle. I felt that I had been given the opportunity to relive each stage of my life, but this time in a much freer, more creative, more fulfilling way.

It reminded me of the Zen expression I'd heard one time:

At first the mountains are mountains and the streams are streams. Then the mountains are not mountains and the streams are not streams. But in the end, the mountains are mountains again and the streams are streams.

As I reflected on the amazing process that life had turned out to be, I realized that I was experiencing the same birth feelings about going back into business that I'd felt getting out of it. I was beginning new again, but from what seemed to be an expanded sense of awareness. Instead of feeling that life was controlling me, I was guiding it. I had added a whole new way of evaluating my choices and had a new courage to act on what I felt—both of which I knew would add entirely new capacities to my business sense.

How everything had changed. What was unthinkable one day was a source of pleasure the next. Nothing was fixed anymore. The freedom to choose without fear had led to greater flexibility, less rigidity, and fewer attachments. Yet at the same time my ability to commit felt like it had deepened.

Ellen was happier now that I was working on something that excited me. Her feelings of security came from everything being in its place, and now that her man was working at something that pleased him and might bring stability and success, she felt lighter and was more content.

All her feminine instincts came out. She began to bake bread every weekend, a wonderful herb bread she had learned to make while living in Vermont. We planted a small herb garden out in the front so the baking herbs would be fresh, and even added basil for homemade pesto. My kitchen had never had such feminine warmth and aromas. And yet beneath the feelings of building a life together, I had the growing perception it would not be here on the mountain. Deep stirrings spoke to me of further change.

When I went down to pick up my stationery, I saw a man in a car who looked like the fellow in the agency who reportedly was instrumental in getting me fired. He had been showing me one face in the office out here, but was quietly poisoning my reputation to upper management in Chicago. When I saw him driving along, I had an automatic urge to reach for my lug wrench and go after him. But in the next instant, I let myself feel a tiny pulse of warmth for him, then even love, and I knew how much I didn't want old fears and anger to affect my new life. Then as I looked closer, I realized that he was not the man from the agency at all.

I immediately recognized what the Subtle Agenda was trying to tell me. It was time to release old resentments and not only forgive those people I felt angry toward, but to take an additional step and let myself see and feel gratitude for what they had contributed to me.

The man at the agency was only doing his job the way he saw it. He might have some frailty, just as I did, but from a larger place, I felt grateful that he had given me a boost when I was too afraid to leave the company on my own. So I got myself together inside and forgave the old bastard, and let bygones be bygones.

In the next instant I recalled how hard Joan and I had been on each other, and how much we had loved one another too. Then I remembered a letter she'd written me just as I was leaving Chicago after the divorce. I had found it again only last week, folded in a book she had given me called *The Portable Jung*. I was not in a forgiving mood when I first received the letter, but when I read it this time, I cried.

She forgave us for the bitterness and anger we both felt toward each other. (Amen.) She offered forgiveness for my leaving (which I didn't know I had waited so long to receive) and hoped that I was able to forgive her. (I had but was unable to speak it). Then she told me she loved me, and for the first time in over ten years, I felt my love for her. Then finally, I felt gratitude for the wonderful life we had before it went awry, and for giving me my daughter Sarah, and for sharing Lynn, her daughter, with me.

And then, in my forgiving mood, I felt gratitude for the Church I grew up in as a child. I thanked it for preparing me to believe in the spirit, for introducing me to Thomas Merton, and for helping me see the invisible in the visible.

Then my parents jumped into my mind. I embraced them and thanked them for giving me the mystery of the Church when I was young and growing up, for the opportunity to experience the beauty of the woods, for the simplicity of our lives together, and for the stability and caring and love they always gave us. I hugged my sister and laughed as I forgave her for having wet her pants when I was carrying her on my shoulders when we were small, and my brother for laughing at my stuttering.

As I drove along forgiving my family, I felt love expanding through my entire body and began to forgive everyone I knew. I slowly went through the succession of people that I held in rows of cells inside of me, keeping them trapped in my anger, and I declared a day of amnesty for them all. It was a kind of Bastille Day of the spirit, and after I cleared the cell block, I closed the place down—except for a tiny cell left empty, just in case I needed a little one, temporarily, some time in the future.

As I got in touch with the gentler side of myself, I saw how much I had always feared these "softer" feelings. I could see now that it was my fear that had created much of what I thought of as "being a man." Forgiving and loving was less manly than holding a grudge or fighting.

I saw how I'd always thought of this sensitive side of myself as forbidden. I knew other men thought this too, but I was sure none of us could remember exactly how we learned it. I was taught somewhere that the softer side of myself was off limits, dark, feminine, and for a man it was the underworld. Perhaps it came from misunderstanding Eastern philosophy, where darkness represents the feminine and light the masculine. But now, having passed through the fear of it, I had discovered that my dark side wasn't feminine and weak—it was kind, responsive, supple, even loving. It wasn't a source of danger at all—but of feeling whole, balanced, tranquil, and complete.

To have denied this part of me for so much of my life was to imprison myself in the fear of it. I never knew that opening to the forbidden was actually embracing my wholeness. The darkness I was once afraid of had now become what I was most proud of, what was most fertile and most passionate in myself.

It was when I was struggling the hardest that I discovered this gentler side. It was when the Subtle Agenda stopped me cold and the male force on which I'd always depended was brought to a halt that I learned the tremendous power in waiting, in being receptive, in sensing. I had to face and finally value the part of me that felt as often as it thought, that waited as often as it acted, that understood as often as it told, that forgave as often as it judged, and that loved quietly as often as it forced.

I had spent more than a few nights learning to be comfortable with this forbidden part of myself, but when I finally welcomed it into my life, I noticed that a living, breathing, loving, real-life woman had come in, too.

THE HAIRPIN TURN

The peacefulness of the after-death was all too brief before another stage was upon me. With my spiritual experiences so heightened, I assumed that I'd reached my destination and that I'd find a simple way of life that would allow me to pursue my inner work. But that was not to be.

This stage was like a mountain road that instead of coming to an end in a peaceful meadow, pauses before it suddenly switches back for a higher view of all that has passed before. In this period I learned the meaning of the saying: Before awakening, you chop wood and carry water. After awakening, you chop wood and carry water.

I saw a brief glimpse ahead and knew that I'd be re-experiencing parts of my life that remained somehow incomplete. But this time I would engage them with a loving heart, caressing the knots and healing old wounds.

The obstacle at hand was to overcome the fear that I'd lose my inner peace by returning to the competitive marketplace. I needed to replace my dread with the trust that I could maintain a loving state even while working hard.

As I visited my fear in an attempt to heal it, the hidden opportunity became obvious—the next phase was not simply about healing the past, or even about building a new life, but about learning to create the future out of conscious, loving choices. It was about doing only work that I loved and continuing my daily meditation of staying in the present with my heart open, walking through any fear that arose.

It was time to try what I knew out in the world.

THIRTY-FIVE

LETTING GO

llen had been staying at the house most nights now, and there was a small collection of her clothes in the closet that she rotated like fresh flowers from a garden. She had left for her office, and I was making the bed. Warm body smells rose up from the rumpled sheets, reminding me of the friendly laundry that I played in as a child. I surrendered to the aromas and climbed back in, pulling the bedclothes up around me. It struck me that I had always been in too big a hurry to ever stay in bed like this.

Now I had two loves. Ellen had reawakened the beauty and enchantment of a first romance. She was love in the shape of a woman's body. How I had longed to love a woman all these years. I could smell her on the pillow as I sank my face into it.

The other love was what I felt for my life. I had never meditated much, but now each day I sat by the pool and attuned to myself, and felt the purity of the deep well inside. My visits were short and very private, as if they were secret trips to a small, wooded cottage. I loved these visits and had them again and again.

Dialogues with my little voice had become exchanges between myself and my feelings, and I tried not to think about what to do next. I preferred to be led by what made me happy and by the messages spoken through the events in my life. When I considered the future and how I would build my company, I felt only that my next steps would be born inside me and connected to where I was now. When I wondered when my life would come together, I felt only the need to be patient. When I imagined how my life would look, I felt only that it was already growing perfectly, even if imperceptibly.

Hearing Stray's toenails on the deck outside the bedroom window forced me back into the moment. As I lay there wondering what my day would be like, I suddenly remembered that I had scheduled my annual tax meeting for that morning. I shot a glance at the clock, and my body charged into motion as I jumped up to get ready to leave.

Traffic was heavy, but it gave me time to think. During the past few weeks I'd found myself writing pieces of sentences in my head. It was as though a writer in my subconscious was working away, and I only got glimpses of his work at odd moments. Even now, as I sat in the long line of cars on the freeway, these sentences were weaving themselves into my thoughts about taxes.

This once-a-year meeting was always a moment of truth for me. The accountant knew all the details of my financial situation, and this year any discussion about taxes would surely involve my plans for the house. The thought sent a chill up my spine.

I walked in a few minutes late and found Milt with my records spread out in front of him. These meetings had been getting more and more difficult as my finances eroded, and I was not looking forward to this one at all. After we nodded our greetings, I was handed a hot cup of black coffee and slid into what felt like a dentist chair in front of his desk.

"How goes the job search?" he asked, getting right to the nitty gritty.

I shook my head and traced my fingers along the sole of my sandal before I replied.

"I think I'd like to start my own company—marketing for small businesses," not telling him I'd already filed for incorporation.

Milt shuffled through several pages, aligning them into a neat stack, took a brief look at me, then turned and punched a few keys on his computer. I watched as he checked my name, address, social security number, and after coming to the word "occupation," he turned back to me.

"You'd probably do pretty well, given your background. Where are you going to get the money to finance the start up?"

"Well, I thought that's one of the things we could talk about."

"How fast can you generate some income?"

I shook my head, knowing which way Milt's mind was heading. He reminded me of a mix between my chairman and my dad. He tried to be supportive, but I never felt completely understood.

"Actually, I want to let things develop organically. I'd like to spend a good part of the mornings writing and handle business the rest of the day. There's a book I want to write."

His lips tightened as he glanced again at the stack of papers in front of him.

"This really forces the issue about your house," he said. "Without an income, a nice, steady income ..." He shrugged letting his voice trail off into silence.

The words stung even though I was prepared for them. For years now, my focus was on knowing when my motivations were coming from my values as opposed to rising from my fears. I'd been trying to make decisions from a positive place, and I didn't expect that to be changing now, even to save the house.

"The good thing in all this is that your house has appreciated substantially since you bought it," he finally continued. "You could sell it and use the money to finance getting your company started, and your writing. Although, if you don't put the profit into another house, you won't like the tax implications."

He watched me patiently as I struggled to make a choice.

"Of course, you could do a lot worse than invest in yourself," he went on. "It's really up to you. What do you want?"

I found it difficult to express my feelings when I was discussing money with my accountant. The two never seemed to quite fit together.

"Well, actually ... I think of myself as a writer first. But I also want to go back into business. Only this time I want to do it the way I want to."

"How's that?"

"I can't explain it very well because I can't quite see what it looks like. But this ... these past few years have changed me. I don't want to go back into big corporations again. I don't want to follow someone else's dreams anymore. I want to build my own life out of what gives me pleasure every day. Writing is part of it and working with small businesses is another. But I want to work only with people I respect and care about, even love, if that's possible. I want to work with products that have the quality and people who have values consistent with how I feel. And I really want to write. I guess you could say I don't want to make compromises anymore."

Not knowing whether I had communicated what I wanted to, I shrugged and looked down at my sandals again. When I looked up, Milt was smiling, I think one of the few times since I had known him. And with a slightly mischievous look in his eyes, he turned to the computer screen and in the blank called "occupation," which called for only one job description, he entered the word "writer."

"I want a signed copy when the first one's done," he said as he leaned back in his chair, smiling.

It was in this way that the vision of writing and building my own company became completely real for me. It was also the catalyst for my finally deciding about the house. Driving home, I pondered my conversation with Milt and felt the house slipping away as if the Subtle Agenda was gently lifting its burden from me. But it also felt like I could keep it if I wanted to. I had two choices. I could fight to save it, or I could let it go.

My emotions were mixed. I was happy to feel the weight being lifted but also felt that I should be fighting to save the house, as if that was the manly thing to do. It was one of those "shoulds" that used to rule my life, but I still couldn't figure out who was being made happy by all those "shoulds."

I found it interesting that the choices were so obvious—like coming to a dead end and having to turn right or left—so obvious, in fact, that I knew the issue wasn't whether to keep the house or not, but how I would make the decision. It was one of those moments where the work of the Subtle Agenda was transparent to the point where I couldn't help but see that the situation was more about my inner work than the drama being played out.

What it boiled down to was whether I would choose from a sense of panic and loss, or from my enthusiasm and trust. And since I could feel the presence of both, it was important that I check the motivations behind each option.

I had plenty of fear about losing the house. I was afraid of any kind of change. I was afraid of what the unknown would bring. I was afraid of no longer living on my own piece of land. I was afraid of the humiliation of living in a small apartment after living in a wonderful house. I was afraid Sarah would be upset or hurt if I no longer had a home for her. I was afraid of not being able to get back into the housing market in California, where prices were skyrocketing and would probably lock me out. I was afraid of leaving my own turf and moving into someone else's territory. I was afraid of not having a home.

But when I thought about starting a small company and having the money to write, I felt buoyant. When I imagined being in a small apartment and living simply, I felt light and eager. When I thought of making ads for people I felt close to and whose products I could get behind, I felt the fun it would be to use what I knew to help small businesses grow.

It was easy to see that I had many reasons to keep the house. Some of them were quite practical, but they all came from fear. I also saw how excited I was about writing and starting my company and about making choices this way. It really was simple, and even though *I* trusted my feelings, all this was too new—or too "airy-fairy" as Ellen would say—for me to be completely candid about it with anyone, even her.

When I got home I walked around the place, feeling it in a new way. The house had a quality of emptiness, like an abandoned cocoon that had completed its work. I no longer wanted the burden of supporting it. I wanted to sell the house and let the money support me.

I was lighting candles on the small table in front of the fireplace when I heard Ellen drive into the carport. I had planned dinner at home that night to tell her I was giving up the house. The news would make her sad, but I was sure she already knew, at least on some level, because we'd talked around the edges of it many times. As she helped me put the food on the table, she must have known something was unusual, because I wouldn't let our eyes meet. Once we were finally seated, I couldn't hold the news back any longer.

"I think I've decided to sell the house," I blurted out, then looked down at my plate a moment and back at her. "I had a meeting with Milt today."

A small wrinkle of disappointment, as quick as lightning, crossed her forehead as my words sank in.

"I thought that's what you'd be doing."

I studied the mood changes in her face for a few seconds before I spoke again. We had talked about all of the issues many times, and now there was little to say.

"We could keep the house, if you really wanted to," I offered. "We could try sharing the cost, and let your apartment go instead."

She thought about it a moment, but I suspected she wouldn't give up her apartment. Even though we were doing well together, she didn't want to lose the security of having her own place.

"It's a tough choice," she said hesitantly. "I'd love to have in a house again ... I'd prefer to keep them both, but I also understand if you want to sell it so you'll have money to get back on your feet."

I felt a momentary sense of relief because I did want to let the house go, but it gave way to sadness about her not trusting the relationship enough to give up her apartment. But not wanting to get lost in my disappointment, I began thinking about where Stray and I would live. There was a long silence before she spoke again.

"You could live in my place," she said.

My heart leapt at the possibility of our actually living together. Having the house and her apartment had been comfortable for both of us. I hadn't wanted to live with anyone since my marriage, but now my desire to live with her felt like it was part of healing old wounds. I knew Ellen hadn't lived with anyone since her marriage and that this was a moment of truth for her too. I could feel my life knitting itself together under the force of change.

In the end, we let our love choose. It felt good that I would move in with her instead getting my own place. As far as the house was concerned, the world was full of houses, and perhaps one day, when my company was stronger, we would buy one together. Her support had helped me to finally let the house go. Without her love it might have been too difficult. So with open hearts and high hopes, our new lives began.

The weight had lifted from my shoulders, but I still had to face the difficulty of telling Sarah about it. Joan had not moved to San Francisco as planned, and after living and studying in several cities, was back in Chicago. So ever since Sarah began school out here in California, my house was her home, and I was her closest parent. She was graduating high school in June, so where she would live was an important issue. We had looked at art schools in Los Angeles to see if she might want to go to college here, but she hadn't found one she liked. There was some talk about her going back to Chicago to The Art Institute, but I also knew she wasn't really happy about living back there.

Ellen had gone east to visit her brother for Thanksgiving, which gave Sarah and me the opportunity to spend some time alone. Sarah had been in Chicago for the last holiday so she was here for this one. I had mixed feelings about her visit because I was having trouble handling my sense of loss about the house and was often depressed. We had some invitations for Thanksgiving dinner, but I preferred that we have the time alone. Sarah and I went out, on what turned out to be a rather dark, drizzly day, to a restaurant overlooking the ocean in Malibu.

On our way back from dinner we drove through Malibu Canyon. Sarah was sitting with her arms crossed on her chest staring out the window at the gray canyon of stone. We had not yet spoken about the house or about how Stray was doing after his surgery, and now felt like the time. As we sped into a dimly lit tunnel, I snapped on my headlights.

"I'm thinking about selling the house."

Her head swung toward me as though she had been slapped, and she took a moment before she spoke.

"Where would you go?"

"I'm thinking about moving in with Ellen. But it's only a one-bedroom apartment, so it's going to be tight for awhile."

She fell back into her silence, and I assumed she was thinking about what this did to her future. An intense sadness welled up inside me at the thought of not having a home for her much longer.

"When would you sell it?"

"I've been waiting to talk with you before I put it on the market. I want your agreement on this. It's been your home too."

As I watched the road I could feel her staring at me a very long time. When I finally looked at her, I could see the disappointment in her eyes. Her life had been hard the last few years, living in a prep school, her mother living in one city and her father in another. Then there were all the economic uncertainties, my career ups and downs, and many mood swings. She'd grown beyond her years just to get by, and I could see both the child in her and the young woman, struggling with all the emotions.

"When you graduate in June, you could go to The Art Institute in Chicago and live with your mother. Or if you prefer to go to school out here, I'll help you get a small apartment near us if you like."

We drove through the light drizzle, silent for a moment. It reminded me of when I left her in Chicago to come out here, and the sadness was hard to bear. We loved each other deeply, despite my not being a traditional father. Yet, I felt like I hadn't given her all she deserved, or what she most wanted, which was my being fully available to her.

"I'm sorry, Sarah."

I was sorry for all the sadness I had brought her. I was sorry about all the dreams I'd shared with her that had failed. I was sorry that I wasn't a good father, strong and successful, there for her just as she was coming into her womanhood. I was sorry that she wouldn't have a home with me for awhile. I felt like I had let her down, that I had made a great gamble with her life, our family, my life ... and I was afraid she might never see the true beauty of what had happened to me.

I wanted to tell her that only good would come from all this because it was chosen from my heart, but I was afraid she wouldn't understand. How could choosing from the heart have any meaning to someone so young, especially when it meant losing her home?

"I'm sorry. I can't keep the house right now, but ... it's a little difficult to describe ..."

"Try me." She wanted to know what I was feeling, and I felt I owed it to her to give it a shot.

"I don't know how to say this, but I can't keep the house anymore without working at a regular job. And I can't go back to work in an agency again. I'd hate it. I just started a little company, but it could be a long time before it's earning enough money to support itself. But if I sell the house, we'll have money to get us through until the company starts turning a profit."

She watched me as I talked, and tears began to gather in both our eyes.

"But something more important than that is happening that I'm not sure I can describe. Even though everything looks like a shambles, actually I feel like a wonderful life is beginning right in the middle of all this chaos. It's not just excitement about the company, it's about how loving I feel deep inside. Does that mean anything to you?"

She shook her head just once, but I knew she was still open.

"I've discovered a new place inside of me, almost a whole new person, and I want this person to be able to decide things in a whole new way."

I kept looking at her, hoping that the force of effort would cause my meaning to leap from my mind to hers. Maybe since she was interested in art, she would understand it in those terms.

"I feel like an artist who has finally discovered how to put his heart into his painting. All my life I've been trying to create things, but I never had the benefit of being completely in touch with myself. The artist in me was never able to be fulfilled painting because he was never able to get deep enough inside himself to own it and hold it in his hands. But because of all the stuff I've been through, I finally feel like I've reached that place, and now I have to be true to it—to build my life from it."

I stopped and took a deep breath, "What that means right now, unfortunately, is giving up our home."

Her gaze left mine for the road. I swung onto the freeway and headed back toward Los Angeles. Tears were flooding my eyes as I reached across and put my arm around her.

"I'll still be able to take care of you. There will be some money because the house is worth a lot more than I paid for it. I don't know what else to say."

She looked at me for a moment, then smiled gently, showing me that she understood.

"I think you should go for it, Dad."

Her release flooded me with gratitude.

"Do you really feel okay about it?"

"Yes, I'm fine."

We smiled, and I squeezed my hand gently on the back of her neck. Once again, Sarah came through a very difficult and painful situation, and her heart was showing the way.

"One last thing," I said. "Hold onto your hat."

"Could it be worse?"

"Stray looks like he's not been healed by the surgery. He seemed fine for a few weeks, but his hind legs are getting wobbly, and the vet thinks he's got no more than a month."

The tears that had welled up in her eyes now began flowing down her cheeks. She slipped down in her seat, folded her arms back over her chest, and stared silently out the window at the mountains moving by.

The morning wind had a slight chill in it, I thought, as I sat by the pool. It looked like rain, but that didn't necessarily mean anything in Southern California. I heard a friend's rooster crowing across the canyon and wondered if she was up writing. Sarah was back at school, and I shifted my attention from the life around me and let it settle inside my chest. My eyes closed slowly, shutting out the world.

I felt like I had put my future together, and it was small and deep inside me. The wild storms I'd been experiencing seemed to have finally ceased, and everything was secure but in a new place. Startled by a splat on my forehead, I realized that a light rain was beginning to fall. Stray felt it too and painfully pulled his hind legs up, trying to get under the roof that covered the deck.

The house sold easily. I put it on the market at a price over four times what I had paid for it, and within a few weeks I had a firm offer, and within a few more weeks, we were in escrow. Ellen was not staying overnight much anymore, not wanting to get more attached to the place. A moving day was set, and I was about to get everything ready to leave.

As if sensing my departure, the house seemed to give up trying to shelter me. As the rains began, the patches on the roof —ones I had fixed and fixed again—were now releasing, and tiny beads of water were coming down steadily in the living room, the bedroom, and even the kitchen.

Through the heavy rain, I went to the building supply store looking for cans of tar, and as soon as the weather cleared, I re-patched the same places that I had patched so many times over the years. But then when it rained again, it was as if I had opened the holes, not closed them, and the water came through with even more fury than before.

The kitchen was hit the worst. The large pots and pans were filling as fast as I could empty them, so I brought in a big green plastic garbage can, and as Ellen arrived one day, I was dragging it, almost filled, to the door. It was both funny and sad, and we didn't know whether to laugh or cry.

I took a break from packing and getting the house ready to leave and went up to Ojai to meet with two young men who were looking for marketing help. They owned a small health food company, and from our phone call, I liked the two of them very much. Since I didn't have to worry about money right away and was determined to work only with small businesses and people I felt connected to, I was very excited about the opportunity. I wanted to work with products that had quality and integrity, and their's did.

I began to spend one day every week with them, helping to position their brands in the way I had with giant corporations. Instead of being big and solvent, they were tiny and on the edge of ruin each month. But we were all committed to making their business as successful as we could.

It was a beginning for them and for me. I gave them the full depth of my marketing and brand experience, and they gave me back my business legs and a tiny fee. My love of the marketplace was reawakening, but this time it was on my terms, with my values, for my company, and with people for whom I felt a strong kinship.

A quiet well of happiness was growing from inside me. I had finally tinkered long enough to fit the components of my life together into a machine that would fly.

In the last few weeks before the move, I began going through each closet getting things together for Goodwill. My whole life in California was thrown out on the bed in the form of sweaters and shoes, shirts and ties, sport coats and trousers, a tux, a fly rod, ski clothes, pictures, and more.

As I went through each cabinet, closet, and drawer, the piles for Goodwill got larger and larger with clothes and household items. They would get most of my furniture too. I marked just a few cherished pieces to go into storage along with some books, photographs, personal records, and some linens. Little of what I owned was going with me. I wanted to release as much as I could.

About a week before moving day, I went looking for Stray and found him under a small citrus tree in the front, unable to get up. He looked at me, totally defeated, and his inability to move told me it was time to let him go.

He had lost control of his stool and his rear quarters were covered with it. With a knot in my throat, I called the vet, then prepared to take him in. I washed him lovingly, the way I would a child, and dried him by rubbing him gently with the best bath towel I owned. His mouth looked dry, but he would drink only a few drops of water, so I put the bowl aside. Then I took a blanket from the box of things I'd packed to keep, and after wrapping him in it, I picked him up carefully and put him on the front seat of the car.

During the long drive over the mountain to the vet's office, I kept looking at him on the seat next to me. He would look back as if he knew that these were our last few moments together. He seemed calm and wasn't panting the way he usually did in the car. Maybe he sensed the oncoming release from his painful body, or maybe he just didn't have enough strength.

I reached over to rub his neck and thanked him for being everything to me. I thanked him for being a friend, for always being there for me, and I told him how sorry I was that everything was ending.

The vet opened the back door of the pet hospital as I was lifting Stray out of the car. Tears were running down my cheeks, and I couldn't even say hello as I carried Stray inside. I put him down on the table, and he looked at me one last time as I kissed him, and I silently turned away. I got into my car and just sat there for a few minutes, sobbing quietly. When I finally felt able to drive, I started the car and slowly made my way back home.

Back at the house, I found a pink flowering plant sitting by the door. I was in tears again as I read the note and discovered it was from Larry. He loved the dog as much as I and had learned from a mutual friend that Stray was about to be leaving. Larry's timing turned out to be perfect, and I appreciated feeling his love at that moment.

By profound coincidence, Stray's remains were delivered on the day the movers arrived. I dug a grave near the fruit tree in the front of the house where he slept when I was away, and planted Larry's shrub over him. That was Larry, I thought, the one person who was there for both of us on that final day.

When the movers were gone, I walked around the empty house saying goodbye to years spent living there. The pool was bright and sparkling in the sunlight. The geraniums were red and pink in their hanging baskets. I touched each one of them as I walked around bidding farewell to everything.

It was an empty nest. A spent cocoon. The caterpillar, once plump with life, had taken refuge here and transformed itself into another kind of creature.

In the beginning, the house and I were one. Now as I was discarding it, I imagined what the emerging butterfly might say, "This new world appears cold and strange, but I feel as though I've learned to fly."

There were no more tears and no bitterness, just a touch of sweet sadness. I was leaving summer camp and returning to school. I was leaving the army and going back to Ohio to start life again. I was graduating school and looking with excitement toward my first job.

Moving in with Ellen was a gift to me and a wonderful way to start again. I was deeply in love and very happy that I would be sharing what felt like the best part of my life with her.

I went out onto the deck and sat down near the pool to look one last time into its surface. I closed my eyes and opened my heart and let any clinging feelings drain away. I released my hold on the house and on the wonderful years I'd spent there. I visited Stray and thanked him for being with me for such a long, precious time. In my imagination I moved around each of the pine trees and knew they would survive the disease now threatening them. I took a deep breath of the mountain air, and grateful tears ran down my face.

I got up and noticed my pink and orange flowering bougainvillea bonsai sitting in the shade. I picked it up gently and set it outside the front door. I exhaled, reached for my keys, and locked the place up. I picked up the bonsai and strapped it into the passenger's seat, making sure the safety belt didn't harm any branches. I settled myself behind the wheel, and without looking back, drove down the driveway for the last time. Below in the city, my new life and my new love were waiting for me.

TAKING FLIGHT

This stage was a final release of the past. Everything not already consumed by the refining fires of my journey was gathered around me for the ceremony. The last weeks at the house were a holy experience.

Surrendering it all was one the most sacred rituals I ever experienced. It was like giving myself in fervent sacrifice to an exhilarating moment when trust so burned in my soul that belongings no longer mattered. An entire life was being consumed in front of me, and rather than resist it, I embraced the moment by casting even my most prized possessions into the pyre.

In the end, everything was in ashes, yet rising from this consecrated dust was an eager spirit. I was ready to begin again, this time from a place made fertile by all that had gone before and with eyes fully opened by the epiphany at the pool.

I was centered in the purest part of myself. I was building my new life and my new work on my own terms, from that most tender place of love. I was reentering the world naked and unprotected, yet stronger and more whole than ever.

I was taking flight.

BEYOND ASTRAL DRIVE

What Worked, What Didn't, and a Few Other Reflections

> *"There is in us an instinct for newness, for renewal,*
> *for a liberation of creative power.*
> *We seek to awaken in ourselves a force that really*
> *changes our lives from within.*
> *And yet the same instinct tells us that this change is*
> *a recovery of that which is deepest, most original,*
> *most personal in ourselves.*
> *To be born again is not to become somebody else,*
> *but to become ourselves."*
>
> Thomas Merton

In the years after selling my house, my desire for material success again stepped forward, not as the primary motivator, not as an end in itself, but as an exploration of living a materially affluent life in unity with spirit. Out of this, I created a successful professional practice helping small business owners—with their marketing and advertising, of course—which has given me a triumphant sense of completion and an abundant financial foundation.

Of even more personal joy and actualization is the rapturous love affair that emerged and continues to blossom after almost three decades of marriage. I didn't set out to attain that. At first, I didn't even know how deeply I wanted that, but now it is who I am. We live and work together in our glorious home in a canyon in the Santa Monica Mountains, surrounded by nature.

Since the move from Astral Drive, I've spent lots of time applying what I experienced to making better choices and helping others do the same. And of course, my learning continues. For instance, I know without question that those who are more open and less stubborn than I don't have to suffer the calamities I did or take large risks to fulfill their most lofty desires.

It's also clear that listening early is just the beginning. It turns on the lights and reveals many secrets, but it takes attentive, skillful navigation to transform and uplift the journey. When you deliberately engage the nudges and whispers and learn to interpret their meaning in the context of your specific situation, the process becomes less confusing, less disruptive, even graceful and well integrated into the rhythms of daily life.

As you know, I did not follow that gentler path.

Back in Chicago, I was so focused on being the successful advertising executive, and so afraid of losing that identity, and so resistant to change, I magnified what could have been minor tremors into significant earthquakes. Thankfully, those quakes had many extraordinary benefits. They forced me to make important choices that I never would have made in a stable, business-as-usual life. The unrelenting pressures kept pushing me to step beyond my carefully crafted life, beyond my fear of loss, beyond the pain, until I noticed I was not alone on my journey and that a larger wisdom was with me.

My passage took on real meaning when I began to trust that this guidance—or the Subtle Agenda as I came to know it—was an aspect of my largest nature. Things got simpler and in many ways easier when I realized I was being called, pushed, and prodded to co-create my life in alignment with my highest nature, even when I was willing to settle for less. One of my biggest learnings was that when life lets you know it's time to change, if you let that knowing lead you, you will inevitably achieve the fulfillment you desire.

A totally unexpected yet cherished outcome of my journey— which many people share—was a transformation in my understanding of religion and spirituality. I can now see that in the early stages of my passage when I struggled so hard to escape religion, I was actually escaping my own parochial fixedness. I needed to transcend the straps and bindings that tied me to prescriptions of any kind so I could find the true self I knew existed somewhere. I needed to unleash my own insights, I needed to establish my own dialogue with the divine, and when I did, it brought me face to face with the eternal goodness that lies within and beyond us all.

In this private unfolding, I explored the mystical teachings of various religions, and as I discovered seeds of truth within each, I rediscovered the sublime essence that lay in my spiritual past. Gaining fresh appreciation for my own faith tradition, which would have been impossible before, has enhanced my life in ways that still surprise me.

As a young man at the beginning of my career, I thought I would express myself in my work. Now I see my career as an arena within which I discovered the even larger game, the ever-refining integration of my material desires with urgings from my soul. Had I remained hypnotized by my singular focus on being a successful executive, my vision would have been too limited to discover this expansive sense of wholeness.

To play off a lovely Zen koan: *First my work was the work. Then my work was not the work. Now my work is an aspect of the real work.*

With the heightened sensing that is just one of the many gifts of this passage, a truth can be glimpsed. The air we breathe, the breath we take, and we who take the breath, are one in loving unity.

To discover the true nature of reality for oneself—and to discover that it is love—is a remarkable experience for one lifetime. It is a journey I highly recommend you continue in the one you live now.

GOING ALL THE WAY

The Language and Meaning of
Three Guided Intrusions

> *"Humankind is being led along an evolving course,*
> *through this migration of intelligences,*
> *and though we seem to be sleeping,*
> *there is an inner wakefulness*
> *that will eventually startle us back*
> *to the truth of who we are."*
>
> Rumi

"In this life, do it in the city." When I heard that voice in the monastery chapel that morning, I didn't fully understand what it meant and wouldn't until many years later. At the time, I simply heard that I was being turned away from a contemplative life, which for me meant going into business instead. I didn't yet have the ears to hear, nor could I grasp the truer, prophetic promise of transformation that would ultimately emerge from that guidance.

After I chose advertising and focused the full force of my attention on becoming successful, my memory of that incident at Gethsemani faded. I might have even abandoned any sense of its being important were it not for the two even more dramatic events that came later: the disaster at Pillsbury, and my epiphany by the pool. With the benefit of more time, I now recognize these three obvious plot points as a trio of inextricably linked *guided intrusions.* Each was, of course, pivotal to my unfolding, but of even more value now is that when taken together, they reveal the lifelong workings of the Subtle Agenda and its persistent urgings toward ultimate fulfillment. Within these events, I was being shown what I needed to fulfill my childhood vow to in this life "go all the way."

This perspective is what prompted the writing of this Afterword. I assume that if you're reading this book, something of this nature has happened or is happening to you, or maybe to someone you love, and I trust that sharing my own sense-making of these guided intrusions might be useful to you too.

First Guided Intrusion: The Voice at Gethsemani

My first major guided intrusion was, of course, the audible voice in the balcony of the Gethsemani chapel. An obvious plot point, it was a distinct resetting of my life's trajectory. In that solemn context, the words, "You've done this and done this. In this life, do it in the city," audaciously suggested that my desire for a spiritually focused, contemplative life was somehow wanting and that I should choose a different direction.

Inexplicably, I accepted this as truth. My heart instantly found meaning in what my logical mind could not fathom. The monastery might be the ultimate path for some, but it was not for me.

Second Guided Intrusion: No Voice at Pillsbury

When I lost my voice at Pillsbury during that major presentation of new Doughboy commercials, that was the Subtle Agenda speaking with a loud and resounding silence—mine! My inability to speak could have been construed as an anxiety attack, or I could have blamed it on too much wine the night before or on the mounting pressures of a troubled divorce. In my heart, however, I knew the truth.

In my success, I had failed.

Stripped naked of pretense by the most savage and public failure of my life, I came face to face with the realization that even at the zenith of my career in advertising, I was empty and unfulfilled. I was miserably unhappy—tormented actually—by the incessant conflicts between my ideals and what I was doing to earn a living, and for my very survival, I had to unhook from my unyielding drive for achievement.

This episode at Pillsbury was a not-so-subtle intervention by the Subtle Agenda letting me know decisively that I had strayed way too far from the spiritual aspect of my life's core quest. I was not just failing to "go all the way," I was in danger of losing sight of my path entirely.

The voice at the monastery said, "In this life, do it in the city." It did not ask me to abandon my deeper calling. It merely suggested I pursue it elsewhere.

Third Guided Intrusion: Epiphany by the Pool

The most profound guided intrusion, and the one that made it possible for me to ultimately understand the graceful linkage of them all, was the epiphany in my meditation by the pool. In this out-of-body experience, I was pulled beyond the normal veil of human perception and shown that the ultimate journey is not a journey at all, but a layer-by-layer opening to the oneness of eternal love. From there, I was taken behind the scenes of my normal walk-around reality and shown the corrosive effects of fear and how I had let it compromise my choices. No wonder my life had become so unbearably heavy.

This transcendent experience also brought me to an even more transformative awakening. It forever seared into my conscious awareness that *love* is the source of all life, the true essence of all fulfillment, material and spiritual. In that luminous merging with the sacred, long-competing parts of myself became unified. The internal split that drove me out of advertising was healed. I became whole. I became myself.

My eyes were opened that day. I understood the Subtle Agenda's lifelong intention for me. Through countless choices both right and wrong, I was supported along a circuitous path to the complete transformation of my self, my work, my life. It revealed the integrated nature of all material and spiritual realities and introduced me to living in wholeness with both. It forever opened my heart to love.

My passage was not just a career quest. It was an initiation into a new way of being in life. It was about learning to live in harmony with the song of my soul. Even if I had been told all of this directly by the voice at the monastery, I could not have understood that my most intimate spiritual aspirations would ultimately be realized through the refining fires of a vigorous business life.

A NOTE TO YOU

If you have similar desires for more fulfillment and wholeness, if you sense any split between your spiritual core and your drive to achieve your version of success, I hope the process illustrated in this book gives you hope and insight. As I've mentioned, I truly believe that if someone had given me a heads up about the twists and turns, and about the importance of developing deep listening, my journey would have been easier, quicker, and much less expensive!

I also hope you won't be dissuaded if your guided intrusions aren't as dramatic or obvious as mine were. (Remember, I was thickheaded and stubborn and needed that.) The full promise of this passage can be attained with considerably gentler input. In fact, Paige's journey has been much smoother than mine. She grappled with signs of dysfunction when they were still quite subtle, and she started sensitizing herself to this multifaceted source of wisdom earlier, before her choices became fully entrenched in confusion.

Everyone receives a constant flow of divine love, and in a multitude of forms, everyone receives a constant stream of communication from their Subtle Agenda. It never commands—although as we've seen it can be pretty insistent—and the choices are always ours. It's all about learning to listen, learning to decipher the unique language of those subtle pulses of wisdom that continually flow to us, within us, and around us.

I was blessed by many teachers along my path, most of whom didn't even know they were teaching me. Leo Burnett, my mentor in advertising, taught me the importance of "listening to that wee small voice." Later, I learned from my life what Rumi said so simply, "There is a voice that doesn't use words. Listen."

When you listen with a sincere heart, when you reflect on what you sense and feel and perceive and intuit, you increase your access to the most profound knowing and wellspring of eternal love. You can put this to work with powerful results in any aspect of your life—in your career, your relationships, your inner life—whatever is meaningful and compelling for you.

In time, the course corrections and resulting sense of pure alignment are achieved with barely perceptible adjustments. This level of mastery gets simpler and less daunting with practice, and at some point becomes second nature as a most healthy and satisfying habit! At the core of it all, it's about healing our fear, opening our hearts, and nourishing our desire to know and truly live our eternal nature in everyday life.

I hope you'll reach out to us via email or on the web, but in case we don't connect further, here's the easy-to-remember mantra Paige and I both use every day:

Make love, not fear.
Do love, not fear.
Be love, not fear.

That's the way we "do it in the city."

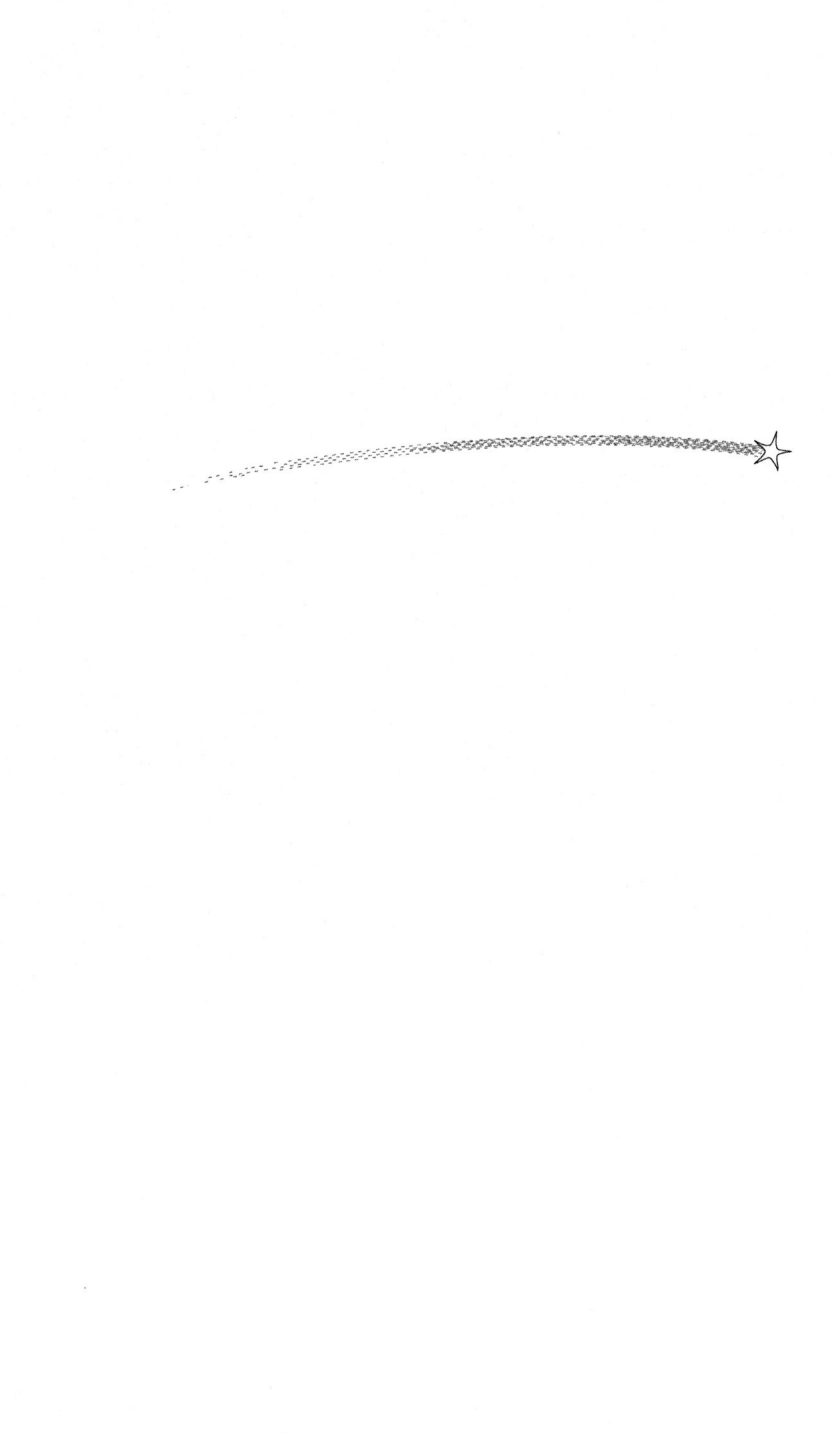

END NOTES

FRONT MATTER

Jalāl-Dīn, Rūmī, & Barks, Coleman. (1995). *The essential Rumi.* (p. 51). San Francisco, CA: Harper.

THE CALL

Campbell, Joseph. (1968). *The hero with a thousand faces* (2d ed.). (p. 51). Princeton, N.J.: Princeton University Press.

Blake, William, Erdman, David V., & Bloom, Harold. (1970). *The poetry and prose of William Blake* (4th print., with revisions ed.). (p. 34). Garden City, N.Y.: Doubleday.

Blake, William, Erdman, David V., & Bloom, Harold. (1970). *The poetry and prose of William Blake* (4th print., with revisions ed.). (p. 35-37). Garden City, N.Y.: Doubleday.

THE COCOON

Klots, Alexander Barrett. (1951). A field guide to the butterflies of North America, east of the Great Plains. (p.45). Boston, Mass.: Houghton Mifflin.

Campbell, Joseph. (1968). *The hero with a thousand faces* (2d ed.). (p. 77). Princeton, N.J.: Princeton University Press.

Ram, Dass. (1976). The only dance there is. (p. 1). New York: J. Aronson.

Lao Tzu, & Wing, R. L. (1986). The Tao of power: a translation of the Tao te ching by Lao Tzu (1st ed.). (p. 18). Garden City, N.Y.: Doubleday.

Lutyens, Mary. (1975). Krishnamurti: the years of awakening. (p. 15). London: J. Murray.

Campbell, Joseph. (1968). *The hero with a thousand faces* (2d ed.). (p. 30). Princeton, N.J.: Princeton University Press.

Campbell, Joseph. (1968). *The hero with a thousand faces* (2d ed.). (p. 10). Princeton, N.J.: Princeton University Press.

Campbell, Joseph. (1968). *The hero with a thousand faces* (2d ed.). (p. 97). Princeton, N.J.: Princeton University Press.

Campbell, Joseph. (1968). *The hero with a thousand faces* (2d ed.). (p. 101). Princeton, N.J.: Princeton University Press.

Campbell, Joseph. (1968). *The hero with a thousand faces* (2d ed.). (p. 109). Princeton, N.J.: Princeton University Press.

THE RETURN

Wilhelm, Richard, & Baynes, Cary F. (1977). *The I ching; or, Book of changes* (3d ed.). (p. 97). Princeton, N.J.: Princeton University Press.

Klots, Alexander Barrett. (1951). A field guide to the butterflies of North America, east of the Great Plains. (p.42). Boston, Mass.: Houghton Mifflin.

Campbell, Joseph. (1968). *The hero with a thousand faces* (2d ed.). (p. 36). Princeton, N.J.: Princeton University Press.

Wilhelm, Richard, Jung, C. G., & Liu, Hug-yang. (1962). *The secret of the golden flower, a Chinese book of life* (New, rev. and augm. ed.). (p. 132). New York: Harcourt, Brace.

Kinnell, Galway. (1980). *Mortal acts, mortal words.* (pp.71-2). Boston, Mass.: Houghton Mifflin.

EPILOGUE & AFTERWORD

Merton, Thomas, Stone, Naomi Burton, & Hart, Patrick. (1979). *Love and living.* (p.196). New York: Farrar, Straus, and Giroux.

Jalāl-Dīn, Rūmī,, & Barks, Coleman. (1995). *The essential Rumi.* (p. 113). San Francisco, CA: Harper.

ABOUT THE AUTHORS

Donald Marrs, by his resume, is a distinguished corporate executive whose career took him into the boardrooms of some of America's most powerful corporations. A closer look at his life reveals an insightful man on an abiding quest to resolve the split he felt between his work and his values, and to  experience deeper meaning through his work. *Executive in Passage*, his first book, describes his treacherous but ultimately triumphant journey out of a painful, disconnected career into a more whole, more meaningful way of being in life. Don coaches private clients out of their discontent and crises into lives of uncommon fulfillment.

Paige Marrs, PhD, is a relationship and communication coach. She teaches clients about the relationship-brain and helps them overcome the hidden "brain mistakes" that are causing trouble in their relationships. Paige's approach is a unique blend of interpersonal neurobiology, cutting-edge  communication theory, and findings from her own research. Her personal sensitivity and wisdom are enhanced by countless lessons learned during years of personal struggle and decades of spiritual searching. In practice for over 25 years, Paige holds a Doctorate in Human & Organizational Systems and a Masters in Human Development.

Don and Paige live, play, and work together happily in their quiet canyon home on the Westside of Los Angeles.

BARRINGTON SKY PUBLISHING
212 26th Street, Suite 239
Santa Monica, CA 90402
connect@bsky.com

Donald Marrs – don@executiveinpassage.com
Paige Marrs, PhD – paige@executiveinpassage.com

Printed in Great Britain
by Amazon

77625146R00183